Daughter of the Cold War

PITT SERIES IN RUSSIAN AND EAST EUROPEAN STUDIES

Jonathan Harris, EDITOR

DAUGHTER

OF ★ THE

COLD WAR

GRACE KENNAN WARNECKE

UNIVERSITY OF PITTSBURGH PRESS

Published by the University of Pittsburgh Press, Pittsburgh, Pa., 15260
Copyright © 2018, University of Pittsburgh Press
All rights reserved
Manufactured in the United States of America
Printed on acid-free paper
10 9 8 7 6 5 4 3 2

Cataloging-in-Publication data is available from the Library of Congress

ISBN 13: 978-0-8229-4520-8

Jacket art: Grace in Moscow. Family photo.
Jacket design by Alex Wolfe

To Charles, Adair, and Kevin
and
in memory of George and Annelise Kennan.

Contents

Acknowledgments

This book would never have been written without the help and encouragement of many people to whom I am deeply indebted.

Foremost was Veronica Golos, the writing teacher who started me on this path and from whom I learned so much. Equally important are the members of my writing group, Gerri Marielle, Mary Marks, Susan Ades Stone, and Rosanne Weston. We have been meeting for the past ten years, initially with Veronica and then on our own. Their intelligent critiques, support, and inspiration remain invaluable. Each has contributed in her own way, but I especially want to thank Susan for hours spent on editing and much needed tightening of the manuscript.

I am grateful to the Woodrow Wilson International Center for Scholars, which provided me with a fellowship and an office in which I could write, and to Blair Ruble and Joe Dresen at the Kennan Institute for their help.

My Russian chapters also benefited from the expertise of Nadezhda Azhgikina, Dick and Sharon Miles, Alan Cooperman, Martina Vandenberg, Viviane Mikhalkov, and the late Catharine Nepomnyashchy and Evgeny Porotov. Ukraine chapters were equally enhanced by the experiences and encouragement of Nell Connors, Marta Baziuk, and Susanne Jalbert.

Many thanks to my cousin, Elisabeth Eide, who corrected and enhanced the Norwegian chapters with her own vivid memories.

Professor Nancy Condee played a decisive role by her faith in my book and led me to Pittsburgh where I am happy to find myself in the expert hands of Peter Kracht at the University of Pittsburgh Press.

My close friends have supported, prodded, and kept me going, especially Laurence Eubank, Meredith Burch, Nancy Eddy, and two who are with us in memory only, Ken Regan and Anna Elman. They would have been so happy to see this book appear.

Thanks to Seth Farkas who was of invaluable assistance during the editing process.

Family, of course, plays a vital part of any memoir. I am particularly grateful to my siblings Joan, Christopher, and Wendy Kennan, my cousin, Eugene Hotchkiss, and my children, Charles, Adair, and Kevin who have put up with me and encouraged me all these years. While they did not want to be a major part of this book, they are always present.

PROLOGUE

An End and a Beginning

Feeling hundreds of eyes on my back, I walked slowly behind a priest carrying a towering and glinting cross up to the pulpit of the National Cathedral in Washington, DC. I was about to deliver a eulogy for my father, George F. Kennan, the diplomat and historian. Those are the titles that are etched into his granite tombstone, but to me he was much more than a prominent actor on the world stage. He was a guide, an icon, and a dominant force, and after days of apprehension about this moment, I felt suddenly calm and ready. To my mind, the cathedral seemed an especially appropriate venue for the memorial service. I had played in its crypts as a ten-year-old while boarding at the National Cathedral School for Girls and had knelt in those pews during many a long Sunday service. The majestic setting was familiar. My role was not.

All my life I had studied, admired, and loved my exceptional father, while occasionally being infuriated and deeply hurt by him. At times my great supporter, he could also be a cutting critic, and his disapproval was withering. He cast an enormous shadow, under which I was both nurtured and hidden. To escape, I ran head-on into some unfortunate relationships and periods of rudderless searching. Living my early years as the "daughter of," I moved on to roles as the "wife of," and eventually the "mother of," as the people in my life never seemed to stray very far from the public eye. Finding a direction in life proved to be a challenge that spanned many decades and many continents.

What propelled me to get up and speak in front of all the distinguished guests—the secretary of state Colin Powell, former secretary of state Madeleine Albright, Senators Biden and Lugar, countless ambassadors, governors, and public figures? I knew that Father would have wanted and expected my brother, Christopher, to represent the family, which he did, but would have been surprised by my participation. Once more, I was rebelling against Father's old-fashioned discomfort with women assuming a public role. But I had to speak, both to honor my father and to acknowledge myself. The routes I had traveled led me very far afield, but now they were circling back, taking me up the long aisle of that familiar cathedral on a sun-warmed day in March 2005. At that moment I recognized myself as someone shaped by forces both ordinary and extraordinary—a daughter with thoughts and feelings to share about a person who was as private as he was public.

I had struggled with the first draft of the eulogy. Writing and rewriting my tribute, trying to shed light on George Kennan as a father, I'd also thought about myself. Sitting down after the eulogy and listening to the strains of Rachmaninoff's *Vocalise*, memories floated in, borne by the music. How much he would have loved this Russian musical send-off.

My father's career in the Foreign Service molded my early life. I was born in Riga, Latvia, and journeyed with him and my mother to Moscow, Prague, Berlin, Vienna, and Lisbon. When his posts were deemed unsuitable for children, I was deposited with various relatives and in boarding school. It was my father who decided that I would go to a Soviet school in war-torn Moscow, even though I knew no Russian. It was he who taught me to revere the power of the written word. He conveyed to me his love of Russia and Russian literature. But his legacy wasn't all formal lessons and books.

The oldest of four children born over a twenty-year span, I was lucky enough to be with my father when he was still young. He taught me skating in Vienna, read aloud to me by the hour, took my sister Joanie and me bicycling through Scotland, searching for our roots, taught me ballroom dancing in a small bedroom of a Scottish country inn. He left a legacy of insatiable curiosity about everything he saw. Every trip was full of adventures, and nothing we did was without a purpose. With our father as my guide, history was alive and I was part of it.

Years later, when he had already celebrated his hundredth birthday, I went to visit him. He was sitting, virtually immobile, in a wingback chair in his bedroom in Princeton, his long, sensitive fingers folding and unfolding a small napkin on the table in front of him. Sitting, facing him, heart thumping, I finally blurted out, "Daddy, I'm writing a memoir—a book about my life." To tell this to him, who had a two-volume memoir among his twenty-one published books, who had received the Pulitzer Prize twice, the National Book Award, the Bancroft Prize, and the Francis Parkman Prize for his writings, seemed an audacious step. He stared at me for a long time with no expression and then answered, "Well, you could."

Daughter of the Cold War

CHAPTER 1

A Nomad from the Start

"Your request for a visa to the USSR has been denied." When I read these words on an official document in the spring of 1985, I felt stomach-punched. My career as a Russian specialist was just beginning to take off, and now what was I going to do and where was I going to do it? I knew what had caused this rejection, and the unfairness of it made me feel even worse.

The previous fall I had returned, feeling both proud and slightly edgy, from an exciting trip to Russia as the associate producer of a Metromedia series called *Inside Russia*. The all-male crew considered this assignment a great adventure, and their escapades, many involving young women, caused us to be constantly followed and observed, always on the brink of some crisis. As the only Russian speaker, I had unusual responsibility in this television medium—relatively new to me. After our return to New York, I sat hour after hour with a Russian-speaking film editor, identifying the reels and reels of footage our crew had brought back. Though it would come to harm me later, I was happy to appear in a brief interview with the film's narrator.

Despite my hours in the editing room, I was not included in the key meeting where decisions were made as to which clips would appear in the final version. I knew that Metromedia would not be content with a lovely travelogue of the Soviet Union, but I was still shocked when our highly critical series appeared on the screen—identifying our Russian colleague as an agent of the KGB, showing an interview with a dissident that we had promised not to air, and in general shaping what we had seen to fit a foreordained concept of Metromedia and our producer.

Some months after the film aired, I applied for a Soviet visa to go to Moscow as a photographer for the San Francisco Boys Chorus. A fun assignment, I thought, photographing young singers. That's when my visa application was rejected. Because of my associate-producer credit and my cameo appearance on-screen, the Russians had judged my role on the Metromedia film to be more important than it actually was. Devastated, I sat glumly in my office, realizing that my future in the Soviet Union might be over.

The director of the Boys Chorus proposed that I accompany the chorus to Hungary and apply for my visa there—the news of my rejection in New York probably hadn't reached Budapest, he reasoned, and as a photographer I could take nice shots of the winsome young musicians by the Danube for the upcoming record album cover. But the Soviet government was more efficient than we anticipated, and my application was rejected again. I had the added humiliation of being asked to brief the choirboys about their upcoming trip to Russia, then waving them good-bye at the Budapest airport.

All this reminded me of my father and his expulsion as ambassador to the Soviet Union in 1952. But my father wasn't the first Kennan to have gone to Russia or to be expelled. My father had been named George in honor of his grandfather's cousin, a famous American explorer of Russia and Siberia at the time of my father's birth in 1904.

Born in 1845 into a family of modest means in Norwalk, Ohio, the original George Kennan had to quit school and go to work for the telegraph company at the age of twelve. Tapping out messages to all parts of the world must have honed his curiosity about foreign travel, so when a job was advertised in 1865—surveying Siberia for a possible trans-Siberian cable for the Russian-American Telegraph Company—this nineteen-year-old telegraph clerk submitted his application and was accepted. He had never been out of Norwalk. My father used to tell me this story, impressed by the adventurous spirit that propelled this relative forward against heavy odds.

The elder George Kennan made his way to Alaska, and in August 1865 he boarded a steamer to Kamchatka. He spent two years traveling through Siberia by sleigh, by reindeer, and by skin canoe (this was before the building of the Trans-Siberian Railway) in temperatures that went down to sixty degrees below zero, and conditions very primitive. He learned to speak Russian on the way. The western part of Siberia was at that point only sparsely settled, inhabited largely by various Asiatic tribes. As a result of this trip, George Kennan wrote a two-volume book, *Tent Life in Siberia: Adventures among the Koraks and Other Tribes in Kamchatka and Northern Asia.* He returned to the United States and gave lectures about this trip in order to supplement his clerical income. He, like my father, had an intense curiosity about the world he was discovering and an ability to keep meticulous notes and card files. However, his Siberian exploration came to naught, as the transatlantic cable was announced at about that time, killing any prospect of a trans-Siberian cable.

George Kennan next returned to Russia in 1870 to do a pioneering trek through Dagestan and the North Caucasus, a wild, mountainous region virtually never traveled by Westerners. This trip led to more lectures and publications. He must have been a charismatic speaker, because eventually he earned some sort of world record, giving a speech every night for two hundred consecutive evenings (except Sundays) from 1890 to 1891.

In his articles, the elder Kennan was rather pro Tsar Alexander II's policies, which led the tsar and his courtiers to assume that Kennan would be a good representative for them in the West. The tsarist government even assisted him in arrangements for a trip to survey penal colonies in Siberia and the exile system. This journey, taken from 1885 to 1887, totally changed George Kennan's mind-set. As he visited Siberian prison settlements, he was horrified and became a strong opponent of the tsarist system of exile. He built a false bottom into his suitcase and risked his life carrying out last letters to their families from prisoners who either knew they were sentenced to death or suspected they would not survive imprisonment. He became close friends with some early Russian revolutionaries and a founding member of the American Friends of Russian Freedom. He wrote a series of articles in *The Century Magazine* that grew into a two-volume book, *Siberia and the Exile System*. When I finally read this book, I understood how grueling those trips were and what unusual physical stamina he must have had.

When the book on the exile system was published, the tsarist government, at the personal direction of the tsar, refused to permit George Kennan back in to Russia. In defiance, my ancestor made one more trip to St. Petersburg, but he was immediately picked up by the police and unceremoniously expelled.

When my father talked about the original George Kennan, it was clear that he felt an almost mystical connection with his great-great-uncle. I have rarely seen my father so pleased as when he, my mother, and I visited Tolstoy's home, Yasnaya Polyana. He was ambassador to the Soviet Union at the time, so we were accompanied by two black cars carrying KGB agents, whom my father jokingly called his "guardian angels." Yasnaya

Polyana, a small country estate, had been left almost untouched since Tolstoy walked out in November 1910 and ended up dying at the nearby Astapova railroad station. Fitting in with the musty museum feeling of the house was the wizened old bespectacled man who greeted us; appropriately, he turned out to have been one of Tolstoy's secretaries, Valentin Bulgakov. When my father introduced himself, Bulgakov volunteered, "Oh, yes, I remember your uncle." He rummaged in the shelves and pulled out an old guest book with crisp, slightly tan paper, and we all looked in awe at the original George Kennan's signature. Even the guardian angels stood respectfully silent, in their black suits, a few steps behind.

The George Kennans shared a birthday, February 16; both played the guitar and loved to sail. The original George Kennan eventually married but never had any children, and I know my father felt he was his spiritual heir. My father told me that the one time he had gone to visit the older Kennans, the wife wasn't very nice to the young relative, but her cold reception never dampened his affection for his great-great-uncle. "I feel that I was in some strange way destined to carry forward as best I could the work of my distinguished and respected namesake," he wrote in *Memoirs*. Years later, when I told my father about my visa denial, he nodded his head. "Ah, you see, it's the Kennan curse." All my life, as my work took me back to Russia again and again, I felt this strange magnetic pull. Russia had always been and would always be intertwined with my life.

Birth in Riga

I always loved the story of how my parents found each other. My father, a young American Foreign Service officer studying Russian in Berlin, met my twenty-year-old Norwegian mother, Annelise Sorensen, at a dinner party, and love followed almost instantly. Within six weeks they were engaged, and the marriage took place in the Lutheran cathedral of her hometown,

Kristiansand, on September 11, 1931. I never questioned why my father didn't take my mother back to meet his family before they married—it was much more romantic to believe that passion propelled these two young people from different sides of the ocean to marry so quickly.

Photographs showed a young, dashing couple, often windswept, who seemed to spend much time climbing in and out of my father's convertible.

A brittle piece of paper with deeply etched creases, written in an incomprehensible language and festooned with stamps, proves that I was christened in St. Peter's Lutheran Cathedral in Riga, Latvia, the city of my birth, in 1932. My father was stationed in the Baltic capital at the American legation immediately after their marriage, and I appeared nine months later. While I have no memories of Riga, I learned about my first two years, in startling detail, because of my father's propensity to record his life. In a long letter composed for me before the war but delivered only when I was twenty-one, he described Riga: "It was a rather sad place. It had never regained all the trade and activity which it had enjoyed in the good old days before the First World War, when it was one of the greatest ports of the Russian Empire. Many factory chimneys, scattered around the far horizon of the flat country, were mute; and downriver, the great timber port lay—for the most part empty and deserted."

We lived on the top two floors of a big old wooden house on Altonavas Isle, in a factory district, across the Daugava River from the main part of town. My father, who had lost all his money in the Depression of 1929, wrote: "We were in desperation about that house. We had lost all our money in the collapse of Kruger and Toll (if you don't know what that was, consider yourselves a blessed generation, and never ask), so we couldn't really afford the house anymore. But we had a year's lease on it and couldn't give it up."

Across the street from their house, a brass band performed each weekend, playing the same five tunes at full volume from three in the afternoon until three in the morning. The music did not entertain but served only to compound my parents' misery. "You couldn't even hear yourself think. We tried to wangle out of our lease. We even enlisted the help of the Foreign Office. All in vain. The landlady stuck to her guns, and we remained for the summer, getting rapidly poorer, and slightly deaf. The last month or two we couldn't even pay the rent anymore; but I made it up to her later, in installments."

Finally, in despair, my parents gave up the apartment. My father moved in with friends, and my mother went back to Norway.

Despite their lack of funds, my parents always had help. Great-Auntie Petra came from Norway to take care of things when I was born, and she stayed a month and a half; then a friend of my mother's, Else Rinnan from the north of Norway, "came to visit us," writes my father, but she clearly came as an unpaid babysitter, and we shared a room. Over time, Else was followed by Sigrid, then Rags, and then, for years after the period of my father's letter, by a parade of nameless nannies.

My mother, nurse Else, and I left my father in Riga and traveled together on a steamship via Tallinn and Helsinki, a trip that took a week. This was before all the child equipment of today, and I simply rode and slept on the lid of the basket that held my diapers and clothes. From then on there was a constant back and forth to Norway. I was six months old the first time my parents left me alone with my grandparents. Three months later my parents reappeared from Riga to join us, as the U.S. government had ordered all Foreign Service officers to take a month's leave without pay owing to the Depression. My father reported of this visit: "You were a friendly, happy baby. . . . We were very thrilled and pleased to see you and to think you were our child."

But thrilled as they may have been, they nevertheless left me with the grandparents while they spent most of the month skiing at my grandfather's hunting cabin, Jorunlid, in the mountains, accessible only by a long car ride and then a two-hour climb on skis.

After this visit, my parents took me with them back to Riga. Despite the family's financial straits, a new nursemaid accompanied us. But, according to my father, I stayed only the summer, and "in the fall you were taken back to Kristiansand again. . . . I did not see you for nearly a year thereafter."

I stayed in Kristiansand with my grandparents while my mother accompanied my father on her first trip to the United States, to meet his family. Shortly thereafter she joined him in Moscow, where as third secretary he was setting up the new American embassy, the United States not having had representation in the Soviet Union since the Russian Revolution of 1917. When my father finally returned to Norway, alone, a year later, he found me: "a grown-up young thing of over two years, speaking exclusively Norwegian. At our first encounter, the family urged you—with much cooing and baby talk—to show some signs of recognition or affection for me, but you didn't remember me, and your only reaction was the fierce declaration: *Jeg vil ikke gaa til mannen* (I don't want to go to the man)."

My mother reappeared a few days later, and my father wrote: "You were about as offish with her. One morning I met you early in the morning and invited you to come up and say good morning to your mother. You replied only with signs of disgust and truculence. I picked you up, carried you to our room, and gave you a sound licking. From that time on, you were again our daughter, and a very affectionate one."

I have always hated that story. I don't know which part bothered me more—my father spanking a two-year-old who barely knew him or my turning into a sweet, obedient child after being punished.

When I was three, my parents took me with them on my first trip to Moscow. An early insomniac, I used to get up at night and stand by the cold window overlooking the Kremlin, developing, as a result, a severe case of pneumonia. At the local Soviet hospital, administrators were afraid to assign a nurse to a foreigner, so American embassy wives stayed up all night pumping air into my lungs with a primitive oxygen pillow, which saved my life.

Soon after that, my father developed bleeding ulcers. He was sent to a sanatorium in Vienna for treatment, and we accompanied him. In time his ulcers were cured, and I picked up Viennese German. We have photographs of my parents and me, all dressed up in Sunday clothes, walking in the sanatorium's manicured gardens and looking like a fashion advertisement rather than a patient and his family.

In late fall 1935, Mother became pregnant again, and the two of us traveled to the United States to await this new child, while my father remained in Moscow. We ended up moving in with Father's sister, Jeanette, her husband, Gene, and their three sons, in Ravinia, Illinois.

Interestingly enough, in my parents' correspondence of the time, the unborn child is always referred to as "he." It must have been a shock when, on April 24, 1936, a beautiful blond baby girl, Joan, was born.

After Joanie's birth, our father came to the States on leave. Our new family of four sailed from the United States on a transatlantic steamer to Hamburg, along with the U.S. Olympic Team going to participate in the shameful 1936 Berlin Olympics. At age four, I had no impression of our famous travel mates on this trip, but I loved these journeys—the smell of the ocean, the slow rocking of the ship, and the screeching of the seagulls. I also loved the undivided attention I received from my parents. There was always a well-equipped playroom for the youngsters, and I was happy amusing myself with other children. After a year in Moscow we were sent back to America, where we moved into a rented house in Alexandria, Virginia, and I went to kindergarten. There are many black-and-white snapshots of me in the garden, decked out in embroidered dresses and Norwegian folk costumes—photos presumably staged to send to my grandmother.

At the end of 1938, we boarded another steamer and sailed back to Europe. My parents were returning to Moscow, and Joanie and I were taken to Norway to spend the winter at my grandparents' apartment. There was heavy snow that year, and Joanie and I played outside on snow banks taller than we were. I had won the heart of my grandfather, known to us as Bessa, and would sit on his lap for hours while he patiently helped me learn my multiplication tables.

Often he would hold my hand and lead me down the stairs into his hardware store, where I relished the smell of sawdust and the hanging pots, knives, and cooking utensils, all arranged by size. I especially loved looking at the smaller pots and implements and wishing that I could play with them.

My grandmother supervised Christmas preparations that went on for days; I remember the baking, the cookie smells, the candlelit tree around which we danced, holding hands, and singing carols on Christmas Eve. My dolls would mysteriously disappear at the beginning of that holiday season and emerge under the tree with newly painted china faces, new clothes, and fresh wigs.

In the spring my parents reappeared to take us to Prague, where my father was stationed at the American embassy as a second secretary. My main memory is being held up to see Hitler from the window of our apartment. He was riding in an open convertible, on his triumphal entry into Prague in March of 1939. I still have my letter to my grandparents, written in Norwegian, about this important event. My father was soon transferred to Berlin, where, although I didn't go to school, I did perfect my German. My parents told me that I would answer the door when they had guests and greet each guest in his or her language—Russian, German, Norwegian, or English.

But despite my linguistic prowess, this was a confusing time for me. There was a parade of constantly changing nurses—some nice and some awful. All of them drilled into me that I had to behave well or my parents wouldn't love me. I started having a recurrent nightmare: I was to be buried alive, and my nurse's job was to dress me up to say good-bye to my parents before I left to be entombed. The nurse said I had to wear a hat, but since I hated hats this was almost as upsetting as the prospect of interment. She then ordered, very strictly, "Whatever you do, you mustn't cry. Crying would upset your parents, and you can't do that." Somewhere after bidding farewell to my parents, I would awake, trembling, relieved at my narrow escape.

In the spring of 1940, Mother, Joanie, and I traveled back to Norway for a spring skiing vacation at Jorunlid. While Joanie was left behind with a nurse at my grandparents' home in Kristiansand, I happily went skiing with Mother and the Norwegian family. There was no telephone in the mountains, but as soon as Mother and I returned to Kristiansand, my father, having heard rumors of an impending German invasion of Norway, was on the phone, telling my mother to bring us back to Berlin on the next train. Mother, who did not like changing her plans, refused, saying, "Oh, George, we are having a lovely time, and the girls are so happy." My father then sent a telegram: I ORDER YOU TO TAKE THE CHILDREN AND LEAVE ON THE NEXT TRAIN TO GERMANY. This time she did not argue, and we left on April 7, 1940. Two days later, the German troops landed and marched into Kristiansand. I was seven years old.

My prescient father was convinced that the war was going to spread. After a few more months in Berlin, he insisted that Mother take Joanie and me back to the United States. Off we went, back to the New World.

Warm Hearth in a Cold Place

During the peripatetic years of my early childhood, my grandparents' home in Norway emerged for me as the one stable base. For my father, as well, my mother's family must have substituted for a kindred life that he had never known. In another letter, he wrote emotionally about the Sorensen home. At the time, he was in Moscow, worrying about the war clouds hovering over Europe.

> I cannot tell at the time of writing whether you will ever see that house again, so I must describe it for you. The family lived on the second floor, above the store and the warehouses. You slept in the little front room, one of the two rooms on a different level, over the entrance driveway. There was an iron stove in the one you slept in. Every morning, early, in the darkness, the maid would come in and build a fire in the stove, and the light would flicker in the dark. The warmth would spread throughout the little room, and gradually it would get light outside and there would be the sounds of early morning in the street.
>
> I wonder whether you sensed, in the world of infancy, something of the note of security and wholesomeness and human warmth in the crackling of the stove in that room, where other children had lived and grown up before you. That, my child, was part of a home, a real home, as people knew them when your mother and I were young—a home in the deepest, most indescribable meaning of the word. It was so much a home that I, who am not a hysterical person, cannot think of it now—and all that has happened to it in the meantime—without weeping.

Unlike the Kennan family, which migrated westward, farm to farm, from Massachusetts to Milwaukee, the Sorensens had been rooted for generations in Kristiansand, an old port city located at the southern tip of Norway. The Sorensen men were house painters, a skill for which nineteenth-century Norwegians had to study and pass numerous tests. Part of the exam was to copy a painting from the art museum to demonstrate how skillfully the applicant could mix colors. Grandfather's painting still hangs in the Norway summerhouse. Painters had special artisan stature in this rather rigid class society. My great-grandfather, Severin, opened a small paint shop that ultimately grew into the hardware store. He must have had other gifts in addition to painting, as he became the vice-mayor of Kristiansand. He died young, of a heart attack while giving a public speech, and according to photographs, half the city showed up for his funeral.

His son, my grandfather, Einar Haakon Sorensen, stopped house painting and raised the family status by becoming a prominent local businessman, owning a lumberyard as well as the hardware store. He joined the Klubbselskapet Foreningen, known as "Klubben," a club for male civil servants and businessmen, which became the focus of my grandparents' social life. It still functions today as a private men's club. Tellingly, my mother never mentioned our house-painting forebears. I only learned about them from my Norwegian cousin many years later, after my mother had sunk into dementia.

The roomy two-story apartment, described by my father in his letter, was above the hardware store on a street called Skippergata. My grandfather was born there in 1875 and lived there with his mother until he was thirty. Only after her death did he start looking for a wife and find my grandmother, Elisabeth. She was from Oslo, and they met at a wedding in the coastal town of Grimstad. They had something in common, as her father was also a master artisan, supervisor of the handicraft workshop in the prison located in the Akershus Fortress. She grew up in a house on the prison grounds, which I thought was strangely romantic. When Grandfather Einar proposed to my grandmother, his older sister, Anna, nicknamed Tatti, cautioned Elisabeth, by now her good friend, against marrying him. She described her brother as "spoiled, demanding, and solitary in his habits." But my gregarious, fun-loving grandmother married him anyway and moved into the apartment above the store, where she bore four children, the oldest being my mother, Annelise.

Always social, my mother appropriately made her first appearance in the summer of 1910 in that Kristiansand apartment the day after a family gathering full of joyous talk, drink, and food. Family lore has it that my grandmother sang a popular opera aria, "Mona, My Handmaiden," so loudly at the dinner that it could be heard out on the street. The next morning she gave birth to my mother. In a letter to my mother celebrating her confirmation day in the Lutheran church, her aunt Petra described the event: "You made your entrance into the world in a house filled with people, and everybody was happy. Your mother called you the 'Sunray' of Sorenhus."

My warm and loving grandmother, whom I called Mormor, was very different from her quiet, reserved husband. Everything about her was ample, including her body. All summer long it was encased in Norwegian folk costumes that she filled to overflowing. She had a loud, infectious laugh, long brown hair that she washed and brushed to dry outside in the sun, and a melodious voice. She loved to sing and to participate in amateur theatricals, but my grandfather vocally disapproved. He did not like her performing in front of other men, and she reluctantly gave up the stage. Her talents were then confined to the kitchen, where she produced, with the help of a young maid, delicious meals. Streams of great-aunts, aunts, uncles, and cousins drifted in and out of both the apartment in the winter and their house on the fjord in summer—mostly, I suspect, to partake of my grandmother's cooking. Both homes were suffused with the smells from the kitchen. I was fascinated by the elaborate ceramic spice rack that hung on the wall in the apartment, each miniature drawer labeled with the name of a different fragrant spice. My grandmother's succulent meals inexorably expanded her already wide waistline. To me she was pillowy, warm, and nurturing—everything my slim, reserved mother was not. Mother, however, described her simply as "fat."

Food played a major role in my life during those Norwegian summers. A favorite activity was picking wild blueberries and strawberries in the woods or gathering cherries from the big cherry tree in the garden. Every day we washed and peeled freshly dug, dirt-coated potatoes, until our fingers wrinkled in the cold water. No *middag*, or main meal, was ever complete without potatoes. Normally we ate fish, but on Sundays, Mormor cooked *ryper*, or ptarmigan, which Grandfather Bessa had shot, and served it with a sour-cream gravy that years later we still try to duplicate. At each middag, we children were measured out a small glass of "Solo," a Norwegian sparkling orange drink, and the meager ration made it especially desirable. In the afternoons at coffee time, Mormor made delicate waffles topped with fresh strawberries and whipped cream, another favorite.

Unlike my tender grandmother, Bessa terrified most children, but never me. When I was three, he built "Sorenhus," a house on a promontory jutting out into the wide Kristiansand fjord. An artificially created flat lawn in front led to rocks that tumbled down to the sea. While all the other houses snuggled into the rocky coast were similar—two-story white wooden buildings—Sorenhus was dark brown, flat-roofed, and low-lying. Our house looked like no other house on the coast and was probably considered an eyesore. I wonder what inspired my grandfather to be so modern and so original, defying local tradition.

Bessa stood out in other ways, as well. Most of our neighbors commuted to town on open, round-bottomed wooden boats with noisy, smelly motors. He, by contrast, had bought a sleek American Chris-Craft with a flat bottom and canvas roof, which made little sense in the rough northern waters of the Skagerrak, the strait separating Norway and Denmark. But the boat was distinctive and elegant, and when the German army occupied Norway in April 1940, the commandant immediately came to my grandfather to commandeer the Chris-Craft.

Clever Bessa had foreseen this and transferred ownership to my father, his American son-in-law. As America was not yet in the war, the Germans could not take possession. After the attack on Pearl Harbor, however, the Germans returned for the boat.

"You can have it," my grandfather said. "But, unfortunately, the motor has been stolen."

The Germans searched his hardware store, the Kristiansand apartment, and Sorenhus, but they never found the motor. Grandfather, again with astute foresight, had arranged for a carpenter in his lumberyard to build a dining room table with a thick hollow base to house the motor, and all during the war the family ate on top of the Chris-Craft engine.

Both before and after the war, my grandfather loved to commute across the sea in his beloved Chris-Craft. Whenever we arrived by steamer from America, we would hang over the railing to see the first glimpse of Bessa, bobbing around the big ship in the Chris-Craft, the Norwegian flag flying, waiting to escort the liner to port. We would descend the gangplank, our belongings would be piled up on the dock and transferred to his boat, alongside baskets of food and provisions already purchased by him, and off we would go to Sorenhus. Because the house was so low and brown, it was hard to see from the water. Always visible, however, was the flagpole on the front lawn. Every day that he was there, Bessa flew the Norwegian flag. The only time he made an exception was on the day of our arrival. Then, in our honor, he raised the American flag.

The boat would dock at our boathouse, located on a little bay a fair distance from Sorenhus.

Bessa then piled all the suitcases and packages into a wheelbarrow, which he pushed down a long path through the woods toward our home. The house itself was simple but light and airy. We had no running water, so we used a two-seater outhouse, which no one ever seemed to share. Water for the kitchen was hand-pumped from a well. When it was warm we bathed in the sea, but on cold days we used a metal tub that Mormor filled with water heated on the stove. Joanie and I loved our

Sorenhus arrivals. We knew that Mormor, smiling and full of hugs, would be waiting, always with a lunch, coffee, or dinner prepared, depending on the time of day. We scanned the horizon as we approached on the Chris-Craft, and as soon as we sighted the American flag fluttering above the rocky shore, we knew we were home.

Family members wandered through our visits to Norway and were an important part of my childhood. These included my mother's siblings, the most dashing of whom was my uncle Einar, the closest to my mother in age and spirit. His exploits during the Second World War became legendary in the family. Heading toward England from Norway in a small boat, he was captured by the Germans and taken to Germany. He made several spectacular escape attempts, helped by the fact that he spoke excellent German, which he'd learned when he attended business school there. But he was always caught. Finally, while being moved to a maximum-security prison camp by railroad, Einar climbed out through an air vent at the top of the boxcar and jumped off the train. He found his way to Hamburg and ultimately to neutral Sweden, after sneaking onto a coal freighter and burying himself under the coal. He almost starved before the freighter sailed days later. From Sweden he set off, again in a small boat, to England. This time he arrived successfully and spent the rest of the war as an officer of the Norwegian army in exile. I loved the stories of my uncle's wartime adventures. Back at the National Cathedral School for Girls, I was awarded the Laura Tuckerman Prize for English for an essay about him.

My mother's two other siblings were still at home in the Skippergata apartment when I first lived in Kristiansand. In keeping with the Norwegian penchant for nicknames, my mother's sister Rigmor, six years younger, was called Mossik. Unlike Mother, who had brown hair and a dark, mysterious beauty, Mossik was blond and outdoorsy, radiating good health. Much more outgoing than my mother, she showed an interest in me. There were many times I would have been more than happy to have her take my mother's place.

When she was eighteen, Mossik came to Vienna, while my father was being treated for bleeding ulcers. There she met a young American, Bob Burlingham, who was living with his mother, Dorothy, daughter of the artist Louis Comfort Tiffany. Mossik ultimately married Bob, and they had five children.

The other sibling to share that apartment was my mother's youngest brother, Per Svein. He became an English teacher in the local gymnasium, or high school. While never close to my mother, he was curious and eager to share knowledge and tell stories that were a treat for his American nieces and nephews. Per Svein took us on hikes, boat trips, expeditions, and, when we returned to Norway after the war, he was the one who reintroduced me to the country.

In common with the Kennan family, the Sorensens displayed a Northern stoicism and a disapproval of showing undue emotion. I always felt that this self-restraint was a definite drawback and wished that we had been spiced up with a little Spanish or Italian blood. But it is to the Sorensens that I attribute my love of the sea and the visual arts, as well as my lifelong appreciation of cooking and good food. More than anything, I received a strong sense of family and of place, without which I might have been forever searching for roots. In a life of many shifting scenes, Norway remained a constant. My father promised my grandmother before my parents married that they would return to Norway every year. He kept that promise. I still do.

The Kennans

I never had the same sense of place about Milwaukee, my father's birthplace and childhood home, as I had about Norway. What I have learned about my Kennan grandparents has been culled from letters collected by my father's closest sister, Jeanette, who shared his passion for historical research. She ferreted out and saved much correspondence from this family of constant letter writers. Very little went undocumented.

The Kennans were Scots who migrated to Ireland and then to the States. For generations, the Kennan men worked as farmers and ministers, moving slowly westward from Massachusetts, but my great-grandfather changed the pattern and became a lawyer. His son, my grandfather Kossuth Kent Kennan—named after a well-known Hungarian freedom fighter of the time, Lajos Kossuth—was the first Kennan to go to college. The name Kossuth may have seemed a little exotic for midwestern tastes, so he was always called Kent. As the family had little money, Kent struggled to earn his college tuition at Ripon College in Wisconsin. He frequently quit school and worked at odd jobs until he earned enough to continue his studies.

By the time he met my grandmother, Florence James, Kent was already in his forties and had been married to a wife who died during childbirth. He lived a simple life, with no social pretensions. Florence, in contrast, came from a socially prominent family. Her father, Charles James, was president of the Northwestern National Insurance Company. When Kent came courting, Florence's parents deemed him too impecunious and without prospects to be an acceptable suitor. So they dispatched Florence off with her sister, Venice, on a six-month tour of Europe, hoping that the trip and the separation would cause Florence to forget Kent.

In fact, the banishment had the opposite effect. The young couple, with Venice's help, engaged in a courtship by mail, with letters that started out "My Dear Miss James" and "Dear Mr. Kennan" and ended up "My Dear Florence" and "Dear Kent." Secretly engaged by the time Florence returned to Milwaukee, they married in January of 1895 at the home of Florence's

brother. Her parents did not attend. Despite the wedding boy-
cott, the James parents did stay in touch with their daughter
and periodically helped the financially hobbled couple.

When my father, George Kennan, was born in 1904,
Florence had already given birth to three girls, Frances, Constance, and Jeanette. Two months after my father's birth, Florence developed peritonitis and died. I was told that in those
days a married woman needed her husband's consent before
an operation, and they could not reach my grandfather, off
on a fishing trip. The story still gives me the chills. But the
truth was worse. While appendectomies were controversial and
considered dangerous, a husband's permission was not legal-
ly required. In Florence's case, the doctors disagreed on what
should be done for the young mother, so they ended up doing
nothing. Aunt Jeanette told me about being brought in with
her sisters to say a final farewell to their mother. In his book
Sketches from a Life, my father wrote of his mother: "We all held
you, in retrospect, in a sort of awed adoration—our ever-young,
dead mother, beautiful, unworldly, full only of love and grace
for us, like a saint."

The family lived in a tall, narrow dark house on Cambridge
Avenue, given to them by the James grandparents after the
birth of Jeanette and described by her as noted for "its gaunt
exterior and lack of sunshine." It didn't even have a yard. She
speculated that the gloomy house was Florence's punishment
for marrying Kent Kennan. Aunt Jeanette added, "They surely
could have afforded to be more generous."

Florence's death left my widowed grandfather saddled with
responsibility for four young children, so a distant relation of
the James family from Massachusetts, a young woman named
Grace Wells—doomed to spinsterhood because of a slight
hunchback—came to live with the family and took care of the
Kennan children for four years. She was much loved by all, so
much so that I am named for her. I knew that I should be proud

of being named for this good, self-sacrificing woman, but as a child I secretly wished for a more dashing namesake.

In the summers the Kennan family packed up and traveled by train to a cottage on Nagawicka Lake in Waukesha County, on land left to Florence by her family. After dark, cold winters in the narrow town house, those summers with swimming, boating, and berry picking were memorable for the four Kennan children. My father, who became a passionate sailor, named one of his first sailboats *Nagawicka*.

Family life was again disrupted when his father married a Ripon College classics teacher, Sarah Louise Wheeler, from Kalamazoo, Michigan. My father was four. Her arrival meant that the beloved Cousin Grace had to leave. The new stepmother was not warmly welcomed by the four Kennan children. Frances and Connie nicknamed Sarah "the kangaroo from Kalamazoo," and all accounts depict her as unaffectionate and lacking in charm. My grandfather was fifty-seven and his bride thirty-five.

Four years after their marriage, Kent and his new wife took his children to spend a year in Kassel, Germany, so that he could study the German tax code and the children could learn German. The family sailed from New York on the Hamburg America liner the *President Grant*, in August of 1912. This trip had an enormous influence on my father, aged eight at the time, who later talked about the time abroad and the voyage as sparking his interest in foreign languages, foreign cultures, and leading to a lifelong passion for boats and the sea. The trip was cut short, however, when Sarah became pregnant, and the family had to return to Milwaukee. A little boy, Kent Wheeler Kennan, was born in April of 1913.

Back on Cambridge Avenue, the family had little social or community life. In *Memoirs*, my father describes the Kennans as having "an obdurate tight-lipped independence, a reluctance to become involved with other people unless in a church community." The stepmother's personality may have added to their isolation.

The presence of a new baby and the influence of three older sisters contributed to my stern grandfather's desire "to toughen George up," so in 1918 he sent his shy, sensitive son of fourteen to a military school, St. John's Northwestern Military Academy in Delafield, Wisconsin, twenty-five miles from Milwaukee. St. John's was derisively known as "the rich man's reform school." My father hated it so much that he ran away from the school and back to his family, but his father returned him with a stern note saying that he deserved any punishment that the school would mete out. When my father told me this story, I was shocked that my grandfather was so cruel, although my father was rather proud of it. After graduating from St. John's, my father never lived at home again and returned to Milwaukee only for brief family visits. I found a startling description of his hometown in his diary: "A raw, dirty wind sneaked out of the railway yards and the dim alleys, bringing clouds of stinging dirt; and over it all lay the familiar flavor of cheap, sinister sin—of back rooms in saloons, of sailors in bus stations, of the stage doors of burlesque theaters, and of dirty picture cards—the same flavor that hung over it, so repulsively and yet so unsettlingly, when I was a youth arriving and departing from this square on my trips to and from the military academy."

My father's one distinction at St. John's was as the class poet. In his junior year, he read F. Scott Fitzgerald's *This Side of Paradise* and decided that if Princeton University could produce such a talented writer, that was where he wanted to study. No graduate of St. John's had ever gone east to college, so my father was excused from drill for his whole senior year in order to study for the Princeton entrance exams, which he nonetheless failed. Undeterred, he moved to Princeton and spent the summer studying, paying his way by trimming trees. He passed the exams in the fall and enrolled in Princeton. An introverted

and vulnerable boy from the Midwest, he was totally unprepared for Princeton. He had a lonely time there but graduated
in 1925. In his *Memoirs*, my father described himself in college:
"I was hopelessly and crudely Midwestern. I had no idea how
to approach boys from the East. I could never find the casual
tone. My behavior knew only two moods: awkward aloofness
and bubbling enthusiasm."

While his description of his Princeton years is bleak, my
father often exaggerated his bad times. Since he spent the last
fifty years of his life living in Princeton and became a dedicated
alumnus, wearing the Princeton jacket and hat and marching
in Princeton P-rades, it's clear that his years in college acquired
a rosier hue in retrospect.

Meanwhile, the family scattered. Constance and Jeanette
married and left Milwaukee. My father's oldest sister, Frances,
ran away to be an actress in New York and advanced to playing
second leads. She never made it to the top. Instead, she fell in
love with an Alaskan and moved to Juneau. I met Aunt Frances
only once, in 1982, when the four Kennan siblings had a reunion at our family farm in East Berlin, Pennsylvania, and she
was already in her eighties. She had been a heroine to me when
I was a young girl. I admired her independence, her unconven-
tional life, and her love of the theater. When I was finally able
to tell her this, she looked surprised and stunned me by responding: "My dear, my life was not at all like that. We had no
money, and your uncle Harry was the town drunk. I worked as
a librarian to make ends meet, but Uncle Harry imbibed much
of what I earned. You can't imagine how we lived."

I was chagrined by how little I had understood and how I
had romanticized her unhappy life.

After my grandfather's death in 1933, the Cambridge
Street house was sold and Sarah Wheeler Kennan moved
back to Michigan, disappearing from our lives. The Kennan
siblings, however, kept up with Uncle Kent, who became a
well-known composer, musical scholar, and professor at the

University of Texas in Austin. Kent and my father corresponded regularly, but we saw Uncle Kent only episodically, as he lived so far away.

The Kennans often found themselves in financial straits. My father even worked as a mail carrier in Trenton during college to earn money to go home for Christmas. But when the James grandparents died, each Kennan grandchild was left a nice inheritance, so, for the first time, the four Kennan children had money.

When my father met my Norwegian mother in Berlin, he was the dashing bachelor and she referred to him as the "super American" who appeared and courted her in a convertible car.

Years later, my cousin Lillebeth gave me my mother's letters to her parents in Norway, written in Berlin at the time she met my father. Mother was looking after a cousin's child, as well as taking a secretarial course, learning how to write business letters in English, German, and French. Each letter home contained a plea to her father asking for more money. Maybe he kept her on a tight leash as a means of control. When she married my father, she was happy to escape that constraint. I don't think that she married him for money, but there is no question that his comfortable financial situation added a little luster.

Their newfound affluence, however, was short-lived. All the Kennan children, except Aunt Connie, put their money in the care of Aunt Jeanette's husband, Uncle Gene Hotchkiss, a Chicago broker, and it was all lost in the Depression. From then on, my parents lived on a small Foreign Service salary, cut by 50 percent in the Depression years. The loss of income was especially hard on my mother, the household accountant, and I have uncovered long lists of even the minutest expenses, such as "one pair of socks—89 cents," and "one pencil—10 cents." To the end of her days, Mother never bought in bulk and was always concerned about money and financial security.

As a young girl I devoured my father's and Aunt Jeanette's stories of growing up in the narrow dark house, dominated by the grim grandfather and haunted by the ghost of the beautiful young mother—it was almost as good as reading *Jane Eyre*. I also inherited some of the moral strictures passed down by the Kennan family, which often tormented me when I strayed too far from the prescribed path. But, on the positive side, my love of books and of writing certainly came from this family of bookworms.

On the Move Again

The constant dislocations of my early years make that period a blur, with only disconnected memories standing out. In 1940, when our father decided it was too dangerous for us to remain in Berlin, mother took Joanie and me back to Ravinia, Illinois, where she left us in the care of my father's sister Jeanette and her husband, Gene Hotchkiss. Mother then disappeared to rejoin our father in Berlin. My cousin Gene later told me that he and his twin brother, Jim, then twelve-year-olds, resented having two little cousins dumped on their family and having to give up their room in the small house. My aunt Jeanette, however, was the warmest and sunniest of human beings, and if there was a resistance to our presence, we were never aware of it. Quite the contrary. When I was with my parents, a succession of nannies and nurses tended to us, but in Ravinia I felt part of a family. I loved Aunt Jeanette's sparkling eyes and engaging smile and boisterous, jolly Uncle Gene, who came home from his work in Chicago and put on a big show of shaking the ice in a silver martini pitcher. An older son, Frank, lived at home, too, but it was the twins that I worshipped and followed around, much to their annoyance.

Sometimes I wonder about my aunt's having taken us in so uncomplainingly. Maybe Uncle Gene's role in the loss of my father's inheritance explained why my parents felt comfortable dumping two little girls, aged four and eight, on a family living in a crowded house with three adolescent boys. Aunt Jeanette even ran a home nursery school to make ends meet. Joanie became one of her pupils. Aunt Jeanette enrolled me in third grade at Ravinia Elementary School.

Scholastically, I seemed to hold my own, despite the fact that I'd never gone to second grade. When I asked my mother about this strange omission, she answered simply, "It wasn't convenient."

A great plus about living with Aunt Jeanette was reading. I had always loved books, but my mother disapproved of her daughter's preference for reading over helpful chores. She rationed how many books I could take from the library. In Ravinia, however, reading was considered a good thing, and I spent happy hours on the screened porch overlooking the ravine, lost in a book.

During the winter, Mother returned and announced that we were moving to Milwaukee. We went to live with Tekki Brumder—a friend of Mother's from Pine Lake, where the Hotchkisses had their summer cabin—in her large Milwaukee house. I never understood this unexplained move. With no apparent trouble I was enrolled in the prestigious, private Milwaukee Downer Seminary. I suspect that the Brumders, heirs to a beer fortune, had something to do with the ease of my admission, and considering my family's lack of finances, they may also have paid the bill. All the other girls had known one another since first grade, so I was especially scared going into this new class, but I was skipped to fourth grade and felt inordinately proud of this advancement. My letters prove that I loved the school, but today I can't conjure up one teacher or student. About three months later, we were just as abruptly moved back to Aunt Jeanette's. I was put back into third grade, and Mother left again, this time for parts unknown. My feelings of upset and humiliation about this demotion are still clear, as I wrote my parents: "How are you? I am not fine. I'm not happy. I cried all afternoon and part of the night. I want to go back to Milwaukee Downer Seminary. Will you please let me?"

Needless to say, nothing happened.

My father remained in Berlin, and we did not see him for two years. In June of 1941 Mother reappeared, and we spent another memorable summer at Aunt Jeanette and Uncle Gene's rustic cottage in Pine Lake, swimming and sailing. At the end of this idyll, Mother announced we were moving to Bronxville, New York. We took the long train trip from Chicago and settled in a yellow hilltop house on Lookout Avenue. I attended fourth grade in Bronxville Elementary School, again the new girl in my class. Why did my mother choose Bronxville? It was close to Riverdale, New York, where mother's sister, Mossik, lived. Mother claimed that she chose Bronxville because it had a good school system, but how did she, who had never lived in the United States except for visits to Wisconsin and Illinois, hear about the Bronxville school system?

In December came Pearl Harbor. Mother sat us down in the living room and told us that America was at war. As a result, she said our father would probably be imprisoned in Germany. She didn't know when we would see him again. To make things worse, she added that communications had been cut off from our Norwegian relatives, because Norway was occupied by the Germans, now our enemy. There would be no more letters to and from my grandmother. That was the only time I saw my mother cry. She must have felt very alone, separated from both her husband and her parents, and only her sister Mossik nearby. We were too young to be much comfort. I understood, however, that war was serious, and I gave our father, serving his country, some kind of hero status.

My mother soon made friends and went out a lot. She had an admirer, a bachelor named Carl, who came to call and of whom I was very jealous. I think I blamed him for the move to Bronxville. Spending a lot of time in the kitchen with our cook/housekeeper, Betty, I began to resent Mother and at the age of nine decided to run away from home. Several nights were spent amassing the appropriate clothes for this trip—how many pairs of underpants did I need, and how many T-shirts? My heart thumping with fear, I stole $25 from mother's dark-green leather purse. I was going to New York City, but where in the city I was headed and what I planned to do when I got there remains unclear. I walked as far as the railroad station with my small suitcase, but then the realization that I had nowhere to go must have sunk in, and I lost my nerve. Slinking back to Lookout Avenue, an unsuccessful escapee, I managed to replace the money and unpack my suitcase, and my venture into the real world remained undiscovered.

Recently, I found in Mother's papers a year-end report card from Bronxville. I read it avidly, looking for clues about this strange year. Much to my surprise, the report card gave a picture of a poised and capable little girl: "agreeable, friendly, and cooperative . . . a conscientious worker, she gives excellent attention and participates freely in situations such as topical discussions, planning class activities, and contributing ideas to help solve group problems." The funniest part is that my teacher, Mrs. Castor, continues, "She has a good memory and uses it to advantage." Yet I remember so little. Why did my mother keep this report card and no others?

The school year's end brought a note of hope. Daddy was coming home! The American diplomats, who had been interned in an abandoned spa in Bad Nauheim, Germany, were sent home on a Swedish liner, the *Drottningholm*. The same ship had brought the German diplomats, confined at White Sulphur Springs, West Virginia, back to Germany. Mother met the ship, but Joanie and I were not included. When our extremely thin father appeared in Bronxville, we looked with awe at this gaunt man we hadn't see for two years. He brought with him a wave of excitement and joy that had been missing from our lives. Unlike my mother, my father had a way of dramatizing life, which was immensely appealing. We soon acquired a Ford convertible and a cocker spaniel. Suddenly we were a family again. We said good-bye to the yellow house on Lookout

Avenue and moved to Washington, DC. My father, who told us how much he had suffered because he didn't know where we were living during his internment, made exciting plans—we were going to buy a farm and finally have a home that belonged to us.

The Cherry Orchard

Because my father had been absent so much, when he returned from internment in June 1942 it was as if a light had suddenly turned on, and family life was transformed from black-and-white to color. My father became my idol. Handsome and energetic, with an infectious smile, he injected music, art, and literature into my life.

With his sense of drama and attention to detail, my newly recovered parent gathered us together one day and showed us a map of the East Coast, on which, with the help of a compass, he had drawn a hundred-mile circle around Washington, DC. We were going to look for a farm, and it had to be within driving distance of our nation's capital and the State Department. He crossed out Virginia because he didn't like the South, but that left quite a bit of Maryland and a slice of southern Pennsylvania open to us. Taking advantage of a month's postinternment leave of absence, Mother, Daddy, Joanie, and I set forth in our Ford convertible to find a permanent home in the States.

We made short shrift of Maryland because, as soon as we drove over the wide Susquehanna River, heading toward Lancaster, and entered the rolling rich Pennsylvania farm country, my parents decided they had found the right region. During our search, we stayed at a bed-and-breakfast, where the owner taught me how to weave simple Pennsylvania Dutch patterns on her loom. Samples of my handiwork still pop up in various houses in the area. We ate corn on the cob, hamburgers, apple pies à la mode—all perfect for my ten-year-old taste buds. This was the first time we had banded together on a family project.

I loved doing reconnaissance, a passion that has stayed with me to this day.

There were challenges, however. Since my father was going back to work in the State Department and we planned to be only weekend farmers, we needed a property with two houses, one for the farmer and one for us. This was not easy to come by. After three weeks, our parents hadn't seen anything that suited our needs. My weaving was improving, but my father's leave was ending and his enthusiasm considerably dampened, as nothing we looked at seemed to work for us. We were about to give up when Mrs. Bechtel, the realtor, said, "Well, there is the old Miller place. Of course, it's been for sale for three years, and the house is much too big, and he died before it was completed." I could see the interest in my father's eyes. "He has six kids, but none of them want a place like that," she continued. "In fact, none of them have been out there since the old man died. But it is different and it has two houses. And he came from Russia. You might want to look at it."

To call the place "different" was an understatement. Jacob Miller, a Jewish immigrant from Odessa, had come to this country at the age of twelve and worked his way up in classic Horatio Alger style, making a substantial amount of money in the cement business in York, Pennsylvania. But in all those years he never forgot the sight of stately country houses around Odessa. He was determined to reproduce one for himself, however incongruous it would seem in the modest Pennsylvania landscape. So he bought an existing farm and went to work transforming an old farmhouse into the manor house of his dreams.

By the time we saw the farm, the house had grown into a twenty-two-room edifice. The roof had been raised and a third floor added, which included a large room we always called "the ballroom," although we never had a ball. Former verandas were glassed in by Mr. Miller and became sleeping porches. Several of the rooms in the house could be accessed only by traversing someone else's room. My aerie was a glassed-in porch, off a guest room. The only way to get there when guests were in residence was to climb through a window from another small bedroom, which I thought great fun. Fitting with Odessa memories, Mr. Miller installed parquet floors in the first floor, unheard of in rural Pennsylvania. He embellished the front of the house with two Southern plantation-type columns, a wide porch, a concrete rococo facade, and a mezuzah. From the front porch, a curving staircase led down to a circular driveway, where I always imagined horses and carriages pulling up to deposit their charges. A grand allée of Lombardy poplars led up to Mr. Miller's folly. As time went on, the poplars had died, the facade was finally taken down, and the circular driveway had become lawn.

In addition to the main house, there was a farmer's house, a huge cow barn, as well as a tobacco barn and a little stone caretaker's house, which my father surmised had probably been a summer kitchen for the original farm. Mr. Miller had added a six-car garage, the home of several horse-drawn carriages.

On our initial visit I gasped as the real estate agent opened the torn screen door to the main house. The inside looked like a rural antiques shop, uninhabited for years. An auction buff, Mr. Miller indiscriminately bought old furniture, glass, china, paintings, and artistic objects. We could barely walk through the house, as the rooms were so filled with junk that we were sneezing from the dust. I loved it. Much to my surprise, my parents did, too. Soon after my parents' first startled look at the farm, the deed was done. For $14,000, the farm was ours. A nervous, proud owner, my father, who was planning to write a biography of Chekhov at the time, decided to call the farm "the Cherry Orchard," but the name never really stuck, and it became simply "the farm." The nearest small town and our postal address was East Berlin, Pennsylvania, which seemed fitting, as my parents had met in Berlin.

After wagonloads of Mr. Miller's treasures were hauled away, we surveyed our new possession. There was a lot to be done. In the beginning (and I realize now that my parents were only in their thirties), the projects were big remodeling efforts, which were gratifying because they showed results. Walls were knocked down, tiny rooms combined to create bigger spaces; a false fireplace was replaced by an attractive, functioning brick one. The Miller clutter that remained was gradually moved up to the third floor and relegated to two unfinished porches, which were now crammed with old paintings, cribs, sleds, discarded dolls, old suitcases with exotic labels, and ornate lamps. The porches were great troves for rainy-day treasure hunts. I delighted in the endless discoveries in our new home.

I reveled in the fact that for the first time we had our father to ourselves. Always a storyteller, he invented tales in which the farm animals were characters with voices and personalities. He dramatized their interactions. Maybe in keeping with the animal theme, he also read us *Winnie-the-Pooh*. He acted out plots from literature, particularly from his favorite author, Chekhov. My favorite story was of the man whose job was to trail the horses in the circus, picking up their dung, and who therefore thought he was important.

My father loved organizing projects, and I loved participating. First he made a plan, then we gathered the materials, and finally we embarked on whatever the undertaking was. At the farm we planted five hundred trees. My father also built a toolshed, with all his work tools carefully arranged and displayed. Just sitting around was impossible for our father. He had to be constantly busy. If he wasn't preoccupied with intellectual activity—where his output was prodigious—he was equally productive building, chopping wood, laying paths, or cleaning out his workroom. Since he didn't play tennis or golf, these physical projects substituted and kept him healthy.

He was very musical and played Russian folk songs on the guitar at night, serenading us with favorites such as "Dark

Eyes," "Kalinka," and gypsy melodies. I was disappointed later when he gave up such songs, which he played by ear, and decided to learn to read music. He then spent hours practicing exercises and elementary pieces on the classical guitar and later the piano. But that was typical of him, never satisfied to rest on his achievements.

Joanie and I mostly lived outside. We invented trips in the carriages left by Mr. Miller; helped Merle, the tenant farmer, milk the cows; rode the farm pony; played hide-and-go-seek in the pungent dusty hay barn; explored the tobacco barn, also full of Miller finds; and climbed up to the top of the silo, with its intoxicating smell of fermented hay. We loved naming the stray cats that were always having kittens. But our early farm period did not last long, as in September 1942 my father received a new assignment, to the American legation in Portugal. My parents and Joanie flew off to Lisbon on a clipper-ship airplane, while I was dispatched to boarding school in Washington, DC.

Walking the Parapets

My parents told me that they were permitted to take only one child on the Lisbon assignment, and because Joan was six and considered "frail," she was the logical choice. They arranged for me, age ten, to live at the National Cathedral School for Girls, in Washington, DC, adjacent to the National Cathedral, which had a small boarding department. I arrived with two distinctions: I was the youngest boarder, and I was the only student with married parents. The other eleven middle school boarders were all children of divorce, and many were clearly suffering the effects.

The daily schedule for this small group of misfits was designed by someone who clearly had forgotten childhood. We started the day with breakfast and chapel, then went to school from 8:30 a.m. to 3:00 p.m. After forty-five minutes of "free time," we had to be back in our rooms by 3:45, getting ready for our first study hall, followed by baths, piano practice, dinner, chapel, and more study hall until bedtime. Needless to say, given so much studying, we all received splendid grades.

Except for an escorted trip to the local drugstore each weekend, we were not allowed off the cathedral grounds. Our main contact with the "outside" was the view from our third-floor windows onto the cars and passersby moving along Wisconsin Avenue. We amused ourselves by playing hide-and-go-seek among the crypts in the cathedral basement on nasty days or in the cathedral herb garden in good weather. For real excitement we would scare ourselves by climbing into the cathedral dome. Fortunately, no one paid any attention to this unsupervised play, and we were allowed to cavort as we wished.

My start at school did not bode well. In the various countries where I had lived, someone always took care of my laundry. I never really considered how my clothes remained clean and pressed. At National Cathedral, there must have been a system for our laundry, but no one thought to advise me of it and, shy and somewhat confused in my new setting, I never thought to ask.

When clothes got visibly soiled, I simply stuffed them under the bed. Finally, the day came when I had no more clean clothes. Incapable of discussing the problem, I stood, embarrassed and silent, when a teacher came up to inspect my room. I prayed that she wouldn't look under the bed, but of course she did, and the dirty clothes were pulled out, one by one. Other teachers were even called in to witness this unusual sight, but beyond the humiliation there was no punishment. Somehow, it probably didn't fit anywhere into the school's lengthy list of rule violations. If it had, I would have suffered the primary penalty— banishment from the next weekend trip to the drugstore.

For the Christmas holidays that year I was sent off to Cousin Grace, the distant James relation for whom I was named. By 1942, Cousin Grace was working as a paid companion to a woman whom I was told to call Cousin Bess, although she was no relation. Cousin Bess was a rich lady who lived in a big old-fashioned house in South Orange, New Jersey. She was chauffeured around the countryside in a long black car. During my visit, I accompanied Cousin Grace and Cousin Bess on those rides, stuck between the two old ladies, a blanket tucked solicitously around us by Arthur, the driver. I felt claustrophobic in that backseat and prayed that no one my age would ever see me.

It was a horrible Christmas. The holiday had always been a high point for my family, but the "cousins" seemed very old to me, and there were no children around with whom to play.

Instead of the big tree that I was used to, there was a very small token spruce. The old ladies towered over it. On Christmas morning I gave my present, an herb sachet, to Cousin Bess, who responded by slapping me in the face. What had I done? I will never know. Later I was told she was crazy, but nobody volunteered such information at the time. I went up to the attic and made myself a calendar, on which I crossed off the days until I could return to boarding school.

Skulking in that attic, I discovered a library of children's books, and I spent much of my time up there reading. I read my way through *Anne of Green Gables,* all the *Katy Did* books, and other Victorian classics. Truth is, I was scared to be downstairs with Cousin Bess. She marched around the house in square patterns and ate that way, as well. Up would come the spoon from the table until it was parallel with her lips, then it would make a ninety-degree turn and follow an imaginary horizontal track into her mouth. She complained loudly about any food she didn't like, and the offending dish was immediately removed. A maid named Bertha scuttled back and forth between the kitchen and dining room in a black dress and white apron, carrying the rejected meal.

Back at National Cathedral, the combination of so little play and almost no exercise made the boarders very restless. I was never ready to go to sleep at night. Normally a goody-goody who was acutely uncomfortable when breaking rules, I would climb up onto a small space on top of the closet after lights out and read by the trickle of light that came through the transom. When particularly restless, I would go out my window and fearlessly edge along on the wide rain gutter thirty feet above the ground, peering into other girls' windows. One night when the vice-principal came to say good night to me—a dubious treat awarded me for being the youngest girl in the school—she almost fainted with shock at seeing my face pressed against the outside of the third-floor windowpane, looking in. After that my windows were nailed shut, and I was hermetically sealed inside for the rest of the year.

In June of 1943, my father arrived back in the United States on consultation and came to retrieve me. I hadn't seen or had contact with my parents all year. His first words were, "My God, she's yellow." Tests revealed that I was anemic, so I left the school, flushed with pride at this tangible proof of the school's mismanagement and also with secret pleasure that I, too, was finally frail. I was also thrilled that I was going to join the rest of the family in Portugal.

CHAPTER 2

The Second World War in Europe

Dear Aunt Connie,

We are still living at the quinta. I am still studying Portuguese and
French. I am also studying geometry. I have quite a few books but
there is no library. I often wish that the White Plains library was
here in Portugal.

Your loving niece, Grace Kennan

In the humid heat of summer in Newport News, Virginia, my
father and I boarded a Portuguese steamer, the *Pinto Basto*, and
crossed the dangerous Atlantic in June of 1943. Since Portugal
was neutral, its ships were not German targets, but there was
a real danger of accidental submarine attacks. My father later
told me that he was convinced that every day would be our last,
that we would be blown up by a German submarine and were
indeed on a "Ship of Fools." He disapproved of the hordes of
unruly, unsupervised English refugee children being repa-
triated, scampering unchecked all over our ship, much to my
admiration and envy. Instead, Daddy and I holed up in our
cabin, where he spent every day reading aloud to me in order
to rid me of what he called the "horrible nasal accent" acquired
at National Cathedral School. While I missed playing with the
other children, I loved listening to my father, as he played the
parts of the characters in the novels, dialects and all. I had never had so much time with him before. As the ship plowed across
the ocean, he read aloud plays by Shakespeare, all of *Treasure*

Island, and polished off *Jane Eyre* just before we landed in Lisbon. I was happy to be released from the confines of the National Cathedral School for Girls but had little idea what lay ahead.

When the ship pulled into the Lisbon harbor, we were both surprised to see, instead of our family, a somber delegation of men, decorated with black armbands, waiting at the dock. The chargé d'affaires—acting head—of the American legation had died while we were at sea, and my young father was now unexpectedly in charge. The legation officers, at that time all men, comprised the black-armband delegation. The next surprise came when my parents, who had an apartment in Lisbon, announced that they, together with an English couple named Coney and Ralph Jarvis, had rented a country villa with the romantic name of the Quinta do Rio de Milho. It was located up in the mountains near Sintra, a forty-five-minute drive from Lisbon. We children were to live at the quinta while our parents would stay in the Lisbon apartment, visiting us on weekends. They tried to sugarcoat this pill by telling us that Joanie and I were very lucky—that living in the healthy hilly air of Sintra would spare us from the heat of Lisbon. I was disappointed, as I had so looked forward to being a family again. My sister and I were going to share the villa with little Antony and Caroline Jarvis, ages six and eight, and be cared for by an English governess named Lucille Armstrong. Her last name said it all.

Nestled on top of a hill, our walled-in quinta was an earthly paradise. The buildings were enclosed by gardens redolent of orange and magnolia trees, camellia bushes, gardenias, and wild geraniums. Something was always in bloom. As the quinta was located on the site of an ancient Roman reservoir system, one of the basins became our swimming pool. In balmy Portuguese weather, the gardens served as a huge playground, perfect for hide-and-go-seek.

The villa came with two maids and a cook, Maria. While the house oozed charm, it lacked electricity, so every day the two maids gathered up all the oil lamps that served as illumination in the evening and cleaned them up for the next night. We children loved to sneak into the forbidden kitchen, with its delectable smells, until we were shooed out by Maria, who was busy holding court with a stream of purveyors bringing fruits, vegetables, and bread up the hill on the backs of their donkeys. It was all lovely, but life wasn't totally idyllic.

The quinta consisted of two houses. Rumor had it that the main house had been built by a bishop for his mistress and contained a secret upstairs room accessible only through a window, which we could see. The second house was adjoined to the main house by a staircase ascending to a second-floor chapel, barred from us because we weren't Catholic. My bedroom, the only one in the second building, was next to the locked chapel, which was frequented by rats. They terrified me. I was convinced that they would find a way into my room through my closet and spent many a sleepless night awaiting the rodent invasion. The flickering light of the oil lamp that I carried upstairs to bed did nothing to quell my fears.

Eleven at the time, full bosomed and tall, I was much older than Joanie, Caroline, and Antony. I ached for friends of my own age and desperately wanted to be in a real school. My misery was compounded by the fact that there was an English school nearby, but my parents refused to send me, saying, "You will get a much better education with Lucille."

Lucille, as we were told to call her, was the poisonous snake in our Garden of Eden. She and her husband had run a school in France, but his death and wartime circumstances had pushed her into teaching our small group of four, augmented in the schoolroom by two other young English boys, from a neighboring quinta, and Lucille's timid little son, Christian. On Tuesdays we had to speak French all day, on Thursdays, Portuguese. We got around it by saying in English, "Lucille, how do I tell Caroline in Portuguese that I will meet her by the big magnolia tree after lunch?" but it still put a damper on conversation. In arithmetic, we spent a lot of time learning to add, subtract, multiply, and divide pounds, shillings, and pence—a particularly useless skill for Joanie and me, the two Americans.

Lucille decreed that activities be competitive. The only one of our games that I remember winning was the obstacle course, which was probably fitting. We had art competitions and botany competitions—who could pick and identify the most wildflowers in an hour? As I was so much older, I was always given a handicap, and Lucille established the handicaps. No matter how hard I struggled, I rarely won.

Another favorite activity of Lucille's was folk dancing. Joanie, Caroline, Antony, and I were all outfitted with Portuguese folk costumes, and Lucille taught us local dances. At least two feet taller than Antony, my six-year-old partner, I towered over the group. As if this wasn't bad enough, we had to perform in local orphanages. I squirmed with embarrassment at each performance and wondered what the orphans thought about being forced to watch this mismatched quartet of American and English children performing Portuguese dances. In fact, my letters to Aunt Connie indicated that these performances were quite ambitious. "We are going to give a show for about a hundred people. We are doing dances and after that two little French plays and one English one. After that we are doing the tableau. I am Joseph."

Poor Grace and poor orphans.

In our free time, Joanie and Caroline took their dolls into the gardens and made up endless games with them. Feeling much too old for this, I read. I read a lot of Dickens and all of Jane Austen that year. Physically I was in an Iberian paradise, but mentally I lived in cold, foggy England.

On weekends, our two sets of parents would arrive in a convoy of cars, usually with friends, for lively house parties, and Lucille's influence waned. Listening to the adults talk, I sensed something of the glamour and intrigue of wartime Lisbon. My mother was the most beautiful of all the women. I have a vivid image of her in a white dress with a square décolleté neckline, a white magnolia in her hair, leaning out of her second-floor bedroom window, smiling and talking to some guests on the patio. She would sunbathe nude by our secluded swimming pool, much to my mortification. Still, I admired her and longed for her the way one longs for the impossible. I don't remember ever really talking to her that year—she seemed faraway and inaccessible to my gawky, self-conscious, eleven-year-old self. My father was often away, but my feelings about him were clear. In the diary I kept that year is an entry in caps that says it all: "DADDY IS COMING! HIP HIP HURRAY! HIP HIP HURRAY!"

Occasionally the outside world and the war impinged on our self-contained little universe. One day, there was great excitement when two French boys named Jean and Pierre, aged eight and ten, thin and bright-eyed, appeared at the quinta. Much to my surprise, I learned they had come alone from France across Spain and that they had mostly walked, being escorted from place to place and smuggled over the borders. They were very shy and spoke only French.

Despite French-speaking Tuesdays, my French remained somewhat rudimentary, so we couldn't converse very well. Only later did I learn that they were Jewish and were on their way to some relatives in England. As mysteriously as they had appeared, they disappeared, and I never learned what happened to them. It was the first time I became aware that the war was about more than battles between soldiers.

One day my father, with his customary dramatic flair, told me that a very famous actor and actress were coming for lunch with my parents. In fact, Daddy added, they might even be the most famous acting couple in America. I would be allowed to greet them and shake hands.

Incredibly excited at meeting this glittering couple, I expected Romeo and Juliet to appear at the door. What a disappointment when the door opened and in walked an ordinary-looking middle-aged couple named Alfred Lunt and Lynn Fontanne. How could this plain couple be so famous? Although my parents both loved the theater, they did not consort with actors, so I assume the fact that Alfred Lunt was from Milwaukee, Wisconsin, may have had something to do with this visit. Such disenchantment.

That year, I learned my first official secret. My father took me aside to say that for the next few days we would see strange men coming in and out of the quinta and that I was to pay no attention and under no circumstances to tell anyone. I watched quietly as men with briefcases, speaking a language I didn't know, entered the residence and huddled in the living room, which was off-limits to us children, anyway. Afterward, Daddy confided to me that the visitors were Italians on a secret mission, beginning negotiations for what would become the Italian Peace Treaty. He never explained who chose the quinta as a place for these historic meetings.

In the middle of 1943 my father was deployed to London as political adviser to the U.S. ambassador. Although I have the letter he wrote, begging her not to come, my mother decided to follow him, leaving us in the hands of Lucille, who now had total control. Sadistically, Lucille described the bombing that was going on in London and warned that my parents had a good chance of being killed in the shelling. She pointed out that if that happened we would be left orphans. Dickens began to seem more and more real. Lucille also informed me about the facts of life. She introduced menstruation with a cautionary tale about a young girl who had ice-skated when she had her period and then died. I found this very alarming but never did dare bring it up with my mother for verification. I ice-skated very cautiously, however.

Years later I found a letter sent to my parents in London from Lucille at the quinta. She reported that all was well, except for Grace. "She is very affectionate and tries to hug me all the time, but I have cured her of that." How she cured me I don't remember. But I also found a little pocket diary with a key in which I sporadically made entries. "I hate Lucille. I hate Lucille. I hate Lucille!" was one, for instance. When Daddy told us that we were moving to Moscow, as he had been transferred to the embassy there, I was glad.

The Long Way to Moscow

Dear Aunt Connie,

We are going to Russia on the 21st of August . . . going from here to Casablanca, then to Algiers and then to Cairo. Just think, we will see the pyramids! After that we will go to Baghdad (I wish I had read *The Arabian Nights*) and then Teheran.

Love, Grace

In the summer of 1944, Father was assigned to Moscow as deputy chief of mission, or second-in-command, under Ambassador Averell Harriman. Our father flew to Moscow ahead of us.

Because spouses and dependents were not allowed in wartime Moscow, the State Department was in a quandary about what to do with our family, stranded in Portugal. Finally we were permitted to travel to the Soviet Union by a circuitous route, with stopovers in Casablanca, Oran, Algiers, Tunis, Cairo, Baghdad, Teheran, Baku, and Astrakhan. The African part of this journey necessitated twelve inoculations—a nightmare for an eleven- and a seven-year-old. To assuage our fear, the kind Portuguese doctor gave us a baby chicken at each visit, but since the poultry couldn't travel, that was small consolation.

The U.S. Air Force arranged our trip across North Africa. At our first stop, Casablanca, we were housed at an air base, where we stayed in a tent with mosquito netting over the beds.

Initially I enjoyed the coziness of the netting, but after a while I felt enmeshed and imprisoned. Mother told us that we could not unpack, as our departure times were a military secret, so we slept with bags ready at our side.

We were awakened in the middle of the night by a man's voice at the door, informing us that we would be picked up in thirty minutes. Sleepy and hungry, the three of us stood outside with our bags in the cool, starry African night until a military escort in a jeep picked us up and drove us out to a camouflaged C-47 twin-engine plane waiting on the tarmac. The planes were outfitted for cargo, so we passengers sat around the edges in a large circle facing a pile of military equipment including jeeps and crates. Each window was blacked out with camouflage paint and had a rubber stopper in the middle, which we could unplug to breathe fresh air while we were waiting on the ground.

Our fellow passengers, all male military personnel, were astonished to find this family of females in their midst. The friendly young soldiers gave Joanie and me candy and chewing gum and tweaked my braids, saying, "Oh, you look just like my sister Janet in Winnetka." Starved for attention, I responded by becoming the social emissary of our group, chatting happily with the soldiers, while my more reserved mother looked on in surprise. Later we were told that we were the first civilian females to fly across North Africa during the war, but I've never confirmed whether or not that was true.

Stopovers in Oran, Tunis, and Algiers were similar to those in Casablanca, but in Cairo we left the U.S. Air Force and moved to the glamorous Shepheard Hotel. An embassy representative took us out to see the pyramids and the Great Sphinx. I was very excited to see these ancient monuments, which I had read about in my schoolbooks. Our embassy escort supplied us with three camels, so large that they looked enormous even when kneeling. My breath stuck in my throat at the thought of mounting this animal. Mother, elegant and calm, was already astride her camel. Being afraid was discouraged in my family. "I can't get up," I stammered, unable to verbalize my fear. After a brief delay, a small donkey was substituted and I ended up ignominiously bringing up the rear of our caravan, which somewhat diminished the pleasure of seeing the pyramids.

From Cairo we flew to Baghdad, but my memories of the land of Arabian nights are dim. The planes flew low and the air was bumpy, and the soldiers were bent over, using their vomit bags. From there we proceeded to Teheran. I was fascinated to see the dirty town water running in culverts on the sides of the street and then drawn from the street into the houses. At the embassy house where we were lodged, I was sternly warned that even a drop of this polluted water could make me deathly ill, and so taking a bath was very scary. What would happen if I accidentally swallowed a sip? Was this slight ache in my stomach because I hadn't closed my lips tightly enough in the bathtub?

After Teheran, our next stop was Baku, its sea of constantly pumping oil wells looking like mechanical birds bobbing up and down, pecking at their food. It was a very curious sight. I had read about oil but had no idea that oil welled up from the ground. One smelled the oil fumes everywhere, so I was happy to leave. In Baku we transferred to a Soviet Aeroflot plane to fly to Astrakhan. Inside the cabin were only a few safety belts and a spare gas tank, on top of which two men sat nonchalantly smoking. My mother watched them in astonishment. She called the stewardess and in broken Russian pointed and complained about the smokers. The stewardess shrugged. "It's normal," she said. It was one of the few times I saw my usually stoic mother upset, and the story became part of our family lore. From Astrakhan we finally flew to Moscow. The airplane trip from Lisbon had taken thirteen days.

Our final landing was in a totally different world. After the picturesque quinta of Portugal, with its flowers, gardens, oil lamps, and donkeys, we found ourselves in a large gray city with wide boulevards designed to accommodate the thousands of soldiers and citizens who paraded regularly into Red Square.

The broad avenues also allowed the cold wind to whistle down the streets. Our father was there to welcome us into the same small apartment at the American embassy, directly facing the Kremlin, where I had lived as a little girl. As the Kennan family was the exception to the rule that dependents were not allowed in wartime Moscow, Joanie and I were the only children living in our embassy and among the few children in the whole diplomatic corps, so we had no playmates. We had lived in different houses in Portugal but now shared a small room at the back of the apartment, where we quarreled a lot. Eventually we drew a line down the center of the room to clearly define our separate turfs.

There was little in the way of normal entertainment for a twelve-year-old. My father worked long hours and was rarely home. My parents compensated for this deprivation by taking me to the theater. They were both theater buffs. Earlier in the war, when there was fear that the Germans would occupy Moscow, all the diplomats and the performers had been evacuated to Kuibyshev. By 1944, actors and dancers were back in Moscow and the theaters had reopened, playing to full houses as part of a campaign to maintain the morale of the population. In a letter to Aunt Connie, I mention having seen *La Traviata*, the *Fountain of Bakhchisarai*, and an operetta, *Mademoiselle Nitouche*, a comedy about a girl in a French boarding school, which was strange fare for such hard times.

I loved going, all dressed up, with my parents to the Bolshoi Theatre. Sitting in the prerevolutionary splendor of the opera house, listening to the first sensuous bars of each overture, usually Tchaikovsky, sent shivers up my spine. My favorite ballet was *Swan Lake*. I was transported into the land of swans, handsome princes, and always-beautiful ballerinas. In those days, before television, the ballet was the leading entertainment for older children in Moscow. Young girls wore their ponytails tied with large bows, and young men were dressed in their best outfits, hair neatly brushed, to go to the Bolshoi.

In the long intermissions, we promenaded politely around the wide hall, sneaking looks at one another.

At that time there were three leading ballerinas: Galina Ulanova, Olga Lepeshinskaya, and Marina Semyonova.

Competition between them was as intense as a World Series rivalry. After each performance, audience members would passionately debate the minutest differences in interpretation. My father was a devoted Ulanova fan, but I adored Semyonova. This was one of the first times that I disagreed with my father, but I was scared to argue with him, as I felt that my father was always right. Instead, I kept my opinion to myself and just dreamed about Semyonova in secret.

The Red Schoolhouse

Dear Aunt Connie,

I am going to a Russian school now. As the Russians do not have enough schools for all their children, they go in two shifts. I am in the second shift, which goes from two o'clock to seven or eight o'clock. They have no sports at all. They teach German, which is very easy for me. Daddy is reading "War and Peace" out loud for me and I like it very much.

Love, Grace

Arriving in dark, solemn Moscow from warm, sunny Portugal in the summer of 1944, we found ourselves in the middle of the war. Nonetheless, in our small apartment in the American embassy on Mokhovaya Square, we had the services of a cook named Klavdia and a maid named Tanya. My mother occupied herself with things other than housework. She had frequent massages, and the masseuse would arrive, go into Mother's bedroom, and close the door firmly behind her. I would sit and stare at the portal, feeling excluded, curious, and jealous about what went on inside the room. Mother was often out, although I had no idea where she went.

Sheltered in the embassy, we had access to a commissary stocked with canned goods as well as powdered eggs and powdered milk. Other than cabbage, potatoes, and onions, for which Klavdia scoured the markets, there were no fresh fruits or vegetables, and there were no dairy products. When my parents occasionally were invited to Kremlin receptions, mandarin oranges, apples, and grapes flown in from Soviet Georgia were offered, and Mother would come back triumphant, her purse stuffed with delectables that she had filched. While I loved the fruit, the puritanical side of me felt uncomfortable because I worried that my mother was stealing.

The big problem in Moscow was where to send us to school. My parents decided that my sister, Joanie, who was still considered frail, should not go to a Russian school, so they ordered a correspondence course for her from the Calvert School, which was often used by diplomats.

Mother, unfortunately, mistakenly ordered fourth grade, while Joanie was only in third. Mother spent mornings teaching Joanie from the shiny correspondence books, but after a while she gave up and delegated much of the teaching to me. At age twelve, I was ill-equipped to homeschool. The worst was trying to teach arithmetic to Joanie, since the material was too advanced for her. Every morning we struggled, and most lessons ended up in tears of frustration from Joanie and anger and exasperation from me. These lessons didn't do much for our relationship.

Although I had forgotten my childhood Russian, my father decided to enroll me in the closest public secondary school, six long blocks from the embassy. In theory he was going to help by giving me Russian lessons, but his busy schedule as deputy to the workaholic Ambassador Harriman precluded that. The first day, my father and I walked to the school up vast Gorky Street. The director initially refused to admit me. But after arguing back and forth, my father reminded her of the law stating that all children of school age were entitled to free education at the nearest school. Moments later I became a member of the fifth class, a rough equivalent to seventh grade at home.

My first day of school, I was marched into my classroom by the principal. A flock of girls stood up as we entered the room. Since I hardly remembered a word of Russian, I had no idea what she said but gathered I was introduced to our homeroom teacher, Nina Yakovlevna, and to the class at large. It was a great relief when I was shown to my desk at the back of the room, where the girls couldn't stare at me without turning around.

As the Soviet Union was going through a short-lived experiment in single-sex education at that time, School Number 131 was a girls' school, located in a two-story prerevolutionary building bisected by a large central hall that doubled as an assembly room and recess area. We congregated in this hall for political meetings, to hear about and cheer the latest Soviet military victory or to receive the latest pronouncement from Comrade Stalin. We also met there in the afternoon for a cup of hot tea with a lump of ersatz sugar. I had written Aunt Connie that there was a shortage of schools, but, in fact, a wartime teacher shortage mandated that schools operate in two shifts.

I dreaded the smell of unwashed bodies and stale air that assailed me every time I entered the school building from our airy apartment. The windows were sealed shut against the cold, and no fresh air entered the building from October to May. Due to a severe housing shortage in Moscow at that time, most people were crammed into communal apartments, with several families sharing a bathroom. The serge school uniforms, worn day in and day out, were rarely washed. My seatmate, Galya, told me that she was taken to the public baths once a week, obviously a major event. As the day wore on, I would adjust to the smell, but entering the school was always a shock. The bathroom, with no toilet seats, toilet paper, or inner doors, was so frightening that I never went there again after my first visit. Later I learned that the Russian girls called me "the Camel" and wondered if Americans had some sort of biological secret.

All the Russian girls were dressed in black or brown dresses with black pinafores, but Mother insisted on outfitting me in American clothes—bright colors, plaid pleated skirts, and matching sweaters. I stood out like a peacock in a cluster of gray hens. On one of my first days, during a recess in the big wide hall, a group of classmates surrounded me and lifted up my skirts to see what kind of underwear I wore. I felt the blood rush to my face and a cloud of shame as everyone stared at my foreign underpants. I never mentioned the humiliating experience to my parents.

I was the only foreigner in the school, other than the daughter of a prominent Chinese Communist. All the desks were two-seaters, and back in the far reaches of the classroom, I shared a bench and writing area with Galya. I sat there five hours a day, struggling to make some sense out this incomprehensible language. I spent a lot of time looking out the window. In the fall I looked at the trees, and in the winter I watched icicles forming both on the outside *and* inside of our windows. None of the teachers knew English. Since I didn't know Russian, I couldn't be called on, or spoken to, so I felt safe. Sometimes I counted the minutes until school would end, but then I had to make my way down cold, dark Gorky Street, as the afternoon shift ended between seven and eight at night. One night a man followed me and tried to jump on me, but I managed to run away. When I told my parents about the encounter, they had me picked up by an embassy car every day until the winter ended, only underscoring my special status.

Monthly, the school received a lice-inspection visit from the dreaded official from the Ministry of Health. The inspector, a large woman encased in a dark-gray suit and white blouse, would arrive with a big black comb that she would run through everyone's hair. When she found lice, there would be tears from the poor victim, who would be sent home to have her head shaved, returning to school completely bald. The rest of us watched in silence, relieved at having been spared. One evening while reading at home, I casually pulled a little insect out of my hair. My horrified mother sprang into action, and the U.S. Army doctor was summoned from his dinner to find an embarrassed young girl standing on a pile of newspapers in a corner. Luckily, army lice powder did the trick, but from then on I was scared to death at the prospect of a recurrence. What if it happened in school? As usual, I felt ambivalent—guilty that I had enjoyed special treatment, and secretly grateful that I didn't have to share my schoolmates' hardships.

Everyone in my class was a member of the Young Pioneers, a quasi-military Communist scout organization, and most students wore their red scarves, the badge of membership. The Pioneers served much the same function as our Girl Scouts and Boy Scouts but included more political education. Galya told me that to belong you had to state that you didn't believe in God. Although my family wasn't very religious, I couldn't imagine doing that, so I didn't join. When the Pioneers held a meeting, I was asked to leave the building and wait outside in the street, often in the snow, my outsider status reconfirmed. In theory, it was not compulsory to join the Pioneers, but I was the only girl in my class who was not a member. The big attraction of being a Pioneer was admission to the beautiful Pioneer centers, usually located in prerevolutionary palaces, where club meetings, special classes, as well as concerts and other entertainments took place. Mother and I went as guests to a New Year's party, where I attended a concert with clowns and dancers, all presided over by Dyed Moroz, or Grandfather Frost. I was a little sorry I hadn't joined.

Teaching was all by rote. That year we studied Russian language and literature, ancient history, arithmetic, German, geography, botany, and military science. The principal apologized that the only language teacher left was German. Military science consisted of a class where a tired old war veteran showed fifty giggling girls how to assemble and take apart a gas mask and a rifle. Unfortunately, he had only one of each, so the forty-eight students who were not working on the gas mask or rifle amused themselves by either talking to one another or throwing paper airplanes the minute his back was turned. I was astonished by this lack of discipline in such a regimented system.

My class was also enrolled in the Young Russian Women's Army and occasionally went out marching in the street. We liked the release from school, but what threat we were to the Germans, I couldn't imagine.

My favorite classes were geography, math, and Russian literature, maybe because they were less subject to propaganda. Even in math we were asked to calculate the days between Lenin's and Stalin's birthdays.

After about three months, I was sitting in geography class one day when I realized that I understood most of what Nina Yakovlevna was saying. I started to speak and ceased being invisible. I even was called on, although, unlike the other students, I was told a day ahead so that I could prepare. By now I understood from Galya, the oldest of three children, that she lived in a communal apartment where her mother lay terminally ill with cancer. Her father was at the front and had not been heard from in months. When her mother died late in that year, Galya found herself struggling at age twelve to take care of her family. One day when she was called on, she was unprepared and stood there mute. She couldn't recite the lesson. The teacher railed at her. "How can you, a Soviet citizen, not do your homework, while this foreigner takes the trouble to study her textbook?" It was not fair, and we all knew it. I felt ashamed.

As the United States and the Soviet Union were allies during the war, it was all right for me to make friends with my classmates, but that did not extend to going to their apartments. However, I had a sophisticated friend named Ira, whose father was the director of the orchestra at the Stanislavsky Theatre, and she and I were allowed to attend dress rehearsals, a thrill for my stagestruck self. Forty years later I learned that Ira had publicly denounced me as an "American spy" after I left the country. My closest friend, though, was a girl named Valya, short for Valentina. Valya and I spent much time together in school and I invited her to our apartment a few times, where she was a big hit with my parents. Many years after this I met her again, but that is a story for later.

Eager to show my father that I was now understanding my lessons, I came home one day and told him, "Guess what, Daddy? We are learning all about the admirable Spartans, who died for their country, and the corrupt, decadent Athenians, who had slaves." I definitely got my father's attention. After that I received two history lessons—one at school, and a revised version at home, where I learned more about Plato and the more-civilized attributes of those Athenian slave owners. To be sent to school to learn and then to be told that what I was learning wasn't true was confusing, to say the least. Why couldn't I go to a school where they told the truth?

Nine months after we arrived in Moscow, on May 9, 1945, martial music and dramatic announcements blared from the omnipresent loudspeakers on every street, announcing that the war had officially ended. While this was news to the entire population, it wasn't news to me. The previous morning at the breakfast table, my father had shared with us the momentous news that the German high command had surrendered unconditionally to the Allies. The fighting was to stop at precisely 11:01 a.m. the next day. "Grace, you mustn't breathe a word about this outside our home," my father warned. "Stalin hasn't officially announced it yet to the country." I went to school that afternoon especially proud that I had been trusted with such an important secret—even bigger than the secret I had kept at the quinta. I ached to tell Galya, whose life had been made so miserable by the war. But I kept my mouth shut and tried to envisage how everyone would react to the news when it was finally announced.

May 9 was declared a holiday. Mother, nevertheless, who

believed that fresh air and routine were more important than special occasions, sent Joanie and me off to play in the garden at Spaso House, the official residence of Ambassador Harriman, as we often did. A few hours later, the driver picked us up to bring us home. As we neared our apartment, a throng of cheering Russians, sharing their joy with their American allies, blocked the car. Instead of stopping, the driver proceeded to drive straight into the crowd, albeit very slowly, with celebrants moving out of the way in the nick of time. Faces were plastered at all the car windows, staring at Joanie and me in the backseat of the black Cadillac. I was terrified that we might run over someone, while at the same time I was embarrassed at being the object of such public interest. There was nowhere to hide. My father came out and stood on a wall outside the embassy and made a few remarks to the crowd, which I've seen quoted in many history books, though through the din I couldn't hear them that day.

The scariest part of the school year was final exams. With the exception of a written test in arithmetic, all exams were oral. When the dreaded exam days came, our classroom was festooned in bright orange satin, with a new and larger photograph of Stalin looking down on us. A board of three outside examiners, unknown to us, sat in a rigid row under his portrait. In front of the triad was a glass bowl filled with little pieces of paper, each with the title of a chapter from our textbook. When called on, a pupil had to pick out a paper from the bowl and then recite that chapter—not just a sentence or two, but ideally paragraph by paragraph. I sat with cold, clammy hands and tight stomach muscles, waiting my turn with the other terrified pupils. But when my turn came, somehow I managed. After our recitation, the marks were entered by hand into our school notebooks. I can still feel the pride at getting fours and fives, five being the highest mark.

On the last day of school, we gathered in our classroom, the exam tension over. We all stood up as the principal came in. "Sit down, girls," she ordered. "I've brought Grace Kennan's notebook, and she can leave now." With no chance to say good-bye to my friends, I was ushered out. In a tearful phone call from Valya, I learned that the class was being sent for a couple of weeks to a collective farm to harvest potatoes. Galya and her siblings were being sent to an orphanage. As usual, I had special status; I didn't have to pick potatoes, but I was torn away from my new friends. I had learned from my mother, however, that we were going to Norway for the summer, and the anticipation of that reunion compensated for being summarily dismissed from school.

Overboard

Floating in the wake of the ship were my pink underpants, white undershirts, a blue-and-pink shirred dimity dress, a hand-embroidered blouse—splayed out for all to see. It was July 1945. I was headed for New York on the first passenger liner to leave Oslo after the war, and I had just thrown all my clothes overboard.

After the war ended, my mother, Joanie, and I headed to Norway from Moscow. My mother had not seen her Norwegian family for five years. After the winter gloom of Moscow, Norway, with its white nights, seemed especially sunny and bright, and memories of that summer remain luminous.

I was happy to be back in Kristiansand, the only real home I had ever had, and back with my adoring grandparents. I was old enough now to listen with fascination to all the war stories: my uncle Einar (confusingly known to me as Besse) told of his heroic escape from a German prisoner-of-war camp; my uncle Per Svein recounted his mad race to beat the Germans to the "Hytte," our mountain hunting cabin at Jorunlid, to hide the family's hunting guns, the possession of which was punishable by execution. It had been a shock to see my grandfather with unfamiliar scars on his face, giving him a strange, haunted look. In bits and pieces over time, and with Norwegian under-statement, the story was told of how those scars came to be.

Considered too well known and too old, my grandfather had not been allowed to join the Resistance, but he was eager to do his part. One day, an enterprising and thoughtless girl-friend of Uncle Einar's came by and asked my grandfather to deliver a letter to a contact in the Resistance. He agreed. On the way, he was picked up by suspicious German authorities. They discovered the missive and took him to the local concen-tration camp. During the interrogation, his interlocutors ex-tinguished lighted cigarettes on his face. Rather than give away the girlfriend's name, he jumped out the window and broke his leg upon landing. As he was now in a different category, the lit-eral German authorities put him in the prison hospital. After his leg healed, he was forgotten and spent the rest of the war in the camp.

Grandfather Bessa never discussed this event, but his face was never the same. He did walk me through town, pointing out the stores belonging to the local merchants who had collabo-rated with the Germans, and warning me never to go into one. My grandparents took me to visit an earlier summer home of theirs that had been requisitioned as a German Army barracks during the war. Smiling blond German pinups in provocative poses still hung on the walls above the soldiers' cots. I peeked at them surreptitiously, trying to hide my interest from my grandparents. One day I saw a column of German soldiers be-ing marched through the streets. They looked young and tired. I didn't know what to think.

In midsummer, my handsome, rakish uncle Einar ap-peared with a beautiful Swedish woman, who later became his wife. At Sorenhus, our summerhouse on the fjord, it was a time of joy, reunion, and celebration.

The only cloud in this joyful atmosphere for me was my mother, Annelise. Her parents may have named her the "sun-ray of Sorenhus," but to me she was no sunray. In my eyes my mother was concerned only with clothes, gossip, massages, and money, while my revered father eschewed such pleasures to save the world. She certainly did not seem interested in me, except to complain about my messiness or my looks. This growing resentment had begun in Moscow, and by the time we reached Norway, leaving my father behind at work, it was full blown. I am sure my sullenness in my mother's presence that summer contributed to my parents' decision to send me back as a boarder to the National Cathedral School for Girls in Washington, DC. I agreed, as after living in Portugal and in Moscow, I worried about losing my American identity. "I hardly know what America looks like," I wailed.

It was arranged that I would sail to America on the first available ship. The North Sea was still full of German mines, so our Norwegian ocean liner was going to be escorted by a minesweeper, making me both proud and apprehensive. But as usual I wasn't allowed to verbalize my fears. My mother, looking especially smart that day in a navy blue dress with a white lace collar, drove me to the Oslo harbor to board the ship. I felt a sudden unexpected pang of separation. As she hustled me on board, Mother said, "I won't be able to wait for the ship to sail; I am having dinner with a friend." I noticed a man standing near her. Apparently, her elegant outfit was not donned for me. Then, with a quick kiss, she disappeared with the stranger.

The other passengers waved and shouted to their loved ones on the dock while I stood alone, tears coursing down my face. Finally, I focused on a sympathetic-looking woman and waved energetically to her until the ship pulled slowly away and the faces on the dock receded to a blur.

Because this was the first ship to leave Norway after the war, the liner was overcrowded. I was put in a cabin with the wife of a Norwegian diplomat, who was on her way to join her husband in the United States. Annoyed at this unwanted thirteen-year-old roommate, she was not very friendly. The second night at sea, I locked the door while I undressed, filled with prudish fear that she might come in and see me naked. I then climbed into bed, forgetting to unlock the door. Later I learned that my cabin mate had pounded on the door, the purser had hammered at it, a sailor, hoisted down on ropes, had banged at our porthole, and the captain had even sounded the steamship's loud whistle. But I slept soundly through the whole clamor. The next morning when I opened my eyes, I was shocked to see the empty bed next to mine. With a sinking feeling, I realized what had happened. Covered in cold sweat, I got up, unlocked the door, and then climbed back in the bed, put my pillow over my head, and lay waiting for life to end. My roommate, who had spent a cold night with no nightclothes in an unheated cabin, came back and told me off in strident tones. "How could you have been so stupid as to lock the door? What were you thinking?" I couldn't explain. By now everyone on the ship knew about me. The voyage had not started well.

My mother may have been a clotheshorse, but my wardrobe, much to my chagrin, was another story. Among other things, I was forced to wear old-fashioned bloomers with elastic on the legs, which I detested. I knew Americans didn't wear them. Having already reached my full height and sprouting a bosom, I also wanted a bra, but Mother had protested, "You are only thirteen. Thirteen-year-olds don't wear bras." The bra problem was exacerbated for me by the fact that Mother's favorite little shirred-top party dresses emphasized my new silhouette.

A few days into this ocean voyage, a brilliant idea popped into my head. What if I just gave all my clothes away? I offered them to the purser for his children, but he seemed strangely uninterested. I sensed that my cabin mate would agree with the purser. So one evening at sunset, when most passengers were at dinner, I crept up on the back deck with my suitcase, took out my clothes, and threw my entire wardrobe overboard. I assumed the offensive garments would all sink straight to the bottom of the Atlantic, but, to my horror, they didn't. Instead, every hated item—underwear and all—was displayed across the wake of the boat in clear sight. I scurried back to my room, anticipating another tirade, but somehow my action escaped notice.

A new crisis loomed. My mother had forgotten to give me my vaccination certificate, an omission that stoked all my negative feelings about her. A fellow passenger told me that without such a certificate the officials would take me off at Ellis Island and I might stay there for weeks. I was worried sick, contemplating such a fate. I shared this problem with friends of my parents, who happened to be returning on the same ship with their flock of children. They invited me to disembark with them and said no one would count vaccination certificates. They turned out to be right, but the worry cost me more than a few nights of sound sleep.

At last at the dock in New York, I was met by Cousin Grace, who took me back to the familiar house in New Jersey, where she was still caring for the crazy rich lady. "My, your suitcase is light," she commented. She looked startled when she opened it. "Your mother didn't send you across the Atlantic without any clothes, did she?"

"Yes," I mumbled, very conscious of my lie. "I had outgrown the lot."

The next day Cousin Grace took me to Sears to buy a new wardrobe for the return to National Cathedral School as an eighth-grade boarder.

CHAPTER 3

An American Education

My father's career in the State Department was peaking at the start of the school year in 1946, while my life was on a downward trajectory. When my family returned from Moscow, my father was assigned as the first civilian instructor at the National War College, located at Fort McNair, an army base in southwest Washington, DC. I had just finished an uneventful eighth grade at National Cathedral School for Girls, where we few boarders huddled together out of necessity.

The next year, for reasons probably financial, my parents did not send me back to National Cathedral but instead enrolled me in the ninth grade at Alice Deal Junior High School, a large public school, miles away from Fort McNair. Every day, as soon as school was over, I was picked up by an army bus and returned to the base, so there was no opportunity for play with my classmates.

The school motto, "You get a Square Deal at Alice Deal," did not apply to me. This was the first coed school I'd attended since the fourth grade. Coming as I did from a family of two girls (my brother had yet to be born), boys seemed like aliens from another planet. I had no idea how to talk to them. Also, by the ninth grade, existing cliques had already calcified and did not welcome newcomers. Even athletics were largely not open to me. I had never played American sports and thus was an undesirable candidate for any team. I concentrated on archery, where competition was at a minimum, and lined the walls of my room with certificates proving that I excelled at hitting bull's-eyes. Unfortunately, they weren't the right ones.

Then there was my wardrobe. In the day of tight ankle-length skirts, white socks, and penny loafers, my mother's insistence on pleated skirts, colored socks, and lace-up shoes drew attention, but of the wrong kind. Attempts to argue with my mother about my clothes would end up with her saying, "But the other girls look awful in those silly skirts. You look nice." Her opinion was no comfort when I walked back into the classroom, isolated by my unpopularity.

My previous three years of education—homeschooling in Portugal, School Number 131 in Moscow, and National Cathedral School for Girls—were all poor preparation for Alice Deal. Jokes and topical references sailed over my head, leaving me feeling slow and stupid. Perhaps more important, all my classmates lived in the Cleveland Park neighborhood and played together after school.

On the Fort McNair base, we lived in a two-hundred-year-old redbrick, white-columned house on what was called General's Row, facing a field where the accomplices to Abraham Lincoln's assassination had been hanged. There were fourteen identical houses: twelve occupied by generals and their families, one by an admiral, and one by the Kennans. My mother liked it, as it came complete with army household help. But I was stuck with the officers' children. This was only two years after the end of the Second World War, and most of the generals had been away fighting the war, leaving their progeny to be brought up by mothers and frequently shuffled from place to place. Maybe the combination of neglect and elite status made these children the brats that they proved to be.

One clique was led by a general's daughter we'll call Joyce. She dominated the school bus and sat near the back, surrounded by a small group of admiring acolytes, none of whom spoke to me. I sat alone near the front of the bus. I couldn't have been more surprised when one day Joyce came up to my seat. "What are you doing here?" she asked. I volunteered that my father was teaching at the War College. "Well, a group of us get together sometimes and think of things to do. Why don't you join us tomorrow? My father's name is Travis, and our house is three doors from you." After total exclusion both at school and on the bus, this invitation buoyed my spirits. Even my mother sounded pleased when I told her about it.

As soon as I arrived at Joyce's house, I found a little group of selected school-bus children.

Joyce announced that we were going to the officers' club. "Are we allowed there?" I asked dubiously. Joyce gave a small smirk. "Do you think that they are going to turn down a general's daughter?"

The enlisted men manning the club in the empty afternoon hours looked a bit surprised to see us, but Joyce was right. We weren't asked to leave. Instead, we sat at the bar, drinking Cokes charged to someone's father. Since my mother didn't allow soft drinks and I had never sat at a bar, this all seemed very daring and exciting for awhile. When the next activity consisted of tying up another newbie and leaving him imprisoned in a dumbwaiter for several hours, I reluctantly realized that being accepted wasn't worth the price and slowly withdrew from the group.

Back at Alice Deal, the low point of this miserable year was the monthly Friday-night ninth-grade dance. To not attend was unheard of. The whole previous week, the girls in my class would gather and gossip about what sweaters they were going to wear, how they were doing their hair, and, most pressing of all, who was going to dance with them. At the gym, which was festooned with paper chains and balloons, boys sat on one side, hair newly washed and slicked back, and the angora-clad girls with matching hairbands whispered and tittered on the other side. I assumed that everyone would dance, but, no, a girl had to be invited. As the music started, a line of self-conscious boys sauntered over to us. A boy would pick the girl to the right of me or the girl to the left, but not me. I'd sit, mortified, doing my best not to look at anyone.

Occasionally, I could find respite away from the dance by going to the bathroom, but, of course, I could stay there only so long. Finally the lights would dim and the welcome strains of "Goodnight, Irene" would be played. The torture was over, and we were released until the next time.

When I told glamorous Mother, the belle of her high school class, that no one had danced with me, she pointed out, "Well, you don't have to go." But I knew that absence would make me even more of an outsider than I already was, and each time I hoped against hope that someone would ask me to dance. Every month I dressed up for these interminable evenings, going through the pantomime of pretending to have a good time. The evenings never got better, but thankfully I graduated from Alice Deal.

And then there was the farm. By now I was fourteen years old. To a teenager unhappy at school, the childhood allure of the farm had worn off, and it seemed to me that the principal activity at the farm was very simply work, work, and more work. Some of my friends went to their family's country places to relax, sail, play tennis; we were engaged in manual labor.

The major remodeling had been completed, but there remained endless upkeep projects—waxing and polishing of the parquet floors, painting outdoor furniture, hedge trimming—all of it in the oppressive heat of the Pennsylvania summers. We did not own a washer, dryer, dishwasher, or air conditioner. A dreamy teenager, I was dragooned into working and even paid for the bigger projects, but my heart wasn't in it.

Trimming the long hedge with heavy metal clippers, my arms aching, sweat running down my neck, and gnats flying up my nose—this was not fun. Instead of the clear sparkling sea of Norway, we swam in the muddy creek, where I was scared of water snakes. My love for our white elephant had waned. This house was just one more thing that made me different from other kids in my school. Oh, how I wished that my parents had a little cabin by the sea. Of course, my visiting school friends claimed to adore the farm, but I thought they were just being polite.

Guests of my parents also gushed over the farm, while I listened suspiciously to the hyperbole. Were they serious? I can hear my mother saying brightly, "Today I thought we would paint the garden furniture," as if that were the most enticing project in the world, and sophisticated Washingtonians would pick up paintbrushes and develop major sunburns.

That work, however, was interspersed with swim trips to neighboring lakes or visits to see local horse shows or the state fair in York. Once, when I was a teenager at the farm, Mother took some guests and me to the Hanover horse show. We paid for general admission tickets, but those seats were crowded and located in the hot summer sun, so without a pause Mother marched us all into a shady empty box. I writhed with discomfort, aware that these were much more expensive seats, but she was unperturbed. When the box holders finally arrived, Mother stood up and graciously greeted the group as if she were doing them a favor by letting them sit in the places that they had paid for. The word "sorry" was never in her vocabulary.

As far as I was concerned, such excursions didn't compensate for all the labor. I begged to go to camp but was told that camp was silly: "after all, we have the farm." I wanted to get a job, but my parents said that I was too young, so instead

I propelled the heavy rusty lawn mower around in the heat, wrestled with the hedge clippers, pushed old-fashioned waxers around the parquet floors, and wished that I were anywhere else. Mother was always right.

By the end of the unhappy Alice Deal ninth-grade year, my father's War College stint had ended and he was back in the State Department, with the impressive job of chief of the policy planning staff. We moved again, this time to a neighborhood called Fox Hall Village, in the Western High School district. My parents seemed oblivious to the fact that Alice Deal Junior High School fed into Woodrow Wilson High School. I had been pleased about the prospect of going to school with classmates from the year before and could not believe we were moving to a new district. I staged a major tantrum. Crying, screaming, I hysterically announced, "I will not go to Western High School." One more new school was more than I could stomach.

This atypical outburst so shocked my parents that they called the board of education, which came up with a solution. Western High did not offer sewing and tailoring, but Woodrow Wilson did, so if I declared that my goal was to be a fashion designer and that these subjects were of paramount importance, I could be given a special dispensation to attend Woodrow Wilson rather than Western. It was a long trip from our house to school, but the two bus rides, pricked fingers, and endless hemming seemed a small price to pay.

Woodrow Wilson High School was a definite improvement after Alice Deal. Along with other college-bound sophomores, I chose the classes with the "hard" teachers and embarked on friendships with similarly motivated students. I made the field hockey team and, in my eagerness, ran up and down the field with such zeal that I became team captain, winning a letter that I proudly sewed on my sweatshirt. There were still occasional reminders of my "foreignness." I was the only girl in my class not invited to a single sorority-rushing tea, and that exclusion rankled for a long time.

I also found God. My parents didn't go to church in those days, but the heavy dose of chapel and church at the Episcopalian National Cathedral School for Girls had left a mark.

Whether my parents attended church or not, I decided, I needed to find a religion. Having always struggled with the concept of the Holy Ghost, I considered converting to Judaism but was greeted with more disinterest than welcome when I presented myself at a nearby synagogue. I toyed with the idea of becoming a Catholic and attended several masses, but when I learned about its index of forbidden books, I realized that the Catholic Church was not for me.

Ultimately, I heard about a youth group called TUXIS (You and I Training for Service through Christ), in a neighboring Congregational Church, that combined prayer and social activism. My new best friend, Sheila, and I joined. My parents looked at my religious explorations with amusement and bewilderment. I took confirmation classes at the Congregational Church; my father and mother refused to attend the confirmation ceremony, saying that they had to be at the farm. In their absence, I was invited to sit with the minister's family. While I liked the honor of being in the central pew, I cringed when people asked me where my parents were. "Out of town," answered the little diplomat, "and they are so sorry that they can't be here." Only I knew that they were a mere ninety miles away. TUXIS became the center of my social life.

A would-be thespian, I auditioned for the school play, that year Oscar Wilde's *The Importance of Being Earnest*. Offered the role of Lady Bracknell, I rushed home to give my mother the good news. "I wonder why they chose you?" she questioned in genuine surprise. But even her tepid response didn't dampen my excitement. I was going to be on the stage! Lady Bracknell was a major role. My parents, both theater lovers, did come on opening night, but the next day Mother stunned me by announcing, "It really hurt to watch you—you were so bad." My dramatic dreams were lacerated. I never acted in a speaking part again.

My resentment of my mother waxed and waned but never went away. Her response to our nomadic life was to instill order and routine in our household. Our constant moves seem to have been accomplished without effort, and I would find myself waking up in a new house with the same sofas, tables, and chairs. Only I didn't fit into her plan. My intense passions and teenage sloppiness were constant irritants to her, and maybe for that reason she so cruelly dampened most of my enthusiasms. Then, to add to our strains, she became pregnant.

It was spring of my sophomore year when Mother stopped me one day in the living room. "Sit down, Grace. I have something important to tell you." I plunked down, sure that I was about to be scolded. "I'm going to have a baby."

I sank deeper into my chair. "You can't be," I answered. "You must have made a mistake." I meant that she was too old, but she thought I questioned their family planning, and she went off in a huff. I was mortified. Nobody else's mother was having a baby. Why did we have to be different—yet again?

By the time I was in eleventh grade, we had moved to a small white colonial house in a neighborhood in the Wilson High School district called Cleveland Park. My brother, Christopher, was born that November, and a nurse moved in to take care of him. Now everything revolved around the baby and even less attention came my way. Despite the new offspring, my mother left us and went skiing with a group of her friends. As usual I was somewhat miffed—why did other mothers join in family vacations, while mine went off by herself?

Adventures on the Side

My choice of college had not been carefully considered. My mother, not even a high school graduate, was indifferent. My

father also lacked interest, as I wasn't eligible for his alma mater, Princeton, which at the time was an all-male bastion. My
first choice was Middlebury College in Vermont. Languages,
skiing, and a coed campus—what could be better?

One spring day at Wilson High, my friend Sheila excitedly
whispered to me in the hall, "Go phone your mother. I rang
mine, and the acceptances from Middlebury have come." So I
called. My mother was out, but my brother Christopher's Russian nanny answered the phone. In halting English, she read,
"We regret to inform you . . ." I was stunned and spent the
next two hours sobbing in a cubicle in the girls' bathroom. As
a good student, a member of the National Honor Society, how
could this have happened?

Fortunately I had a second choice. In the summer of 1949,
my mother had taken me to visit friends of hers, the Porter
family, at Great Spruce Head Island in Maine. To be included
on such a trip was a rare occurrence in my young life. The crisp
bracing air, the rocky coast overlooking the ocean, reminded
me of Norway. I felt I had come home. Not only did I fall in
love with the island, but I was smitten by a sexy, dark-haired
Porter cousin, a Harvard freshman called Bebo. He took me
for walks and swims, and on top of a hill he kissed me—my
first kiss; I relived that moment for months. One day as we sat
swinging our legs on the pier, we made a bet about what time
the mail boat would arrive, with the proviso that if I lost the
bet I had to apply to Radcliffe College. After losing, I dutifully
applied. Still smarting from my Middlebury rejection, no one
was more surprised than I was when the Radcliffe acceptance
letter appeared. Later, I liked telling people I went to Radcliffe
on a bet. The same year I started Radcliffe, my family moved
to Princeton, New Jersey, where my father had been appointed
a scholar at the Institute for Advanced Study, an independent
research center where minds such as Einstein and Robert Oppenheimer were also scholars.

Radcliffe changed me and changed my life. At Wilson, I

American Education

had been shy, self-conscious, and utterly lacking in social skills. At Harvard and Radcliffe, where the ratio of men to women was about five to one, having a normal social life was effortless, even though my summer romance with Bebo petered out in the cooler air of Cambridge. My courses, especially cultural anthropology and intellectual history, opened up new worlds. I also enrolled in an intensive Russian class, ashamed that I had forgotten the language.

The extracurricular side of life loomed just as large as my courses. I started what became a lifelong pattern, jumping into new experiences with great enthusiasm and little preparation. I was always ten feet ahead of myself.

As a freshman, I signed up for an intermediate Harvard–Radcliffe ski trip to Vermont, neglecting to mention that I hadn't skied since I was six, when I cross-country skied in Norway with my grandfather. While the nominal purpose of this trip was fresh air and exercise, my unspoken goal was to meet Harvard boys. Huddled, shivering, outside the Radcliffe dorm at 5:00 a.m., our little group of would-be skiers was picked up by a chartered bus and driven to Stowe. I noticed quite a few candidates for my attention. The next day on the chairlift, sharing a seat with a handsome Harvard man named Spencer, I thought everything was going according to plan—until we reached the top of the mountain and I looked down at the precipitous slope.

My seatmate was obviously an experienced skier, while I didn't know how to downhill ski. "Ladies first," Spencer offered.

"Oh, no. You lead and show me the way. I'll follow," I answered, with false bravado.

Making crisp, graceful turns, he slid away and was soon out of sight. I stood and pondered. I felt sick. Reason dictated that if I pointed the skis downhill, gravity would take me, and the worst that could happen was a fall in the beautiful soft snow. I started down, going faster and faster, for a minute exhilarated, and then terrified. Soon I was flying, blinded by snow in my eyes, until some invisible obstacle caused me to go tumbling head over heels, leaving me in a pile with one ski sticking up as a marker to this disastrous descent. The other ski, having come loose, was making its solitary way down the mountain. Although stunned, miraculously I was unhurt. When rescued, I sheepishly accepted praise for my courage. The next day I enrolled in beginning ski classes. I never heard from Spencer again.

A short waitressing career during the Radcliffe years had a somewhat similar beginning. I desperately needed money for something—a new coat, a radio, or another ski trip, who knows? The student-employment flyer printed that "experienced waitresses" could charge double what babysitters earned. Calculating that my childhood living overseas, where we always had a cook and maid, would constitute experience, I immediately signed up and soon was assigned a job. To my acute embarrassment, the employment agency outfitted me in a little black dress, crisp white apron, and, worst of all, a small white crown that fitted on my head. Slipping on my worn blue coat, I crept out of the dormitory, praying that none of my classmates would see me.

All I knew was that I was going to serve at a dinner party for a family named Putnam, who lived in one of the large wooden Victorian houses of Cambridge. Mrs. Putnam pointed me to the big old-fashioned kitchen, introduced me to Bridget, a weathered Irish cook, and told me to set the table for twelve. I set it quite nicely, I thought, until Bridget pointed out the omission of salts and peppers, candlesticks, napkins, and dessert forks. As I stumbled about in the unfamiliar kitchen, a thin, nervous man tiptoed in. To my surprise he turned out to be Mr. Putnam, about half the size of his formidable wife. He stealthily reached into a cupboard for a jar of peanut butter and, with a look of sensual delight, stood and spooned the forbidden treat into his mouth, until footsteps sounded and he scurried away. With Bridget's coaching, I managed to get through the dinner and was soon engaged again. We went through the same routine, peanut butter and all. By now I felt the three of us had formed some secret circle.

On my next foray, going around the formal dining room table, serving peas from a heavy silver bowl, I heard a guest telling an anecdote about his friend, Charles Bohlen, whom I had known as Uncle Charles when he served in the Moscow embassy with my father. I was mesmerized. Focused only on the conversation, I kept circling the table, offering people more and more peas, oblivious to the fact that I soon had no takers. Finally I heard my name and saw Mrs. Putnam giving me semaphore signals from her end of the table. "That is enough, Grace," she said loudly, in her clipped, upper-class East Coast accent. As soon as the guests left, she fired me. Evidently I had gone around the table four times. My waitressing career ended, and with considerable relief I turned in my dress, apron, and cap.

During my freshman year at Radcliffe, I read about a summer school at the University of Oslo, run in English. It seemed perfect for me. I would find out about my mother's homeland and brush up on my forgotten Norwegian so that I could talk again to my grandparents, who spoke no English. Strangely enough, my mother was against the summer school plan, but my father, who always believed in the value of education, prevailed. My tuition was paid, but Mother, who controlled the household purse strings, doled me out an even smaller allowance than usual in revenge.

On the steamship *Stavangerfjord*, sailing from New York to Oslo, I met my fellow students in the summer program, mostly from St. Olaf College in Minnesota. While not unfriendly, they were an inbred group, and my Norwegian American heritage was too different from theirs to qualify me as a member. So I roomed with two other outsiders: exotic, black-haired Betsy from North Carolina, and lively, redheaded Sarah from

Connecticut. Academic requirements were hardly onerous. We attended two courses a day, one on Norwegian history, one on Norwegian culture. I dutifully practiced Norwegian in the language lab, but my roommates and I spent the rest of the day on expeditions: to the Viking Ship Museum, the Kon-Tiki Museum, the Munch Museum, and the Holmenkollen ski jump. We thought Vigeland Park, with its nude statues, extremely racy and spent an enormous amount of time sending postcards to friends, hoping to impress them with our new sophistication and daring.

Betsy and Sarah decided that a fitting cap to this experience would be a trip to Copenhagen, and I readily agreed to go along. None of us had enough money, but Sarah came up with the idea that we could earn it. Since the summer school had no laundry, we decided to set up a pressing service for men's shirts. We approached the director of the summer school for a loan of irons and ironing boards. Although very surprised by our request, he finally produced two irons and two ironing boards, and we set up a business in our bedroom. The results were dramatic. Male students lined up, ostensibly to have their shirts pressed but mostly to meet Betsy and Sarah.

Leaving behind a trail of burned shirts, we ultimately learned to iron. Our pressing service earned us just enough money to go to Copenhagen if Sarah and I hitchhiked. Betsy went ahead by train. We didn't ask our parents' permission, as we knew that they wouldn't have approved.

Two men offered to go with us for protection. One was Sarah's faithful admirer, Jim, and the other was Jim's friend, Sam, a "colored" graduate student and a radical Socialist, whom I had never met before the Copenhagen trip. Growing up in Norway, Portugal, Russia, and Germany, and then attending segregated public schools in the States, I had never known a person of color before as a friend, much less a traveling companion. We decided to split into two groups, get rides as far as the Swedish coastal city of Malmo, stay overnight at the youth hostel, and then hitch our way to Copenhagen. With Sarah's flaming red hair serving as a beacon, she and Jim immediately got a ride, while Sam and I had a longer wait. When we reached Malmo, we found the youth hostel but no sign of Jim and Sarah.

Sam, all of age twenty-eight, immediately took charge. Saying that it made sense to pool our resources, he proposed that I give him all my hard-earned money. Stupidly obedient, I handed it over but kept a small amount in reserve. I ventured the opinion that Sarah and Jim had gotten a ride straight through to Copenhagen, but Sam pooh-poohed that idea. "No," he said. "Our deal was to meet in Malmo, and Jim would never have gone on without us. They just haven't gotten here yet."

The next day, as we walked around Malmo, he made me stop every person we saw on the street and ask in halting Norwegian, "Excuse me, but have you seen two Americans—a redheaded woman and a man?" For a shy girl, accosting a stranger on the street was a form of torture, especially as my questions were often met with bewilderment and even laughter. For three days, we continued our fruitless search, interspersed with Sam's lectures on socialism. By the time Sam and I reached the three-day limit at the youth hostel and were asked to move on, I had begun to dislike him for his bossiness and rigidity. Sam found us a new place to stay within our limited budget, a very modest pension about five kilometers outside Malmo. The only available two rooms were adjoining, and you had to go through Sam's outside room to reach mine. I thought that Sam looked at me in a strange way, making me feel entrapped, and I decided that I had to escape. Certain that Sam would never give me back my money, I calculated that my small stash of hidden cash would just pay for the train to Copenhagen.

Night fell and we settled into our separate rooms. I didn't unpack my bag but lay awake until about four in the morning, when the sound of Sam's even breathing ensured that he was asleep. With my heart thudding in my chest, I tiptoed through his room with my heavy suitcase. He didn't wake up. As I was walking down the long road to town, a passing driver took pity on me and gave me a lift to the station. I bought my ticket, which left me with about twenty-five cents, and crouched behind a bench in the waiting room for three hours until the first train left, terrified that Sam would wake up and try to find me.

In Copenhagen I had just enough money to take the bus to the nearest youth hostel, where I met Jim and Sarah, who, as I thought, had found a ride straight through. After two happy days with them, I left for Kristiansand. I couldn't bear to see Sam again. When I told my parents about the hitchhiking, they were so angry that the rest of the trip was never discussed and remained hidden under their cloud of disapproval. That Sam was black never came up.

CHAPTER 4

Fits and Starts

At the end of my junior year at Radcliffe, my mother informed me in a puzzled voice, "We've been invited to the British embassy in Washington to attend Queen Elizabeth's coronation ball, and the funny thing is that you've been invited, too. I can't imagine why they invited you."

I had never been included in parties with my parents in Washington, since I was only a high school student when we moved there. Mother took me to a thrift shop, and for $5 she bought a yellow evening dress with a tulle skirt. I thought it looked swell. We drove down to Washington from Princeton and stayed with my parents' very social friends, Polly and Frank Wisner. The ball started at the fashionably late hour of 9:00 p.m., but I was included in the pre-ball dinner party at the Wisners' impressive Georgetown house. My escort was Joe Alsop, a much older columnist, known for his sardonic wit and passionately held political opinions. He was visibly unimpressed by his shy young dinner companion and spent the evening talking to the lady on his other side.

When we arrived at the ball in the palatial British embassy on Massachusetts Avenue, my parents went off to dance, leaving me standing alone, a stick figure in yellow tulle. As I looked at the elegant women swirling around, my dress, which I had thought so pretty, suddenly seemed more appropriate for a senior prom. I felt very out of place. My father finally reappeared on a rescue mission. "You don't know anyone here, do you? Well, let's see. Oh, there's that young senator from Massachusetts." He took my arm and propelled me over to a young, handsome, sandy-haired man. "Senator Kennedy, I want you to meet my daughter Grace. She's a student at Radcliffe." My father left us, and the senator smiled.

I knew that I had to say something, but I lacked the skill to make small talk. I realized that I should have known about Senator Kennedy, as I was studying in Massachusetts, but I didn't. I heard his pronounced Boston accent, and all that came across my mind was that he was Irish. Boston College reputedly had a lot of Irish students. "Oh," I volunteered, "you must have gone to Boston College." There was a long moment of silence before the senator responded, a bit coldly, "No, I went to Harvard." Realizing that I had made a horrible gaffe, I stood speechless, not knowing where to proceed with this unfortunate conversation. The senator rescued me by saying he wanted to sit down and invited me to go out with him to the garden. I wondered why anyone would want to go to a garden in the middle of a ball, but I trotted along after him.

We had barely sat down at a table when we were spotted by Joe Alsop, suddenly delighted to reclaim his date. Alsop had just come from Harvard, where he served on the board of overseers, and that day they had chosen a new president to replace the retiring James Conant, but the decision had not yet been announced.

"Well, Joe," needled the senator, "tell us who you chose."

"A dusty cat from an even dingier barrel," Joe replied dramatically, referring to Nathan Pusey, from Appleton, Wisconsin. I felt a tingle, thinking, "This is real grown-up conversation, and I'm a part of it." At that point, a tall glamorous lady in a clinging satin dress came out and sat on the senator's other side. Startled, I saw her put her hand on the senator's knee. Good heavens. Was this what grown-ups did? The rest of the evening receded to a blur. I know I never wore that dress again.

Seven years later I was married to C. K. McClatchy, a political reporter for the *Sacramento Bee*, and living with our firstborn child, Charles, in Northern California. C. K. came home from the office and told me that Senator Kennedy, then running for president, was flying in to Sacramento early the next morning. "Do you want to go to the airport with me?" Of course I did, so early the next morning about thirty of us stood around shivering in the cold morning air, watching a small white private jet land.

Out stepped the very recognizable senator, followed by six or seven men. He strode over to our group, smiling his unforgettable smile, and started going around shaking each person's hand and saying something. But when he came to me he stopped. He paused and then pointed at me with his forefinger. "I remember you. We met in Washington at Queen Elizabeth's coronation ball." I flushed, embarrassed by the attention. C. K. was impressed. Little did I know that this was the beginning of an involvement with the Kennedys that would last many years.

The Ambassador's Daughter

By the spring of my sophomore year at Radcliffe, I acquired a serious boyfriend. Letters brought us together. A prolific correspondent, I had to mail every letter the second it was written. On one of my frequent trips to the corner mailbox, a distinguished-looking older couple asked me directions to Moors Hall. While I escorted them there, we started talking and they discovered that I was studying Russian. "Oh, so is our son, Lee," they said. "You two would have so much in common. Please come over for drinks on Thursday. Our names are Manley and Janet Hudson." So on Thursday, dressed in my best blue dress, I walked down the street to their big, old-fashioned Cambridge home. It was my first cocktail party.

Lee opened the door. A Nordic-looking blond whose blue eyes lit up as he smiled, he immediately engaged me in conversation. We soon discovered that we shared a passion for literature and a love of the outdoors. Both of us spoke Russian and French. He, too, had lived abroad, when his father, a Harvard professor, served at the Permanent Court of International Justice in The Hague. That night, and as long as I knew him, Lee dressed in crisp, freshly ironed Brooks Brothers shirts. To me he was suave, sophisticated, and brilliant. I had found a hero to admire.

We began to date. With Lee leading the way, we soon created our own language, full of literary allusions. Nabokov was our favorite author, and *Speak, Memory*, the author's memoir of his prerevolutionary childhood in Russia, was our favorite book. We liked using Nabokov's arcane vocabulary, such as, "Oh, look, she's wearing that refulgent dress." In front of others, we showed off by talking to each other in Russian. Soon Lee became number one among several boyfriends, and we began to see each other more and more frequently.

Both of our fathers were distinguished in their fields and both came from the Midwest—my father from Milwaukee and his from St. Peters, Missouri. Manley O. Hudson, a distinguished professor of international relations at the Harvard Law School, was twice nominated for the Nobel Peace Prize. Although short and balding, with a Midwest accent, he commanded attention wherever he went. Lee and I each strove to meet our fathers' expectations, and both of us were fearful of falling short.

In December, Mother made a momentous phone call: "I

have big news. Your father has been appointed U.S. ambassador to the Soviet Union. We will be moving to Moscow." This meant our house in Princeton had to be rented, Joanie had to live with family friends to finish out her school year, and I no longer had a place to go home to. But I was very excited. On April 2, 1952, Mother, Daddy, and I met in Washington for the swearing-in, the first public event in which I had ever participated. The *Washington Post* photo of my parents and me at the ceremony shows me with the solemn, startled look of a deer in the headlights, while Mother looks lively and pretty. The caption under the photo reversed us, to my mortification and my mother's pleasure. I was Mrs. Kennan and she was Grace. I was especially embarrassed as my mother was again visibly pregnant, a fact the photographer cleverly hid.

My father's appointment began a lifetime of introductions as my father's daughter. "Yes, I'd like you to meet Grace Kennan. She's the daughter of George Kennan, head of the policy planning staff in the State Department." He had just written an article for *Foreign Affairs* magazine but, on instruction from the State Department, signed it only as "X," although the authorship was soon discovered. My more sophisticated friends called me "Miss X" to show that they had read the article outlining the containment policy toward the Soviet Union. The article was later reprinted in *LIFE* magazine and attracted even more attention and notoriety. I'm ashamed to say that I didn't even read the famous piece at the time, but I liked being called Miss X.

My mother's age, forty-one, and the primitive condition of Russian hospitals at that time led my parents to decide that my father would go alone to Moscow at the beginning of May and Mother would stay in Bonn, Germany, with three-year-old Christopher, to have her baby.

Mother's imminent new arrival embarrassed me yet again. How could my mother be pregnant when I was a sophomore in college? None of my classmates' mothers were having babies.

My friends admitted they thought it strange, although none of us verbalized the embarrassing part, that my parents must be having sex.

One day, when I returned to Briggs Hall after a dramatic Saturday of sailing off Marblehead, where our boat narrowly missed being upended by a large whale, the switchboard girl handed me a telegram. The yellow page informed me that a new baby sister, Wendy Antonia, had been born in Bonn. My parents never considered using the long-distance telephone. I was convinced that the action of the giant cetacean had some cosmic connection with Wendy's birth, as both seemed equally incredible.

Joanie and I sailed to Bremen on a steamer and took a train from there to Bonn to unite with Mother, Christopher, and baby Wendy. On July 1, the five of us flew from Berlin to Moscow on a U.S. government plane. On the road in from Sheremetyevo Airport, we were startled by a line of huge advertising billboards. Since everything in the Soviet Union was owned by the government, the messages were very terse: DRINK MILK, EAT BREAD, AND PUT YOUR MONEY IN THE STATE SAVINGS BANK.

We settled into Spaso House, a prerevolutionary sugar baron's fifty-room mansion that still serves as the American ambassador's residence in Moscow. As a young Foreign Service officer, my father had outfitted the house when diplomatic relations resumed between the two countries in 1933. The central part of the mansion was built around a large white marble ballroom, and all the big bedrooms on the second floor opened onto a balustrade overlooking that ballroom—a wonderful perch from which to spy on those below. A butler, a cook, the nanny, and maids took care of us—we didn't lift a finger. In fact, the kitchen was more or less off-limits to us, as were a myriad of rooms in the basement and mezzanine. One morning I opened a door and stumbled across a seamstress hard at work on a Singer sewing machine, with swaths of silk curtains around her. I hadn't even known she existed. Joanie, however, was not happy in Spaso House and was dispatched to Norway to spend the summer with our grandparents.

Much to my excitement, I was given a job working in the U.S. embassy. My assignment was to type up incoming telegrams in the morning and to assume the duty of protocol clerk in the afternoon. Surely a Radcliffe student—the ambassador's daughter to boot—would know about protocol.

Working with the incoming telegrams was exciting. They came in from all over the world, encrypted, then were decoded and given to me to type up. I felt a direct involvement in all global crises as they occurred. But the protocol job! I had to initial each embassy officer's calling card and transmit the batch to various embassies, depending on whose national day or special event it was. As an example, when Eva Perón died that summer, I wrote "pc," for *pour condoler*, on each card and sent them off to the Argentinian embassy.

When a new Ethiopian ambassador arrived and was accredited as the official representative of the country of Ethiopia, I asked my predecessor, who had another job in the embassy, what to do. "Go into the files, find an appropriate letter, make a copy, then send it up to the ambassador's office for signature," she told me. I followed instructions. The next thing I knew, there was an unexpected visit from the Ethiopian ambassador to see my father, the U.S. ambassador. It turned out that the file contained two different congratulatory letters—one to countries with whom we had friendly relations, which was written in the first person and ended, "I look forward to the continuance of the happy relations that have always existed between our two countries," and the other letter for countries with whom we did not have such relations, written in the third person and omitting the final sentence. Unknowingly, I sent the latter letter to the Ethiopian ambassador. The

Ethiopian government decided that America was breaking off friendly relations with Ethiopia and sent its ambassador to express the country's alarm about this sudden rift between the two countries. The offending letter was traced to me, and my father gave his deputy chief of mission, Counselor Elim O'Shaughnessy, the unfortunate job of relieving me of my protocol duties. From then on, I was relegated to spending my afternoons filing book cards in the embassy library. So much for being the ambassador's daughter!

The United States' involvement in the Korean War was in high gear that summer. Plastered all over Moscow were anti-American placards, such as a cartoon of a grimacing American soldier injecting germs into the arm of a cringing Korean woman. But even in the tense summer of 1952, Moscow had its charms. The roses were in bloom, and the parks were full of Russians eating ice cream and basking in the good weather. I had made friends with the younger officers from the British and Dutch embassies, and we would meet after work to stroll around the formal paths of the Park of Culture and Rest and to sample an occasional ice cream. It was forbidden to sit on the grass. We also took the few trips permitted to us, as foreigners were confined to a twenty-five-mile radius from Moscow. One excursion was an overnight boat trip down the Moscow River and through the newly built Volga–Don Canal, the sole purpose of which was to view a giant statue of Stalin. This permitted us to have brief, furtive conversations with Russian passengers. "Where are you from?" they would ask, and when we answered, they would whisper, "Welcome. We are glad that you have come to our country." This friendly response was in direct contrast to the official hostile propaganda, and every encounter had the thrill of contraband.

About a month into my Moscow stay, Lee arrived from Geneva, where his family was vacationing, for a prearranged week's visit. The sojourn that was so exciting when planned in May looked totally different in August, now that I was working in the embassy and mingling with my new group of older friends. I had asked my mother if we could cancel Lee's visit, but she adamantly refused. "You can't un-invite someone once you have asked him. And you must act glad to see him." So Lee arrived, but now he seemed young to me. The Brooks Brothers clothes looked out of place; the literary allusions were too precious; I didn't feel the same. I counted the days until he left.

This was still the Stalin era, so we also bumped up against the harsher realities of Soviet life.

My father was followed at all times outside Spaso House and the embassy by five KGB plainclothesmen—the "guardian angels"—who had been assigned by the Soviet government "for his protection." If my father went on a walk, two angels walked on either side of him, one behind, while the other two cruised alongside in a car.

One night, my parents and I were seeing the Chekhov play *Uncle Vanya*. The angels as usual commandeered the five seats behind us, telling the occupants of those seats to leave the theater. They rose, without protest, and silently filed out. During the first intermission a young man sitting next to me started a conversation. Listening to him and practicing my Russian was fun. I soon learned that he was a student at Moscow State University. During the second intermission I was shocked to see the student being hustled out of the theater, surrounded by gray, unsmiling men. My father felt so badly for those ejected that he stopped going to the theater.

As the summer wore on, my new friends suggested I stay in Moscow and not go back to Radcliffe. "Just think, this is a unique opportunity for you, and you can always go back to college a year later," urged an appealing British cohort, Robin. I was sorely tempted to stay, but to me, at age twenty, it was more important to be with my friends and to graduate with my class. I had changed, however. The world seemed a much bigger place than Cambridge, Massachusetts.

Persona Non Grata

Returning to Radcliffe after the heady, intense atmosphere of Moscow was a cosmic shift. With images of the Kremlin still floating through my head, I resolved to break up with Lee before settling down to my studies and the demands of junior year. I went to see him at his parents' house. In the formal living room, I took a deep breath and ventured, "I don't think we should see each other anymore. We're too young." Instead of arguing, he threatened to commit suicide. His reaction scared me. Feeling the responsibility of his very life in my hands, I was enormously conflicted. I thought he must love me very much, to the extent that he thought he couldn't live without me. But nonetheless I wasn't ready for such an intense commitment. So we broke up and I started seeing other men, enjoying myself skiing, exploring jazz clubs, and attending amateur theater.

As I chatted up a date on our way to a concert in downtown Boston only a few weeks into the new term, the shrill call of a newsboy caught my attention. I heard the word "Moscow." Jerking on my date's sleeve, I said, "Wait a second, I want to know what they're saying." I walked to the newsstand, where a boy stood on a pile of evening papers, vigorously waving one in the air. It was then I heard him yell in his flat Boston accent, "Get your paper! Ambassador Kennan kicked out of Moscow!" Stunned, I fumbled through the paper, but all I could learn was that my father had been declared persona non grata by Soviet leader Josef Stalin. What was going on? I rushed to the nearest pay phone and called my dorm, but there was no message. How could this be? Somehow, I sat through the concert, but I didn't hear a note, my mind racing and my head throbbing with worry. What could possibly have gone so wrong so fast? "Persona non grata"—it sounded so grave. Only the next afternoon did I receive a telegram from my father from Geneva, confirming the news. The message was brief, but he added that Mother and the younger children would be leaving Moscow to join him in Germany.

The morning papers mercifully contained more detail, enabling me to piece together the news item. The facts were simple, the underlying story much more complex. My father had left Moscow on September 19, 1952, on a U.S. plane assigned to pick him up and take him to a NATO conference in London. A stopover in Berlin was included. Because any word from Moscow was news at the time, the Germans organized a press conference at the airport. At the end of the event, a young journalist asked my father what it was like living in Moscow. My father, disenchanted by the Cold War atmosphere in Moscow, where he had no contact with high-level Soviet officials and was constantly trailed by five KGB agents, answered that life in Moscow reminded him of his internment in Bad Nauheim at the outbreak of the Second World War. There, too, he had been isolated from the local population, but in that situation he had been detained in a guarded residence, along with the rest of the American diplomats. No more questions were asked.

My father attended the NATO conference in London and returned through Germany. But before he was able to complete his trip to Moscow, *Pravda*, the official Soviet newspaper, printed a long article on September 26, viciously attacking my father, describing him as "a slanderer" who "lied ecstatically." The hostility was obviously a harbinger of something to come, so my father remained in Western Europe and passed the time visiting my sister, Joan, at her Swiss boarding school. It was there a week later that an officer from the American consulate presented my father with an official edict from the Soviet government, stating that in light of the events at Tempelhof Airport, the government "considers Mr. Kennan as persona non grata and insists on Mr. Kennan's immediate recall from the post of Ambassador of the United States of America in the Soviet Union."[1]

---

1. George F. Kennan, *Memoirs, 1950–1963* (New York: Pantheon, 1983), 164.

The official reason for my father's banishment was that he had compared life in the Soviet Union with life in Fascist Germany, a highly undiplomatic association. I couldn't understand how my adored father, during my whole childhood held up as an example of diplomatic excellence, could have made such a faux pas. Could his pedestal really be cracking? Unanswered questions swirled in my head, and here in faraway Cambridge, Massachusetts, there were no answers. To compound the trauma, most of my friends acted as if nothing at all had happened, obviously embarrassed for me. I felt very isolated from what was going on in my family.

A proviso of the persona non grata declaration was that now ex-Ambassador Kennan could not return to Moscow, leaving my mother and the younger children stranded in the Soviet capital. From what I later learned, Mother's departure from Moscow was undoubtedly her finest hour, but with her typical reserve she never spoke about it. She had been informed by the State Department of my father's ouster before the announcement in the press. And during the intervening days, she continued her official role, hosting a formal lunch and attending a black-tie dinner. After the public disclosure, she had only three days to pack up all the family possessions from the large residence. Although helped by a nurse, she was also busy with the usual demands of caring for four-month-old Wendy and nearly four-year-old Christopher.

The State Department received permission to send an official U.S. government plane to Moscow to fly Mother, the children, and the Danish nurse, with all the Kennan belongings, to Germany. This being at the height of the Cold War, the entire Western-oriented diplomatic corps based in Moscow assembled at the airport to say farewell, as a gesture of support for my mother and a public expression of outrage at my father's expulsion. To add dramatic weight to the occasion, the military attachés of the various countries appeared in full regalia, gold braid and medals shining.

My father's longtime secretary, Dorothy Hessman, described a comic footnote to this emotional departure in a letter I later received at Radcliffe. In those days of light airport security, the farewell delegation was allowed to stand outside on the tarmac to wave good-bye, while the family climbed onto the plane and the luggage was loaded. Everyone had boarded, except the American crewmember still on the ground to ensure that the propellers started properly. U.S. Air Force personnel had few chances to see the Moscow airport, since the United States and the Soviet Union were virtual enemies at the time, so this older and visibly paunchy crewmember was undoubtedly a high-level air force officer. After the propellers roared, he signaled for the ladder to climb up onto the plane. "No," the Soviet agent in charge replied, "it is only permitted to have the ladder once." Obviously the plane had to leave but could not do so without the air force officer, so again he requested the ladder, and again the Soviet official, standing amid a group of equally stony-faced colleagues in military uniform, denied the request. The stupidity of the moment was glaring, but what to do? Finally a rope was lowered to the poor American on the ground, who had to shimmy up into the plane, not an easy feat for the overweight flier. With much flailing around, he ultimately succeeded in reaching the plane, but not before the farewell delegation, still standing at attention to observe the departure, broke into unofficial laughter, spoiling the solemnity of the moment but emphasizing the silliness of the Soviet bureaucracy.

When my parents finally returned to the States from Germany in late November, my father gave me his more intimate version of the ouster. He had thought the airport press conference was over when he made the remarks in question, and he had stated that they were off the record. But he admitted that the airport noise might have made his statement to that effect inaudible. More important, he considered that his unique role as unofficial leader of the diplomatic corps in Moscow had played a major part in his expulsion by Stalin. A Russian speaker, and an exhaustive reader of the Soviet press, he kept thousands of file cards, written in his meticulous penmanship, tracking the whereabouts and public statements of all Soviet political and military leaders. This card system allowed him to connect the dots, using both his painstakingly thorough research and his uncanny intuition, which earned him a reputation as a brilliant soothsayer. As a result of his analysis of the Soviet press, he always had a much better picture of what was going on than did his diplomatic colleagues, who routinely visited him at the U.S. embassy to pick his brain before writing their dispatches. This ambassadorial traffic was clearly visible from the Kremlin across the street, because an ambassador's car always flew his country's flag. My father was also convinced that Stalin still resented the fact that he had come out and spoken to the crowd in front of the American embassy the day that the war ended in May 1945.

My father felt that what really tipped the scales was his role in removing the KGB listening device discovered in the United States seal at the embassy. American embassy officials had suspected that there was some sort of bug in the upstairs living room at Spaso House, recently remodeled by an unsupervised Soviet painting crew. As the white-marble ballroom on the main floor was hardly cozy to sit in, the family always gathered upstairs. Two technicians were brought in from Washington under the pretense that they were fur traders. One of the "fur traders" asked my father to telephone his secretary, Dorothy, and ask her to come to the residence so he could dictate a dispatch. My father made the call with considerable reluctance, as he saw his role as a diplomat, not as a player in a spy movie. While my father dictated to Dorothy an old telegram already sent weeks before, a very small device, later described as smaller than a pencil, was traced to the U.S. seal hanging on the wall of the living room. The microphone was both a transmitter and a receiver of messages and could be activated by remote control. The device had not been previously discovered because the KGB had turned it off when the room was routinely tested for listening devices. This tiny bug was technologically more advanced than anything we Americans had at the time. I was told about the little eavesdropper while I was living at Spaso House but had been sworn to secrecy and pushed it to the back of my mind.

What I did not know was that the U.S. State Department had asked my father to conceal the bug in his pocket when he left Moscow for the London NATO conference, since ambassadors could not be searched. Convinced by my father that this nasty small apparatus (now on display at the International Spy Museum in Washington) had cost him his career as a diplomat, I was very frustrated by this mandatory silence. Eight years later, Henry Cabot Lodge, the U.S. ambassador to the United Nations, dramatically displayed the bug and the seal at the United Nations as proof of Soviet espionage, and we Kennans finally felt a bit vindicated.

My parents and the younger children were reunited in Germany, but they were not allowed to go home. Instead, the State Department requested that they stay in Bonn, where the U.S. High Commission was based, until after the November election. Dwight Eisenhower was running against Adlai Stevenson. My father's diary entry at the time reflected his miserable state of mind: "Just what dangers my presence in the country would have added to the fortunes of the Democratic party I was unable then to imagine, nor can I easily picture them today; but I was thoroughly humbled by what had just befallen me, and was in no mood to argue."[2] My parents moved into a government apartment in Bonn.

Back at Radcliffe, I kept up to date about their life only by what I read in the paper or snippets from letters. My parents still considered that the telephone was to be used only for

2. Kennan, *Memoirs, 1950–1963*, 168.

matters of life or death. But the fact that they weren't allowed to come home added to my feeling that something shameful had occurred. Having earned some recognition just for being a Kennan, I felt this public denouement was my undoing, as well.

In the beginning, there was still hope of another post. Every few weeks the *New York Times* or the *Washington Post* would print speculation about a possible new assignment. Kennan was going to Switzerland, or to Japan, or to Israel. I dreamed about skiing in the Alps, learning Japanese, seeing the Dead Sea. Perhaps fearing competition, Secretary of State John Foster Dulles did not want my father in the State Department any longer, and after three months my father had to submit his resignation. He was only forty-nine years old.

Our future was uncertain and a bit frightening. For one thing, we had no income. I filled out a scholarship form for Radcliffe and in the income column wrote "$00.00." Thankfully, the scholarship came through. Whenever I was home, I'd find my father bitter and angry. He felt betrayed not only by Stalin but also by the Department of State, to which he had dedicated his life. A sarcastic snarl occasionally appeared in his voice, and a certain embarrassing self-pity lingered for some time. It hurt me to see him that way, but it seemed disloyal to share this pain with my friends. In time, my father did receive a diminished pension, but our family's life had been irrevocably changed. I was no longer "the ambassador's daughter."

During the time Lee and I were separated, I had gone to dinner with a Frenchman who kissed me when he brought me home. For some reason, I felt obliged to tell Lee about this when we reunited. He startled me by reacting with cold anger. "How could you? You behaved like a slut, allowing him to kiss you. You're no better than a whore."

I was shaken by his reaction. Could he be right? Why had I allowed this presumptuous kiss?

I was strangely affected by his unfair criticism. Other people thought I was a nice girl, but Lee understood the bad, easily tempted, real me. I was almost pathetically grateful that he wanted to keep seeing me.

Soon Lee and I became a couple again, much to the approval of our friends. My classmate Thalia said that we made a good-looking pair, like matching bookends. Both of us lived with roommates, so opportunities to be alone together were rare. Most of our private time was spent in his room at home, supposedly studying, with his tall, brainy New England mother hovering nearby. When we finally had sex, it was only occasional, hindered by roommates, and contaminated by guilt and inexperience. Although all my girlfriends were preoccupied with sex, discussion of the subject was taboo, and I had no one to talk to.

While Lee opened up new literary horizons, so that Tolstoy, Dostoyevsky, and Turgenev were almost members of the family, in other ways he closed me down. An idealist and a joiner, I always felt that I had a mission to do good and help save the world. I was chairman of the campus United Way; I was the Briggs Hall fire marshal and ran unsuccessfully for class president. But in my junior year my grades fell to Bs, and I received my only C, ironically, in a Russian-language course, which was so easy for me that I had stopped working. Instead, I was happy to be accepted into the kick line of Drumbeats and Song, the Radcliffe version of the Rockettes. At last I had a chance to be back on the stage. Lee didn't share my excitement. "How can you go out in that cheesy costume, kicking your legs for all to see? Don't you realize how cheap you look? I was ashamed to watch you." He also chided me for not having a straight-A average. His criticisms rankled, but again I thought that this must be real love—he cared so much. Dutifully, in my senior year I dropped out of all extracurricular activities and received straight A's.

By the time Lee asked me to marry him, it was an anticlimax. The big moment seemed more of a conversation than a proposal. He explained that we could be engaged, but we would have to wait three years to marry, because he was going to law school, planned to be on the law review, and would not have time for a wife. He would give me a family ring when his mother had it cleaned. I accepted this not-very-romantic proposal. My parents seemed pleased, though, and I still cared a great deal about pleasing them.

At my graduation a year later, in 1954, my father was the commencement speaker. As usual, I was very uneasy; whenever my father spoke at my schools, I was afraid that he would say something embarrassing or I would overhear my classmates criticizing him. When I posed for photographs with him in my black robe and mortarboard, I looked self-conscious but happy. I had my diploma and I was engaged. My future life had been decided, or so it seemed.

A Fractured Future

Until my marriage to Lee, I had to support myself. My job search dragged on for three months, as I stubbornly refused to go to the Katie Gibbs secretarial school to learn shorthand— recommended by many—or to take the various typing jobs offered to me. My parents funded this economically barren period by doling out small loans, but they became increasingly annoyed at what they perceived as my laziness in nailing employment. Each month, my debt grew. Frugality had never been my strong point. For the next two years, every letter from me to them started with the status of my insolvency. Finally, to everyone's relief, I landed a job as a researcher at the MIT Center for International Studies.

At MIT, my boss was an older Russian naval engineer, Alexander Korol, who was writing a book titled *A Qualitative Analysis of Soviet Scientific Education*. The first week was a disaster. Mr. Korol handed me a 250-page Russian textbook on Soviet education and asked me to return in a week or so with a summary. Sitting in my windowless office, lit by the flickering of a fluorescent tube, I took out my dictionary and went to work, looking up the unfamiliar words in the Cyrillic alphabet. By the day's end, my head ached and I had read only three pages. The next day stretched out the same way, but the headache was even worse. By the third day it was clear that my college Russian was not up to the job.

I went into Mr. Korol's office and took a deep breath. "I'm afraid that you've hired me under false pretenses. My Russian isn't nearly as fluent as we thought. I've only read six pages. You probably should let me go and hire someone else."

Mr. Korol stared at me through his rimless glasses, and my heart sank even lower. Katie Gibbs loomed in my future.

"Never mind," he said. "You go back and keep reading. I don't care how long it takes. When you've finished the book, write a summary and bring it to me." It took two months of sitting under the sickening blue light with no one to talk to—a form of torture for a social animal like me—but I did it.

Another Radcliffe graduate, Thalia Poleway, and I moved into a tiny two-room apartment in Cambridge, where we shared the bedroom. We took great pleasure in furnishing the flat with discarded orange crates and painting the bathroom purple. Meanwhile, Lee, as predicted, made the law review at Harvard Law School. He lived with three roommates and worked around the clock, practicing moot court sessions until late at night.

Lee's and my social life for the next two years consisted mostly of study dates in the Harvard Law School library (he studied and I read books), with a stop for an ice cream frappé on the way back to our separate apartments, occasionally enlivened by a law school party. Was I in love? I certainly thought so, although now I wonder. In a sense, both Lee and I were programmed, and we were doing what was expected.

At the end of my second year at MIT, preparations went

into high gear for our June wedding in Princeton. Mother and I picked out a wedding gown and blue bridesmaid's dresses; a family friend caught salmon in Canada and froze it to serve at the reception; presents piled up at Hodge Road in Princeton. Shortly before the wedding, my parents went off on a holiday trip down the Connecticut River with some friends, planning to return a week before the big day. Meanwhile, the lease on my apartment lapsed, so I moved into the guest room in Lee's family house. The Korol project had ended and I was working for a new boss, writing a paper on Chinese Communist infiltration of middle schools in Singapore and Malaysia, a job that had come my way because my attendance at a Soviet school had categorized me as an expert on Communist education. I was rushing against a deadline to finish the paper before I left on our honeymoon to Biarritz.

One hot afternoon about ten days before the wedding, Lee took me to his bedroom and said that we needed to talk. "Sit down. We have to have a serious conversation. I can't go through with our wedding. It has nothing to do with you, but I'm not ready to take on the responsibilities of marriage."

My head spun. The white chenille bedspread on the single bed, the old-fashioned floor lamp, and Lee's Milton School ribbons—all seemed etched in place. I could barely breathe. But why? "What's wrong? Have I done something?" I asked. I thought if I could just keep talking, this nightmare would go away.

But Lee inserted the final cut. "I really can't explain. But I discussed this with my mother, and she agrees that we should wait." The word "wait" afforded a thin thread of hope, but I still felt totally betrayed.

My world had collapsed, and my future, as I saw it, had vanished. My parents, cruising down the Connecticut River, had left no phone numbers. The house in Princeton was locked. I had no key. Neither Lee nor I knew how to deal with the crisis that he had created, so, both paralyzed, we spent the week until my parents returned pretending that we were still getting married. My red eyes hidden by dark glasses, and my face shadowed under a big hat, I attended Lee's law school graduation parties and accepted good wishes on our upcoming nuptials. My stomach froze shut. I lost twenty pounds that month.

I did insist that we go to see a therapist and found one in Boston. Everything about him was roseate. Redheaded with a red beard, he had a snappy red MG sitting in front of his office. After our joint session, the doctor met with me alone and gave me a blunt, and not rosy, prognostication. "You're well out of it," he said. "Your fiancé is immature, a mama's boy, and emotionally cold. You'd be better off with a loving truck driver than with him."

I was appalled. It was clear that the doctor didn't understand how smart and sensitive Lee was and how much he really cared for me. I knew that this was just a bad dream and someday we would wake up.

When my parents returned and heard my voice sobbing out the news on the telephone, it was clear to them that I couldn't get myself to Princeton. My mother drove up to Cambridge and brought my belongings and me home. For the next few days we sat in the living room, frantically looking up addresses and composing telegrams to the 125 invitees, "postponing" the wedding.

Since I was obviously unable to function, my new boss at MIT suggested that I take a few weeks off before I returned to the world of Singapore and Malaysia. Lee, meanwhile, took our tickets and went to Biarritz with his younger brother, another stab to my heart. As consolation, he left me his convertible to use.

Mary, another classmate, and I drove the car to Chicago, left it with Lee's roommate, and boarded a train for California, sitting up and eating oranges for two days and nights as we rode across the country. It was my first trip to California. Although I still burst into spasms of uncontrollable crying, San Francisco was exhilarating, and my spirits slowly lifted as we spent ten days riding cable cars, admiring the views, and eating in colorful little ethnic restaurants. But I kept touching the diamond ring hanging on a chain hidden under my sweaters, and I clung to a forlorn hope that someday I might wear it again.

Arriving back in Princeton in sultry, humid August, I found the unopened wedding presents stacked in the stifling hot attic, which lacked both air-conditioning and insulation. Mother instructed me to open each gift, write a personal letter to each guest, rewrap the present, and take the packages to the post office. The monogrammed towels and jewelry case couldn't be returned and hung around for years as unwelcome reminders. Mother's lack of participation in this horrible project made me feel in some way responsible for the broken engagement. My father just ignored the subject, which added to my feeling of inadequacy. To rub it in, after my sweltering days in the attic, we ate the wedding salmon every night for dinner.

The first day back at my office at MIT, I sat down at my desk and stared at a blank lined yellow pad. Every Chinese name I had ever learned had vanished from my mind, and I had almost no memory of the half-written paper. At the end of the day, I was still staring at the empty pad. I had to start again from scratch. Nothing like this had ever happened to me.

My new boss was surprisingly sympathetic. "Don't worry. You've had a horrible shock. Take your time and I know you'll do it." A Yale graduate, he conveyed a sort of "Boola Boola" attitude toward the project.

So for six weeks I lived in a temporary basement sublet with the bathtub in the kitchen. When the paper was finally completed, I moved to Washington, DC. Since I already had a security clearance for some classified work I had done at MIT, it was easy for me to transfer my skills. I couldn't wait to put Cambridge behind me.

CHAPTER 5

California, Here We Come

I found a job in the intelligence service of the Department of the Army and settled in to a tiny row house with a postage-stamp-size backyard in the Foggy Bottom section of Washington. In 1956, Foggy Bottom was a transitional neighborhood, although my roommate, Nancy, and I liked to call it Bohemian. Drunks staggered home, passing young bureaucrats going to work.

Living by day in the clandestine world of military secrets, at night I jumped into the Washington social scene with gusto. My father, who had been designated the Eastman Professor at Oxford University, was pleased about my job, but his letters from England kept reproving me for "burning the candle at both ends." My mother, struggling with young Christopher and Wendy, may have been secretly jealous.

An unexpected phone call changed all this. "Hello, this is C. K. McClatchy. You may not remember me, but I met you at Adlai Stevenson's house in Libertyville, Illinois, the night that Eisenhower accepted the Republican nomination for president."

"Oh, yes," I dissembled, groping to remember this man, known by his initials, although the evening in question remained vivid.

Eight months before, returning by train to Washington from my California trip, I stopped off in Chicago to join my father, who was staying in Aunt Jeanette's house in Highland Park. My mother had arranged for me to cook and launder for him while he did research for a new book at the University of Chicago. Aunt Jeanette and Uncle Gene were away on vacation. As usual, my father's needs were foremost in my mother's mind and took precedence over my broken heart.

While I stood over the ironing board one day, pondering my murky future, the telephone rang. The caller introduced himself as Mr. Stevenson from Libertyville, Illinois, phoning to invite Ambassador Kennan for dinner the next night. After hanging up, I realized that it must be Adlai Stevenson, then the Democratic nominee for president.

When my father returned, I told him eagerly and then begged, "Please, please, ask if you can bring me, too."

"Why?" he asked. "You weren't invited." But, after ardent pleading on my part, he called back and I was included in the evening.

My father and I drove to the old Stevenson family home in Libertyville. Our visit coincided with the last night of the Republican convention. The dinner turned out to be an intimate one, including two of Stevenson's sons, Adlai and John Fell, as well as a couple of staff members. Adlai Stevenson's wit and charm matched up well with my father's erudition and brilliance. Verbal sallies flew back and forth across the table. I soaked it all up, especially when the press, which had been camped outside the front door, was let in to photograph Adlai watching Eisenhower's acceptance speech on TV. I only vaguely noticed a young deputy press secretary with initials for a name, who had been with us at the table.

When C. K. called six months later, he had moved to Washington, DC, and was now working for John Secondari at ABC News. He asked if I would join him for dinner, and we started going out. Unlike my previous boyfriend, who preferred to spend most of the time at home, interrupted by occasional trips to the movies or to eat Chinese, C. K. inhabited a larger world. Bright and kind, he had lots of friends, and his career as a journalist was one that I admired. He came from an old and distinguished newspaper family in California that owned the *Sacramento Bee*, the *Fresno Bee*, and the *Modesto Bee*. In fact, the Central Valley was often jokingly called "The Valley of the Bees." C. K. squired me to fancy restaurants and glamorous parties. In light of my father's decision to attend Princeton after reading *This Side of Paradise*, the most impressive for me was a dinner party at the home of Scottie Lanahan, F. Scott Fitzgerald's daughter.

At the same time, my work—classified and interesting—was a far cry from my job at MIT, where I worked for older men with few young colleagues. In Washington, I was happy to be with people my own age. I became torn between my job and my social life. A letter to my parents conveyed contradictory messages as well as some gender preconceptions with which I must have been struggling:

Work has been tremendously interesting and demanding. The last two weeks, due to a resignation and a vacation, I had three people's jobs; and while the pace was terrific . . . the responsibility was very exciting. They have given me just the type of work I love, and I am for the first time doing almost a good job at something. It is wonderful to feel that there are some things one has a talent for. There is only one trouble with this kind of work, which is that it is really a man's work and it takes so much out of you and is so emotionally rewarding that it can easily become a substitute for other things. Now that they are giving me real responsibility, I can imagine becoming a career girl, and frankly there is nothing more unhappy for women in the long run. The majority of the 35- and 40-year-olds around the office are not happy people.

We had known each other for only six months when C. K. took me to California to meet his mother at Lake Tahoe and his friends in San Francisco. We skipped Sacramento, where the family newspapers were based, and instead flew to Reno and then drove to Lake Tahoe. The fabled deep-blue lake, the pungent smell of pine, and the crisp mountain air were intoxicating. However, despite C. K.'s and my shared pleasure in hiking and water skiing—a new sport—the vacation was not idyllic. The atmosphere in that small rustic cabin, the second-oldest house on Lake Tahoe, was cold.

C. K.'s mother, Phebe, with whom C. K. had a distant, wary relationship, was charming, well-read, and intelligent. She was also demanding. A late arrival for dinner was met with an icy look from her penetrating brown eyes. The household was run on rigid, hourly schedules. Hugs and kisses were not in evidence. In our separate rooms, C. K. and I whispered to each other through the thin, splintery wooden walls, but he didn't approach me physically beyond stolen kisses. I yearned for more affection but attributed his restraint to the inhibiting influence of his mother.

Instead of drawing us together, the trip made me question our relationship. Back in Washington, I proposed that we stop seeing each other for a while, but that barely registered with C. K. He responded by asking if I would see him again in six weeks. I accepted, convinced that six weeks was an eternity and C. K. would become a distant memory. I returned to the single life.

Six weeks to the day later, C. K. called. "I need to see you. Will you have dinner with me tomorrow night?"

Mostly because I couldn't think of a good reason to refuse, I accepted. After all, a dinner was just a dinner.

When C. K. walked in the door, he handed me a big bouquet of roses, then blurted, "Will you marry me? I can't live without you."

Standing in my small entryway, I felt as if the air had suddenly been sucked out of the room. "No, I'm not ready," I stammered.

But C. K. paid no attention and swept me out the door to a smart, posh restaurant. The china glittered, the wineglasses sparkled, the crisp white napkins stood up by themselves, and the flutes were filled with champagne. We had barely touched the entrées when C. K. launched into an emotional speech about how unhappy he had been without me, how much he loved me, how impressed his mother had been with me. I absorbed it like a sponge. This worldly, experienced journalist, six years my senior, needed me. That was a powerful aphrodisiac, and the champagne undoubtedly helped. Surely he wouldn't leave me in the lurch, like Lee.

It must have been sometime during the second bottle of champagne that I heard myself saying yes. On a cloud of excitement and champagne bubbles, we floated back to the house. "We have to call my mother," C. K. said.

"So soon?" I asked. "Can't we wait until tomorrow?"

"No," he insisted. "There is a time change between Washington and California. Now is the perfect time." His mother seemed genuinely happy with the news. At age thirty, C. K. was the youngest of three unmarried sons. Phebe's joy was very encouraging.

When we reached my parents in Oxford, England, they were not as ecstatic as my future mother-in-law. They said that it was selfish of us to plan a wedding for March, just three months away. Couldn't we wait until they returned? It would be both inconvenient and too expensive for them to make a special trip to Washington for the wedding. I also knew that my father thought of Californians as some sort of American subspecies—healthy and athletic, but not our kind. I interpreted their negativity as a familiar lack of support. "They'll come around," my friends said, and I chose to believe them.

Our engagement took on a life of its own, totally beyond my control. An announcement of our engagement, submitted by C. K.'s mother, appeared in the *New York Times*.

There was a tradition in old California families of sending a demitasse cup as an engagement present. Miniature china cups piled up in the Foggy Bottom house. Letters flew back and forth to England. My parents now wanted us to be married in Oxford. Despite their expressed wishes, I thought it unfair for C. K.'s family to have to travel to Oxford and knew that few of our friends could afford the long trip. C. K. and I remained adamant about being married in Washington. Finally, my parents' friend Polly Wisner offered to give the wedding reception in her elegant Georgetown house. As usual, I felt slightly out of whack. My married classmates, wed at home, were given away by their fathers, while I was being married at a strange house with no parents in sight.

C. K.'s pals gave us a series of parties in Washington, and Barklie and Margaret Henry, friends of my parents from Princeton, gave a dinner party there in our honor, as well. At the formal seated repast, I found myself next to the atomic physicist Robert Oppenheimer, a close colleague of my father's at the Institute for Advanced Study and a national hero, as well, for his work on the atom bomb. He had a beautiful sensitive face, melting brown eyes, and a poetic manner of speech. We were just finishing the entrée, however, when he turned steely. "How can you do what you're doing? You can't get married without your parents. Don't you know how much you are hurting them by not going to England?" I tried to explain how difficult it would be for C. K.'s California family and friends to travel so far, but Oppenheimer persisted. He said we were being selfish; that convenience was no excuse. "Your parents are much more important than friends. Don't you know that?"

Of course, he hit a nerve. I excused myself and, in tears, hurried down the hallway to a bedroom, where I threw myself on the bed. Kitty Oppenheimer, Robert's wife, found me there and said, "Don't pay attention to him. He does this to me all the time." She helped me pull myself together and I returned to the company. I felt like a fallen soufflé that night and, by this point, I had developed doubts. Something didn't seem quite right.

I started to have nightly fantasies of a knight on horseback, who would pick me up on a beach and swoop me away. But the wedding machinery was in full gear. My roommate, Nancy Boardman, would be getting married two weeks before me, and I was to be maid of honor in her wedding. The two wedding dresses hung side by side in the living room. Evenings in the snowy winter of 1958 were busy with addressing invitations, opening and listing presents, and accepting good wishes from friends and family. Due to the presence of roommates, C. K.'s work, and the taboo of premarital sex in the days before the sexual revolution, my fiancé and I managed to make love exactly once during our engagement period. So I was shocked when I discovered that I was pregnant. Now there was no going back.

On March 1, 1958, C. K. and I were married at St. John's Episcopal Church, in the shadow of the White House. My parents' friend Barklie Henry gave me away. As the reception got under way, I still hoped that my parents would make a surprise appearance. But when I was called to the phone and heard their voices, all I could do was cry.

A Domestic Life

When C. K. and I moved to Sacramento from Washington in the summer of 1958, I thought that I had landed in another foreign country. Sacramento was different from anything I knew. In those days, it was a low town—the high-rises had yet to come. Its center was made up of wooden Victorian houses with stairs going directly to the second floor, as the first, or ground, floor was used as a basement because of periodic Sacramento River floods. Palm, camellia, and magnolia trees abounded. A friend, another transplant to the area, referred rather sarcastically to "moral, floral Sacramento."

Seven months pregnant when we moved, I began to feel invisible. Having been accustomed to men looking at me, I was aware that eyes no longer lingered. Because of my pregnancy, my doctor had forbidden me to travel cross-country with C. K. in our new Mercedes convertible, so I rode to Sacramento alone on the train. During the three-day train trip, the only people who spoke to me were some nuns. I wondered, "Is this my new life?" When I disembarked and lumbered out of the station, the sweltering, dry summer heat practically knocked me over.

While C. K. and I house-hunted, we lived in his aunt Eleanor McClatchy's guesthouse. A formal garden, tiled fountains, and a profusion of orange trees and oleanders connected our house with her Spanish-style hacienda. Aunt Eleanor had become publisher of the family newspapers after the death of her brother, Carlos, C. K.'s father.

Increasing my sense of isolation, I began to dislike Aunt Eleanor. Everything she did annoyed me. I would hide in my room behind the pages of a book or retreat into writing letters—a great solace. My parents, who had heard little from me, were suddenly deluged with mail. My obvious unhappiness made C. K. miserable.

Aunt Eleanor was imposing but painfully shy, a woman plagued with a frequent stutter. She was acutely conscious of the family legacy, responsibilities, and reputation, which she upheld by contributing generously to local restoration projects and theater events. Almost every evening Aunt Eleanor attended a play or musical, which was her escape from the newspaper business.

Not much happened on the Sacramento stage without her approval. I perceived this as her dictatorship of the local drama scene, not admitting that without Eleanor's generosity there wouldn't have been a drama scene at all. She had little social life beyond that.

Highly self-conscious, Eleanor used storytelling to settle into social situations. She liked to serve a fish house punch when she entertained, accompanied by a long shaggy-dog story about the origins of the punch. Every time I heard the story I cringed, wondering how people could pretend to be so fascinated by this rambling tale. I also disliked the sweet taste of the punch.

Finally, C. K. sat me down and said that my obvious resentment of Eleanor was putting him in an impossible situation. After all, she was both his aunt *and* his employer. Couldn't I find a way to look at her differently? Strangely enough, his plea worked. From then on, I approached her repertoire of stories with a fresh attitude, knowing that C. K.'s very livelihood depended on it.

My new mother-in-law was something else. A tall, articulate Vassar graduate, Phebe came from a wealthy banking family based in Marysville and San Francisco. Phebe and Carlos McClatchy had moved to Fresno when he started the *Fresno Bee*. They lived in a large old-fashioned house complete with swimming pool and tennis court. Carlos died when C. K. was only nine. After her husband's death, Phebe purposely remained in that agricultural valley town and created her own life far from the McClatchy fiefdom in Sacramento. While well-traveled and sophisticated, she was emotionally unreachable. My husband was never close to his mother, perhaps because it was evident that his older brother, James, was her favorite.

Intellectually brilliant, Phebe dominated social situations with her erudition and wit but also with her quick criticisms and put-downs, especially of C. K. She clearly resented that Eleanor had taken over Carlos's position at the newspapers, believing she, Phebe, would have been better equipped for the job. I rarely saw the two women together except at weddings and christenings.

We moved into our new little house on Coleman Way. Within weeks our son, Charles, was born. My parents did not visit for the event, as they were vacationing in Naushon Island. I missed them terribly. At the hospital, I not only nursed the baby—unusual at the time, and against C. K.'s wishes—but also annoyed the nurses by insisting on having my newborn sleep in the room with me. Nurses didn't like this arrangement, as calls from nervous new mothers added to their workload. But I was adamant. I had read about it in a magazine and knew better.

Charles was a tall, well-formed baby, and both our families were thrilled by the arrival of the first grandchild on either side. Smugly, I felt I had finally done something right, but my confidence wavered at home when Charles soon turned into a screamer. His piercing cries made me feel inadequate, and our temporary baby nurse reinforced this idea. "Mrs. McClatchy, it must be something in your milk. Are you sure you haven't been eating onions or chocolate? You can tell me." I hadn't, but she clearly didn't believe me. When I finally took Charles to the pediatrician, the doctor discovered that Charles had an intestinal problem and indeed had been suffering the entire time, his pitiful calls for help unheeded.

My tilted life, however, righted itself. I became friends with other young mothers. In hindsight, nearly all my Sacramento friends were also East Coast refugees or San Francisco transplants trying to adjust to new marriages, new children, and Sacramento's staid and stodgy culture. None of us had families in the area, so we became an unusually close group.

I had a harder time with the old Sacramento families. Many of them paid off their social obligations by giving an annual dinner at the Del Paso Country Club. At my first such soiree, my dinner partner turned to me and said, "Oh, you're from back east. I was there once. It's all so run down back there." Controlling my astonishment and a sudden urge to giggle, I turned to the man on my other side, as he asked, "How did a nice girl like you get to be a Democrat?" Everyone assumed that I must be ecstatic about my good fortune at ending up in beautiful Sacramento. I could hardly share my homesickness.

Moscow, Vienna, Portugal, Norway, Berlin, Washington, and Cambridge all seemed very far away.

Even the vocabulary was strange to me. People talked about a "family room" and not a large kitchen, "drapes" instead of curtains, "passing" instead of dying. Everyone had gone either to "Cal" (the University of California) or my husband's alma mater, Stanford. When I mentioned Radcliffe College, most had never heard of it or mixed it up with Bradford Junior College—a humbling experience. I stopped talking about my past and concentrated on adjusting to the floral paradise that was my home, like it or not.

Holidays, especially Christmas, accentuated my homesickness. The Christmases of my youth, wherever we found ourselves, were Norwegian and had a bit of magic. We celebrated the holiday on Christmas Eve, originally trimming the tree with real candles, which soon became sparkling electric lights. For Christmas Eve we all dressed in our best clothes, and Mother was resplendent in a long dress, often a rich red silk or satin. We would sit down for a salmon dinner in the dining room, the table decorated with special Christmas angels and reindeer. After, we would dim the lights, form a circle, and, holding hands, walk around the tree, singing all the carols we knew, my sister Joan's beautiful voice rising from the chorus. The next-to-last song was always Mother's favorite, the Norwegian carol "O Yule Messen Glede," followed by "Silent Night," the beauty of which still makes me want to cry.

In those early married years, we spent the Christmas holidays in Fresno with Phebe and her new husband, a nice judge named Philip Conley, whom she married shortly after my wedding to C. K. The warm weather in Fresno often caused the wreaths and the Christmas trees to wilt, and references to Santa and his sleigh seemed ludicrously out of place. Instead of magical Christmas Eves, we assembled after breakfast in the harsh light of Christmas Day in front of a desiccated tree, its desultory needles falling. Presents were sorted out and piled up in front of each recipient, to be opened alone by each of us. Since Phebe was an agnostic, she made sure that there were no references to God or the birth of Jesus. There was nothing spiritual in the McClatchy Christmas.

After my third Fresno Christmas, I wrote my parents: "Our Christmas was perfectly awful. Phebe was as one possessed the entire weekend, playing one person off against the other and sending cruel shafts in C. K.'s direction."

Two years later, Charles was followed by a beautiful little girl, whom we named Adair. Bedtimes, diets, and toilet training filled my life. Dr. Spock was my bible. But it was not my whole life. All the time I had wanted to keep up my Russian. Finally I found a job translating periodicals from Russian to English for the Library of Congress. I wrote my parents: "My first assignment was satisfactory, and I'm going to be paid! It will keep up my Russian and my knowledge of the area and what is going on. It has been wonderful to feel my intellectual energies harnessed in some direction."

C. K. also wanted and expected me to accompany him to the many social events to which we were invited. I was happy to do so, but life was hectic. All this necessitated child care, so a stream of au pair girls came and went. After Adair's birth, I wrote my mother to excuse myself for not having written sooner: "Life has been AWFUL. Not really awful, just frightfully busy and horribly disorganized. The help situation really got us down. As we all know, I am a very poor housekeeper, so I feel miserably my shortcomings. I can keep the house going all right (cooking, laundry, dishes, children) if everything is calm, but any calamity or break in the routine occurs and suddenly everything piles up, and there are the unwashed diapers on the floor of the john." Needless to say, the confusion only increased when, two years later, Kevin joined the family and we had three children under the age of four.

Then there was tennis. C. K., who loved tennis, had given me lessons as a wedding present. Since tennis had not been part of my childhood, I started from behind but worked like mad to catch up. Soon I became an avid player and competed in interclub matches.

My son Charles's adventures were a leitmotif woven into my letters of this period. A hyperactive child, he was constantly in trouble. Only when he was an adult was he diagnosed with attention deficit disorder (ADD). Typically, I put a good face on it and hid my feelings behind humor. "Charles is fine, too, except that he has perfected his climbing talents, which are considerable, and it is now like having a human chimpanzee around the house. I walk into the bedroom and find him on top of the bureau. . . . Next day Charles is having a tea party in the kitchen with my best demitasse cups." Anything that he could pull down on his head, he did. Charles and I were familiar faces in the emergency room.

Summer weekends, we went up to Lake Tahoe to stay in my mother-in-law's old summer cottage, located on a fifteen-acre piece of land on the lake. In addition to charm and historic significance, the house had paper-thin walls and antique bathrooms. As far as sound was concerned, we all might as well have been sleeping in one room. The crowding intensified after Adair's birth.

Ironically, despite the fact that in the Tahoe house you could hear everything, the McClatchy family was full of secrets. Carlos's premature death was probably due to alcoholism, but that was an issue never mentioned. In fact, I found out only years later, from a doctor. Maybe as a result, Phebe's cocktail hour lasted about fifteen minutes, and anything alcoholic was measured out by the spoonful. When C. K. and I had guests at Lake Tahoe, this made life difficult. We found our guests sneaking off to a local bar, making us feel very inhospitable. C. K. started to agitate for permission to build our own house on the property, where there was still plenty of space.

C. K.'s older brother Jim and Phebe joined in opposition: "Everyone else has been happy in the main house. Why do you have to strike out on your own? You will clutter up this beautiful property with unnecessary buildings."

But C. K. was resolute, saying that we would stop coming if we could not build our own house. We finally received permission to build, with the proviso that we use Phebe's friend, the distinguished Bay Area architect Bill Wurster. I resented the fact that we couldn't choose our own designer and found Mr. Wurster quite intimidating. At our first meeting with him, he warned, "I hope that you have a strong marriage, because if not, building a house together will tear it apart."

Our home turned out to be a lovely symmetrical shingled house with a warm, spacious living room, large decks, and a welcoming kitchen with antique Dutch tiles. I ended up loving it and later told my parents, "I feel like the bride who fell in love with her husband after the marriage." While we had reassured Mr. Wurster that our marriage was solid, in fact, cracks were appearing with amazing speed.

Things Unravel

One night we were sitting around our dinner table with guests, sated and happy. I had cooked roast duck for the first time and was feeling proud of this culinary accomplishment. C. K. began to reminisce about a well-known beauty in Washington, Deeda Blair, married to William McCormick Blair, his former boss on the Stevenson campaign. C. K. was extolling her appearance when one of the guests, a bachelor renowned for his romantic escapades, interrupted: "C. K., never mind Deeda. The most beautiful woman is here in this room—it's your wife." There was dead silence. I was stunned, as my husband never complimented or mentioned my looks. Soon after this, C. K. was invited to participate in a study program in Germany for six weeks as a guest of the German government, and he invited the bachelor to amuse me and keep me company while he was gone.

Well, the bachelor amused me so much that I fell in love. Our romance, however, was short-lived. Not only did the man live far away, he was also a rolling stone and soon moved on. What had drawn me to him, besides strong physical attraction, was the warmth that I so badly missed in my marriage. In reality, I had few illusions in describing him to my best friend: "He's rather like an Irish poet—fantastic imagination, fantastic humor, fantastic warmth, will charm the leaves off the trees, and at other times is feckless, lies, drinks, and undoubtedly seduces any girl that's near."

My letters to my father in Yugoslavia, where he had been appointed ambassador by President Kennedy in 1962, took on a different tone, becoming more introspective: "I have a compulsion to keep busy to a certain point outside the house—too much inside makes me feel the emptiness of it all. And oddly enough I seem to amuse C. K. more. I sometimes think that my chief value to him is as diversion, a hostess, and a link with the outside world."

Soon the letters became more unhappy: "This is a hellish time—like a squirrel in a cage, my mind goes over and over the litany of our marriage, and I keep wondering if it is me that has failed us or whether the situation is indeed unbearable."

My unhappiness was camouflaged by constant activity. I was asked to translate for the first Soviet women's delegation that came to Sacramento, and as a result was invited to accompany the first American women's delegation on the return trip to the Soviet Union in 1962. Four months' pregnant, but with my doctor's reluctant permission, I flew off with the group. I felt comfortable back in Moscow. I also made my first trip to Riga since my birth. Far from Sacramento and my family, I was a successful translator and facilitator, but I couldn't reconcile this competent person with the insecurity I felt as a wife and mother at home. The pressure was increased after the birth of Kevin, in January 1963. The more I tried to fill an empty personal life with volunteer work, the more in demand I became. "The phone rings all day long," I wrote in one of my letters. "The poor old house and family sort of bounce along between rings."

However, when I was offered a job at the local television station as production assistant on an interview show, something that I would have been good at, C. K. was adamant about my not accepting. In those days, volunteer work was okay for a young matron, but a real job was not. A month later, when I was asked to join the Junior League, I wrote to my parents:

> I can't think of anything that I would less rather do and it seems to me a spurious way to do good works (i.e., by forming an exclusive and discriminatory club) and I am already doing good works.
>
> However, no one has ever declined in the history of the Sacramento League, and C. K. fears that if I do, it will add to the legend of the antisocial McClatchys.

So I joined.

C. K. was a kind, decent, bright man with a good sense of humor and a deep capacity for friendship, but he had no interest in our sex life. We had twin beds on our honeymoon in the Barbados, and he never slept with me during the trip. My assumption was that pregnant women were repellent to men. I was too ashamed to discuss this, so no one disabused me of this idea. When we resumed sex after Charles's birth, it was lukewarm and very obviously associated with my ability to get pregnant, which I seemed able to do at the drop of a trouser. Early on, when I had reached out for C. K. in bed, he turned me away, saying, "Never touch me unless I touch you first." I listened to my friends' marital stories and realized that my marriage was different.

Painfully uneducated about male–female relationships, I decided the problem was my fault. I was too fat. I wasn't attractive. I launched ferociously into one self-improvement campaign after another. Diet followed diet; every new form of exercise was tried; I read "Can This Marriage Be Saved?" in the *Ladies' Home Journal* every month, hoping for a lifeline. Every now and then, I look back at old photographs and see pictures of an attractive, vivacious young woman who does not seem in any way to be related to the person that I thought I was.

As many of our friends were from San Francisco, we entertained them at Tahoe, which was a relatively short hop for them. One weekend, about seven years into our marriage, we were hosting five male houseguests. After dinner, when most everyone, including C. K., had gone up to bed, I shared a nightcap with one of the guests. Suddenly he blurted out, "Don't you realize who your husband is and what he is doing? Don't you know he's gay?"

His words echoed in my ears. I stared at him, dumbfounded. "How do you know?" I asked him, almost hoping he wouldn't answer.

"Well, for one thing," he answered, without a bit of hesitation, "he chased me around the shower this afternoon."

No, I didn't realize. And I didn't want to believe that what this guest was saying was true. I feared that life would never be the same. Why hadn't I thought of this possibility when C. K. and I didn't even have sex on our honeymoon? Why hadn't I realized how acutely lonely I was?

Homosexuality at that time was such a taboo that it never crossed my mind. I did know that C. K. had been seeing a therapist in San Francisco but had no idea why. Maybe he would give me the confirmation or denial I needed.

I called C. K.'s doctor and demanded to see him. He grudgingly agreed to meet me, on the condition that he wouldn't reveal any patient information. I drove to San Francisco, and the doctor listened to me with little reaction for about forty minutes. When I concluded by saying that I thought our marriage was over, he suddenly engaged, leaning forward. "Oh you mustn't leave him," he said. "It would be bad for his therapy."

I felt my stomach turn. "Then what am I to do?" I asked. "Play more tennis," advised the doctor, looking at his watch.

I climbed into the car and drove the ninety miles back to Sacramento with tears streaming down my face, matching the rain hitting the windshield. I felt very sorry for myself. I should have felt emotion for the hell that C. K. was in, being a member of a prominent family and having to bear such a big secret, but I was too young, and that compassion came years later. The one thing I knew for sure, however, without knowing how or when, was that my life in Sacramento was coming to an end.

Divorcing C. K. was easier decided than done. When I asked for a divorce, he was shocked and upset. He didn't ask why and I didn't volunteer. I was consumed with guilt about my action. What had seemed so logical to me became a prolonged battle, with more and more people drawn into the fray. My parents, from whom I had hoped for a modicum of support, had grown very fond of C. K., and although my mother knew that C. K. preferred men to women, she took a firm stand: "You can have affairs, and everyone will be satisfied. No one in our family has ever been divorced, and you can't do it, either. Don't break up a marriage. It hasn't been easy living with your father, but we stayed married. If you leave C. K., you will be responsible for ruining your children's lives."

There was a clear implication that she had suffered and I should, too. My father, while a little more understanding, also seemed to think that this was in some way my fault. Mother even invited C. K. for Christmas, which that year lacked the usual holiday spirit.

The worst was telling our children. "You tell them," C. K. said. "This is your idea." Not wanting to tell the children in front of the au pair girl, I took them—ages three, five, and seven—out in the car to get an ice cream so we could be alone. I told them that C. K. and I were separating but that they would still see their father frequently. Charles was devastated and not to be consoled. Adair was quiet. Kevin asked, "Now can I have my ice cream?"

GRACE IN NORWAY. FAMILY PHOTO.

GRACE AND HER MOTHER. FAMILY PHOTO.

GRACE IN MOSCOW. FAMILY PHOTO.

GRACE IN AUSTRIA. FAMILY PHOTO

GRACE AND HER FATHER ON THE BERGENSFJPORD. FAMILY PHOTO.

GRACE AND JOAN IN KRISTIANSAND, NORWAY. FAMILY PHOTO.

GRACE AT PINE LAKE, WISCONSIN. FAMILY PHOTO.

GRACE AT THE QUINTA, PORTUGAL. FAMILY PHOTO.

131-ая школа Советского р-на г. Москва

VI Класс.

В этом классе в 1944/45 уч году училась
б. Кеннон.

GRACE'S CLASS AT SCHOOL NO. 131, TAKEN THE YEAR AFTER SHE LEFT.
GRACE'S PHOTO.

VALENTINA, GRACE'S MOSCOW SCHOOL
FRIEND. VALENTINA'S PHOTO.

THE FARM, EAST BERLIN, PENNSYLVANIA. FAMILY PHOTO.

GEORGE KENNAN BEING SWORN IN AS U.S. AMBASSADOR TO
THE SOVIET UNION. ASSOCIATED PRESS WIRE PHOTO.

GRACE AND HER FATHER AT RADCLIFFE GRADUATION, 1954.
PHOTO BY GORDON N. CONVERSE (NOW DECEASED), STAFF
PHOTOGRAPHER FOR *CHRISTIAN SCIENCE MONITOR.*

GRACE'S WEDDING PICTURE AT HER MARRIAGE TO C. K. MCCLATCHY,
1958. FAMILY PHOTO.

KEVIN AND JOHN FELL'S CHRISTENING. FROM LEFT TO RIGHT: C. K. MCCLATCHY, GRACE, KEVIN, ADLAI STEVENSON, JOHN FELL JR., NATALIE, AND JOHN FELL STEVENSON. ORIGIN UNKNOWN.

ANNELISE ON THE SAILBOAT. FAMILY PHOTO.

GRACE AND HER
CHILDREN. FAMILY
PHOTO.

GRACE AND JACK AT
WARNECKE RANCH.
PHOTO BY MICHELLE
VIGNES (NOW DECEASED).

GRACE WITH TED KENNEDY AND FAMILY IN BREZHNEV'S OFFICE.
PHOTO BY KEN REGAN/CAMERA 5

JOAN BAEZ IN MOSCOW. PHOTO BY GRACE WARNECKE.

GEORGE KENNAN IN INSTITUTE OFFICE, 1982.
PHOTO BY GRACE WARNECKE.

GEORGE KENNAN AT THE BRANDENBURG GATE, BERLIN, 1982.

PHOTO BY GRACE WARNECKE.

GEORGE, KENT, AND THEIR SISTERS FRANCES, JEANETTE, AND CONSTANCE.
FAMILY PHOTO.

GEORGE KENNAN RAKING AT THE FARM. FAMILY PHOTO.

GRACE AND RENEE VOLEN ON THE WAY TO MOSCOW, 1989. FAMILY PHOTO.

GRACE AND VOLKHOV INCUBATOR STAFF. PHOTO BY STAFF MEMBER.

OPENING OF CHERNIHIV WOMEN'S BUSINESS CENTER, 2000.
ORIGIN UNKNOWN.

GRACE AND HER CHILDREN, PITTSBURGH, 2001. FAMILY PHOTO.

ZHENYA POROTOV. PHOTO BY GRACE WARNECKE.

KENNAN SIBLINGS AT INSTITUTE FOR ADVANCED STUDIES.

FAMILY PHOTO.

GRACE AND SECRETARY OF STATE COLIN POWELL. FAMILY PHOTO.

GEORGE KENNAN AT 101. PHOTO BY GRACE WARNECKE.

A COLLAGE OF GRACE IN RUSSIA. COLLAGE BY ALEXANDRA CHALIF.

CHAPTER 6

Marriage: A Second Act

If C. K. hadn't gone to Cuba, my life might have turned out quite differently. In 1965, when we were still living in Sacramento, C. K. arranged to go to this communist Caribbean island to write a series of articles for the *Sacramento Bee*. He invited me to go with him. I accepted with great enthusiasm, as a trip to Cuba was a rarity. Also, C. K. and I both loved traveling, exploring new places, and I enjoyed getting out of Sacramento.

We arrived in Mexico City full of excitement and curiosity about Cuba, only to learn at the last minute that the Cuban government had turned down my request for a visa. C. K.'s visa had come through. So he flew off, leaving me to spend three dismal days fighting bureaucrats in Mexican government offices to change my transit visa to a tourist visa. Only through a bribe was I permitted to exit Mexico. Having made byzantine arrangements for my children to stay with their grandmother in Fresno during our absence, I decided to spend the remaining days of the aborted Cuban trip in San Francisco with friends.

Two good Washington friends, Barbara Gamarekian and Meredith Burch—both journalists who had worked in the Kennedy White House press office—happened to be visiting San Francisco at the time. When I called Barbara, she was delighted. "Oh, I'm so sorry about your trip to Cuba. But what perfect timing," she announced. "Our friend Tom Page, a consultant to Warnecke Associates, is giving a party for his boss, Jack Warnecke. You know, the famous architect who designed President Kennedy's grave. Tom will want you to come." Jack and I had met three years before at a dance during the Goldwater convention in San Francisco, which C. K. was covering for the *Sacramento Bee*. Jack had danced most of the evening with me, but I had never seen or heard from him since. "You must come," Barbara continued. "The party will cheer you up. I'll call Tom." Considering this a well-deserved reward for the canceled trip, I accepted.

When Barbara and I arrived at the party in a glamorous Nob Hill apartment with a view of the city, Jack had not appeared. Later I learned that he was always late, even if he was the guest of honor. I was happy catching up with good friends, listening to lively chitchat and hearing Washington gossip. Suddenly there was a slight lull—and a very tall, handsome man with intense blue eyes strolled in the door. It was clear he was our honoree.

Jack had a feline walk that reminded me of a tiger stalking his prey. A fitting musical accompaniment might have been the cat music in *Peter and the Wolf*. Jack slowly made his way around the room, until he came to me. We were reintroduced and started a slightly flirtatious conversation. A tingling sensation took over my body.

"Why haven't we met before?" he asked.

"We have," I answered. "We met at the Vietor Dance during the Goldwater convention." "No, you're wrong," he said. "I danced all evening with a girl in a pink dress."

"Yes, you did," I answered, "but I was the girl in the pink dress."

The current that I felt jumping between us frightened me. I was dying to see him again, but at the same time I suspected it would lead to trouble. I was reassured by the fact that he lived in San Francisco with a country house on the Russian River, and I lived in Sacramento and vacationed at Lake Tahoe. In three days I would be back in the family nest, and chances were good that we would not see each other again.

The next morning Barbara called, full of excitement. "Guess what? Jack Warnecke has invited eight of us out to his ranch tomorrow for canoeing and dinner and to spend the night. He has an incredible house that he remodeled for himself in an old barn. There is also a main house, a guesthouse, and tent platforms for guests. So there's lots of room."

"Well, I don't think I should," I faltered, my saner side weighing in.

Barbara persisted. "He specifically asked me to invite you and said that you and I can have the guesthouse, so you will be properly chaperoned."

I capitulated. My curiosity to see the place and the host were both intense.

I later discovered to what lengths Jack would go when he was pursuing a person or project, but at the time I couldn't conceive that this entire party was part of a calculated strategy directed at me. When Barbara and I arrived, we were greeted by Jack's four good-looking teenage children, John, Roger, Margo, and Freddie. Handsome Roger escorted us to our guesthouse at the top of a hill. After we reunited with our friends at the main house, Jack picked us up and took us on a tour. First we saw the tent platforms—complete with electricity, reading lights, and well-stocked small refrigerators. Then we visited his house, which was always called "the Barn," with its cathedral-ceilinged main room.

After changing into our bathing suits, we piled into waiting cars and were driven up the river, where a ring of canoes, driven there by Roger in a truck, awaited us. We paddled and swam down the wide, rather shallow Russian River to the ranch. Later that night we met on the porch at the main house for a long, lazy cocktail hour, followed by a dinner under the stars. I was not surprised to be seated next to Jack. The setting, the guests, Jack's intense gaze, and the moon—it seemed magical and romantic.

As the other guests departed for their platforms, Jack walked Barbara and me back to the cottage, but, after a quick kiss, I ran inside.

The next day, guests were led to a cavalcade of cars for the trip home. Barbara was placed in one car and I, not surprisingly, in Jack's. As we drove from the ranch to San Francisco, we talked about our lives. He talked about architecture, about his travels. He spoke in curious circular patterns so that I never knew where he was going until he reached the end of his story. I was enthralled. At one moment he reached down and touched my ankle. I could feel a vibration running from my foot to the top of my head. I knew there was trouble ahead.

With much scheming on our parts, Jack and his children came to Tahoe a few weeks later. There were meaningful glances, conversational innuendos, occasional touches—all the preludes to an affair, so banal to the observers and so exciting to the lovers. We were surrounded with six of our seven children—Jack's oldest having been left home. Late one night we snuck off to an unused maid's room, but such rendezvous were rare. After Lake Tahoe, we mostly talked on the telephone.

A few months later, I told Jack I was planning to ask for a divorce. Ever since I had learned about C. K.'s sexual preference, separation had been in the forefront of my mind. But Jack assumed that he was the cause of my decision and quickly withdrew. "You don't know what you're doing. I don't want any part of this. I am not interested in getting involved with a woman with three children. I think we should stop seeing each other."

Somewhat to my relief, we did. The physical passion that Jack had stirred up in me was so powerful that it scared me, and my more rational self knew a divorce would be difficult enough without another person involved.

Despite Mother's dismal warnings, I moved forward with the divorce. I moved to San Francisco and spent my time house-hunting, enrolling the two older children in new schools, and dealing with the details of an endless, painful legal procedure. I didn't see Jack again for another fifteen months, although I received a letter from Hawaii, where Jack seemed to be spending a lot of time. Ultimately I was consoled by a wonderful older widower, a local politician, who showered me with love and attention and nursed my spirit. I assumed that Jack had left my life.

San Francisco was a new world. I haunted museums and art galleries. When I noticed that there were no art reviews in the San Francisco Art Institute newsletter, I offered to write them for free. While I doubt my readership was very large, among my fans was a new friend, Grover Sales, the music critic of *San Francisco* magazine. Grover introduced me to jazz, took me to the Purple Onion to hear Mort Sahl, to another venue to see Lenny Bruce, and definitely expanded my provincial horizons.

One day Grover approached me and said, "You know, Grace, Blair Fuller, *San Francisco* magazine's book critic, is going to Morocco for a year. Why don't you apply for his job?"

"I couldn't possibly," I answered. "I don't have any experience. I've never even written a book review."

"Yes, you can do it. Write a letter and submit some of your art reviews." Grover pushed, nudged, and encouraged, and ultimately I applied. Much to my surprise, I was hired. The fact that I was willing to work for $50 a month and free books undoubtedly had something to do with my landing the job. Now I had work, token pay, and a certain status. To my naive surprise, famous authors were very happy to meet with me. I had left Sacramento behind.

The legal wrestling match dragged on, however, with the children visiting their father every other weekend. Meanwhile,

I was entering a new and different life as a single mother in San Francisco. San Francisco at that time was the home of Beat poets and the mecca of the flower children, but my life had been on a different track. My days were filled with traditional volunteer work, tennis, shopping, child activities, and worrying about my son Charles. He was making a difficult adjustment to the divorce and had endless problems in school.

One night I gave a dinner party for some new literary friends, and a literary agent named Michael asked if he could bring his client, a Hells Angel named Freewheeling Frank, also a poet. I had never heard of Freewheeling Frank and had some reservations, but Michael convinced me that Frank would be well-behaved and would add a dash of spice to this Pacific Heights evening.

I told my children in advance about Frank, and to my surprise they were thrilled. When Frank walked in, Charles was sitting on the stairs with something that resembled an autograph book. Frank took time to talk to him, and we saw the kinder, gentler side of the bearded, weathered motorcycle man. Everyone had a good time. Politicians were talking to writers, and everyone spoke with Frank, and I went to bed feeling as if I had produced a successful evening.

But the next day C. K. phoned, and my rosy picture quickly faded to gray. "What were you thinking of, exposing our children to the Hells Angels? Don't you realize that they could be in danger?" he asked. "If this is what is important to you, maybe I should take the children."

A call from his lawyer made the message even clearer. For weeks I lived in fear. C. K. and I were already battling in the divorce court, and my prospects for an amicable divorce seemed dimmer and dimmer. How could I have done something so thoughtless?

My life was changed again by an unexpected phone call. Jack Warnecke's sexy, languid voice drawled, "I heard that you are now the book critic for *San Francisco* magazine. I'm calling to congratulate you." But that wasn't why he was calling. He invited me up to his ranch for dinner. The same frissons ran up my spine. I guardedly accepted.

As Jack drove me up to the Russian River, there was a letter propped up in front of me on the dashboard. Addressed in very distinctive feminine handwriting, it was from Hammersmith Farm, which I knew as the home of Jacqueline Kennedy. Soon I learned that Jack and Jackie had been together in Hawaii. "Imagine a man who romanced Jackie Kennedy, the nation's idol, wanting to date me" was all I could think.

I still had reservations. Jack kept pursuing. He invited me to the dedications of the University of California, Santa Cruz Library and the Henry Meyer Memorial Library at Stanford University, both of which he had designed. I saw his work, his creativity, and his originality, as well as his charm. I also saw his free spirit, seemingly untethered by the usual worries and concerns of most people. I ended my relationship with the supportive older politician and plunged into what turned out to be a tempestuous courtship with Jack. Taking care of my children by day and seeing Jack by night was exhausting. I survived only because Jack spent much time working in his New York office, as well as traveling on frequent business trips. During his absences, I pulled myself back together. I kept reading and writing book reviews, since I knew that was my identity and sensed I was in danger of losing it.

A seductive side of Jack was that he introduced me to many glamorous people I would never otherwise have met. After my conservative life in Sacramento, this was very appealing. Among these was Senator Ted Kennedy. Although I had met Ted in college, Jack had designed his house in Virginia and knew him quite well. Each had a playboy side to his personality, and those sides meshed.

While Ted's marriage was going through a rough patch, he invited us to join him on various sailing expeditions—to the Bahamas, Nova Scotia, and Hawaii. Each trip was made without his wife and included an attractive woman guest. On these excursions, a lively and bibulous Ted would regale us with amusing stories about his friends and family, often at his own expense. He once told us that his father warned him about driving too fast and said prophetically, "You better watch out, Teddy. You are the kind that will always get caught."

In Hawaii, we joined Ted and friends scuba diving in the ocean off a large boat, an activity at which he was proficient. I had never scuba dived, but Ted insisted that I try it. "Go on," he urged. "I mastered it the first time I tried. Come on—you will, too."

The Kennedys not being the only competitive ones, I agreed to this ridiculous proposal.

After being outfitted with a heavy tank and a breathing mask over my mouth, I jumped overboard, dove straight down, and immediately panicked. I felt smothered by the mask, so I tore it off. But with the heavy tank I couldn't rise to the surface. Fortunately, there was a strong current that day, and when Ted jumped in, the same undertow bore him toward me and he could see me flailing. He tore the tank off my back and pushed me upward to the air. After endangering my life, he saved it. I have never gone scuba diving since.

Our friendship with Ted grew closer; I think he trusted us because we were not involved with his Senate life. That year—1968—Ted's brother Bobby was running for president, but his competitor was Eugene McCarthy. I was a strong McCarthy supporter, which embarrassed Jack. Jack introduced me to Bobby at that time by saying, " . . . but she's for McCarthy."

Shortly afterward, on April 4, Martin Luther King Jr. was shot. As it happened, that evening I went to hear McCarthy speak. To my surprise, he devoted only a sentence or two to King's death and then went on with his canned speech.

A few days later Jack invited me to hear Bobby talk at one of the local universities. Looking slight and vulnerable as he walked out on the stage, he announced, "In light of the Martin

Luther King shooting, I am throwing away my prepared speech and will spend the time answering your questions." Bobby's compassion pierced my heart. From that day on I was a fervent Bobby Kennedy supporter. I volunteered to help organize one of the first fund-raisers for Bobby in San Francisco and enlisted Ted as the speaker. Soon I was named Women's Chairman for Northern California of the Robert Kennedy campaign.

Jack and I kept seeing Ted in California. The night of the primary—June 5, 1968, coincidentally, my birthday—we had been invited to go to Los Angeles for the election party, but, because of Jack's legendary lateness, we missed our plane, and the later ones were sold out. Driving back from the airport, a bit deflated, Jack said, "Oh, well, let's call Ted and see what he's doing." He was having dinner with a lady friend and asked us to join him. We had a lively evening, as the news from Los Angeles was good. We parted early, however, and returned to our separate abodes.

Jack and I turned on the TV to watch the latest from Los Angeles and were stunned to see the shocking footage of Bobby Kennedy being shot and rushed to the hospital, where he lay near death. We knew that Ted was not in the hotel where he was registered but in a borrowed apartment, so Jack decided he had to call Ted in case he had not seen the television.

Jack telephoned Ted with the tragic news, and we all raced to meet at the Fairmont Hotel.

Jack went off to be with Ted in his room and told me to stay in the lobby and organize a Coast Guard plane to fly Ted to Los Angeles. Never questioning this challenging order, I started dropping quarters in a pay phone, until I was finally helped by a senior local politician, who took over. Between us, we did procure the plane that flew Ted Kennedy to Los Angeles.

After Bobby died, Jack immediately flew to New York. He had no intention of including me. But because of my work for Bobby, I also received an invitation to the funeral mass at St. Patrick's Cathedral in New York and to ride on the special train that would take Bobby's body, his family, and his supporters to Washington for his burial at Arlington National Cemetery.

I called Jack and told him that I had decided to come to New York. Bobby had been my political hero, and I wanted to honor and mourn him. I also felt that if Jack didn't acknowledge me as his special friend, our relationship was over. I think Jack knew it, too, because he immediately invited me to go with him to the cathedral.

My most vivid memory is the singing of "The Battle Hymn of the Republic," with almost all the mourners in tears, and pregnant Ethel coming down the aisle followed by her ten children. I was also awed by Ted's speech. It was both simple and moving—a new Ted that I had never seen before.

The trip on the funeral train was an extraordinary journey—in the end taking almost eight hours, as the train traveled at a very slow speed. Hundreds, thousands of people, many of them black, holding up their children, gathered all along the way to pay tribute to Bobby. They lined the tracks with American flags and homemade signs, such as SO LONG, BOBBY.

Jack went around the train, talking to friends and Kennedys, but I sat alone, looking out the window. Intensely sad, I wanted to live in that historic moment and was not able to make casual conversation. My reverie was broken when I looked up to see Ethel and her oldest son, Joe, who had walked the entire length of the train, thanking each rider for coming to honor Bobby. It was dark by the time we arrived at the cemetery, where we stood holding candles and saying our last farewells.

However, the Jack that was enriching my life and introducing me to a much larger world had another side. He was controlling, insanely jealous, and wanted me to be at his beck and call, regardless of my children or other commitments. He had an explosive temper and when angry would frequently keep me up most of the night haranguing me, although he knew I had to get up in the morning with my children. Sleep deprivation became a constant part of my life.

Once, when he invited me on a business trip to London, he refused to allow me to take time off to write a review for *San Francisco* magazine, due that weekend, which I had put off to the last minute. "You should have written it earlier. You are here to be with me," Jack said. Instead of fighting with him, I waited until he fell asleep, then tiptoed into the bathroom and stealthily wrote the review of a San Francisco poetry anthology, lying on my stomach in the cold bathtub at the Dorchester Hotel.

I had no confidantes. While Jack liked my friends who had recognizable accomplishments, he had no use for the others. Many of my friends were leery of Jack, a hesitation I should have paid more attention to. My family did not like Jack, so I did not share these concerns with them. But I was in love. Jack and I had a busy social life, were constantly in demand, and took numerous trips, and so, by and large, things went well.

Svetlana Stalin

My new, busy, Jack-centered life was interrupted by a phone call from my father. Since he disliked the telephone, when he rang me in California in March of 1967, I knew it was something important. He was calling to announce that the State Department had asked him to go to Switzerland on a secret mission to establish the bona fides of a woman who had defected in India and claimed to be the daughter of Josef Stalin. Although long retired, my father had been chosen for this mission because he knew the Stalin history and the right questions to ask. I could tell that he was pleased and liked being back in the fray. The next day he flew off to Geneva on a special plane.

When he returned, he told me about his trip. It was clear that Svetlana Stalin had unexpectedly touched him. Forty-one years old, she was Stalin's only daughter. My father, although not a churchgoer at the time, had been impressed both by her energy and her claim to newfound spirituality. Always gallant to those in need, he also succumbed to Svetlana's helpless-and-alone-in-the world facade. He offered to provide her with peace and quiet at the family farm in East Berlin, Pennsylvania, but Svetlana turned him down. She had made plans to live with her translator, Priscilla Johnson, on Long Island, while Johnson translated Svetlana's manuscript *Twenty Letters to a Friend*. I was certain that Svetlana would have expired of boredom at the farm after a week but kept these feelings to myself.

Svetlana's defection to the West was world news in 1967. I flew from California to be with my parents and Joanie at JFK Airport for her arrival on April 21, which was kept secret until the last minute. Our parents were whisked off to be part of the official welcoming committee standing on the tarmac, while Joanie and I were seated on the high balcony of a building, with a more distant view of the scene. I was astounded by the tight security and especially by the sharpshooters on top of neighboring buildings.

I tingled with excitement at the dramatic sight of this red-haired, young-looking woman coming down the airplane stairs, escorted by a man I later found out was her lawyer, Alan U. Schwartz. She went up to the waiting microphone. "Hello, I'm happy to be here," she said, with a big smile.

The press could not get enough of Svetlana. Her dramatic defection, newly found religion, abandonment of her two teenage children, and her condemnation of the Soviet Union were all grist for the mill. After an initial press conference at the Plaza in Manhattan, she refused all interviews and was guarded on Long Island by a police car parked outside the Johnson home and by two private security men. Her inaccessibility made her even more like catnip to the media.

A few months later, Svetlana's friendship with Priscilla Johnson came to an abrupt end, an event that foreshadowed the pattern of most of her relationships. My father renewed his invitation for Svetlana to stay at the farm for the summer.

However, since he and Mother would be making their annual summer trip to Norway, he asked Joanie, who was living in nearby Princeton, to be her hostess. Joanie, a natural caregiver, agreed with enthusiasm to this assignment. She and her husband, Larry Griggs, with their two boys, Brandon and Barklie, lived with Svetlana for six weeks. Joanie and Larry took her on expeditions, and Larry barbecued on the warm summer nights. Joanie cooked and cleaned; she bought Svetlana clothes. Svetlana thrived on all this love and attention, and she and Joanie became good friends. During the daytime, Svetlana worked on her voluminous mail and her new book.

But after a while, Joanie and Larry, who had received an assignment with the Peace Corps, had to go into training, so my father recruited me to take care of Svetlana for the remainder of her stay. Joanie called to request an additional favor. "Would you mind also taking care of Brandon and Barklie?" The boys were then aged six and eight. "They won't be any trouble; they're used to the farm and will play outside all day."

At the time of these requests, I was knee-deep in children's problems, volunteer work, and the challenges of dating Jack Warnecke, all of which required me to stay put in San Francisco. But as a former Russian history and literature major, the opportunity to get to know Stalin's daughter and to have an inside glimpse into historic Kremlin politics was priceless. My father also weighed in strongly in favor of my coming to Pennsylvania. "It will be no problem," he said. "All you have to do is include Svetlana in your meals and drive in to East Berlin for her mail, which is being sent to an assumed name at the post office."

So my children and I joined the family project. Despite much grumbling on Jack's part, I knew him well enough to know that he would get over his feelings of abandonment, since I would be associated with a world-famous woman who was on the cover of countless magazines. I promised that as long as he kept her stay a secret, he could come visit.

Youthful and blue-eyed, Svetlana had a girlish, ingénue-like quality that endeared her to many, especially to men. Shortly after I met her, she confided, "The State Department proposed to provide me with protection, but I turned the offer down. Finally I am free!" She literally twirled with joy.

Her independence worried me. My father, from his secure perch on a Norwegian fjord, had warned that there was real danger that the KGB might kidnap her and spirit her away. He reminded me of Trotsky's assassination in Mexico after he fled the Soviet Union. I was taking care of a possible Trotsky, and her visit had to be top secret. Not only did this mean I couldn't tell my friends, it also dictated that we couldn't have any help in the house. The people of East Berlin must not know that they had a mysterious visitor in their midst. Joanie had faced the same challenges, but she was a better housekeeper than I and had only two children to worry about, while I had five.

What I had foreseen as an intellectual exchange and a chance to practice my Russian had turned into a different kind of experience. We had no washer or dryer, so the laundry for seven people had to be carted to the East Berlin Laundromat, a steam oven in the summer heat. The nearest big store was ten miles away in Hanover, and my new collective required lots of food. Endless trips were made, sometimes with two or three children in tow. Father's idea that we would all eat together proved unrealistic, as the children got up long before Svetlana. I would feed them and, after doing their dishes, then feed Svetlana a second breakfast. The "Kremlin Princess," as some tabloid had named her, had done little housework and was not starting to learn on my watch.

Then there were the meals. When Svetlana had gone to scatter the ashes of her Indian lover in the Ganges, she lived for a while with his family before she defected; there she adopted their vegetarian diet. She wouldn't eat the hamburgers, hot dogs, and chicken that the children liked. Instead, I had to whip up risottos and other filling vegetable dishes for Svetlana;

I desperately worked my way through *Joy of Cooking* to stay ahead of the game. A lifetime dieter, all this food preparation turned me into a compulsive nibbler, tasting a little of this and a lot of that. To add to the housekeeping nightmare, Svetlana's translator from England, Max Hayward, a noted Russian scholar, soon moved in with us to work with Svetlana. A recovering alcoholic, Max craved sweets. I had to add cake baking and pie making to my culinary repertoire: more hours in the sweltering kitchen. We had no air-conditioning.

Svetlana's lawyer, Alan U. Schwartz, also appeared for a few days. Sometimes we were nine for every meal. Realizing that the children were not getting enough attention, I enlisted Simki Page, the teenage daughter of Washington friends, to come and help. She, too, was pledged to secrecy but was another mouth to feed.

A confirmed bachelor, Max Hayward was not interested in women, an aspect of his character that Svetlana did not grasp. In fact, she took quite a shine to him. One summer evening, the three of us were outside sipping wine before a late dinner. Svetlana, in a white dress I had washed and ironed, stood up and flirtatiously flitted around the garden. She looked like an actress in a Chekhov play, catching fireflies in a glass jar. She became distinctly cold to me during Max's visit, as she saw me as competition.

Despite her girlish quality, she had strong feelings about people. Either they were faultless and wonderful, or they were all bad. She saw no shades of gray. She claimed great love for her mother, who died from a gunshot wound when Svetlana was only six. It was supposedly a suicide or, according to some rumors, could have been murder at the behest of Stalin. Svetlana dedicated her book *Twenty Letters to a Friend* to her mother, but the parent she mostly talked about—and not entirely pejoratively—was her father.

Max was reading galley proofs of *Journey into the Whirlwind*, an autobiography of Evgenia Ginzburg's life and time in the gulag, and he kindly shared them with me. As soon as we started discussing the book, Svetlana quickly curtailed all discussion and wanted to switch the conversation to her book. When she did mention the purges, or other former horrors of the Soviet period, they were all the fault of Lavrentii Beria, a fellow Georgian and head of the KGB from 1938 to the year Stalin died, 1953. According to Svetlana, Beria had made Stalin into the cruel dictator that he was and was responsible for the horrors that went on. Her father, she implied, was more of a hapless bystander.

In time Max and Alan departed, and Svetlana and I were the only adults at the farm. We resumed our budding friend-ship. One day, in her usual impulsive manner, she grabbed my arm and said, "Grace, I have to have my hair cut. This heat makes me itch where my hair touches my neck. Can you get me an appointment right away?" I was nervous about taking her out in public but realized that this was not a request but an imperative. So I found a hair salon in a neighboring town where I wasn't known, and off we went. As soon as I walked in, I saw a *Ladies' Home Journal* with Svetlana's familiar face staring up at me. I grabbed the magazine and pressed Svetlana's image to my breast as I gave instructions on the haircut. Luckily, none of the ladies there recognized her. They couldn't conceive that someone on the cover of a national magazine would end up in Abbotstown, Pennsylvania.

By the time Jack arrived for his promised visit, I already knew that his stay would be a disaster. He and Svetlana both demanded center stage, and there wasn't room for two. They eyed each other warily, like circling dogs. The first night after dinner, Jack took me aside. "Look, darling, this is ridiculous. You are doing all the work. For God's sake, you're acting like her maid." I explained the importance of her anonymity, and he snorted, "If it's dangerous to have normal help here, call the State Department and let them help you out. And look at you. What's happening to your figure? You're gaining weight."

When he left abruptly after two days, ostensibly for an urgent business meeting, I was secretly relieved. I badly needed support, and Jack provided nothing but criticism.

A few days later, Svetlana came downstairs, breathing heavily. "Grace, you must help me. I am having a heart attack," she gasped.

"Heart attack—oh, my God," I gulped. "I'll take you to the hospital!"

"Oh, no, I don't need that," Svetlana replied. "I just need some brandy—you know, the kind with a pear in the middle of the bottle. I had it in Switzerland, and it is very good for the heart."

I have learned since that Russians label as "heart attacks" all sorts of breathing problems that would not be categorized as such in America, but I did not know this then. After checking with the local Pennsylvania State Liquor Store and learning that they did not stock a brandy with a pear in it, I got on the phone and called everyone I knew in Washington, pleading, "Please, please this is a crisis—I absolutely must have a bottle of pear brandy." What my friends thought, I can't imagine. Finally I persuaded a busy lawyer to drop all he was doing and drive out to the farm with a forty-dollar bottle of the lifesaving liquid.

Svetlana drank some of it every night. I don't know what the brandy did for her heart, but she started to talk about her childhood, her children, her two husbands. She told me about how Stalin slapped her so hard that she fainted when he learned about her Jewish lover, Aleksei Kapler, who was shortly afterward sentenced to the gulag. Just as her stories would get really interesting, my eyes would start to close and I would have to go to sleep. I was exhausted after flying around at top speed from 7:00 a.m., cooking, shopping, cleaning the eighteen-room house, and taking care of its seven inhabitants. My new notebook, in which I had planned to write every night, remained largely empty. Afterward, I always felt that in some way I had failed. I had squandered this great opportunity to get to know the daughter of one of the world's most cruel dictators and had ended up, instead, mostly in the kitchen.

Svetlana in time turned against everyone in the Kennan family, but I was the first. We were only six years apart, and she was by nature competitive. I was reluctant to assume the role of a handmaiden. I knew that I played second fiddle to her favorite, my sister Joan, and I was distracted by the demands of five children and phone calls from an angry Jack. Still, I was shocked when I first read the book she had been working on while at the farm, *Only One Year*. Eager to learn her version of our time together, I picked it up and raced through the pages, only to discover that I wasn't there. According to Svetlana, only Joanie and Larry had been at the farm. My photographs of that trying summer reveal otherwise, however. As they say, "A picture is worth a thousand words."

An Astrological Wedding

I returned to San Francisco after my sojourn with Svetlana, and Jack and I resumed our tempestuous relationship for another two years. But when Jack started being unusually distant, both psychologically and geographically, I decided that I couldn't stand the last-minute phone calls, the constant change in plans, the fights, the tears, and the roller-coaster ups and downs of our long courtship anymore. When Jack went off on a long trip to London, I sent him a lengthy telegram breaking off our relationship. I added that while my children stayed with their father during summer vacation, I was going to visit in Washington for a few days with my friends Patty and John Bankson, after which I would depart for an unknown destination. I was determined to be out of reach.

On the last day of my visit with Patty and John, we were polishing off pastas in a small Italian restaurant in Bethesda, Maryland, when the maître d' appeared. "Is there a Mrs. Mc-

Clatchy here? There's a phone call for her. She can take it at the desk."

My heart lurched. I knew right away it was Jack. Only Jack would be crazy enough to find me in this restaurant. We had left the name of the restaurant with Patty's babysitter. I went to the desk and picked up the phone.

"Hi. You won't believe where I am. My plane couldn't land at Kennedy Airport, so we've been diverted to Niagara Falls." Was he telling the truth? Was there an airport near Niagara Falls? "But I'm glad I found you. What are you doing on July thirtieth? Will you marry me?" The maître d' was still within earshot, obviously listening.

"But, Jack, it's so soon. That's in a week! And my parents are in Norway, and my children are with C. K."

"I know, darling," Jack drawled in his seductive voice. "But I've been thinking it over while I've been in England, and I've decided that we are meant for each other. I consulted Carroll Righter, the famous astrologer, and he said that our signs are incompatible. You're a Gemini and I'm a Pisces, both twin signs, so if we marry it will be as if there were four people in bed. But when I told him that you are the one and I have to marry you, Righter said that there was only one day this year when the stars are auspicious, and that's in a week, on July thirtieth. I love you. Please say yes."

Nervously clutching the phone as diners went in and out and the maître d' glared, I hesitated. "Can't I call you back?"

"No, we have to decide now—it's only a week away. Think of all we have been through." "Well, then, yes," I finally answered.

"Good," he replied. "I have to run. They're calling my plane. I'll call you tomorrow. But promise me you won't tell anyone."

I promised.

In our next conversation, Jack explained that the wedding had to be secret, as it wasn't convenient for him to tell his children, who were all scattered for summer vacation at that point. He forbade me to tell my family or children, either—a decision that started us off on the wrong foot and that I later deeply regretted. He arranged for us to be married in Mexico City through some officials that he had met the previous year at the Mexico City Olympics.

I was happy nonetheless and thought our troubles were over. Now we were going to settle down to marital bliss. No longer would I have to worry about Jack going out with other women; my children, Jack, and I would finally all be under the same roof; our social life would become orderly. And I would stop suffering from the terminal fatigue caused by constantly running from Jack's bed in the middle of the night to go to my house and wake up in the morning with my children.

Even in the short term, things did not turn out as planned. I was greeted on our wedding day, July 30, 1969, by a headline in the *San Francisco Chronicle* announcing that American Airlines, on which we were flying to Mexico, had gone on strike. Jack called, frantic about the astrological deadline, and told me that by pulling every possible string he'd rebooked us on Mexican Airlines, with three stopovers en route to Mexico City.

He took advantage of the four flights to confide in me the devastating news that during the last months he had been living in his New York apartment with a woman named Eleanora, whom he had previously described to me as a beautiful, former Uruguayan girlfriend. It turned out that the relationship had only been "former" for about a week. Every time I had reached him on the phone, another woman had been listening; another woman had shared his New York bed; he had lied to me right up until the wedding. My new contentment was quenched. I felt trapped. This was not the marriage I had envisaged. I didn't have the money to get on the next plane back to San Francisco, and I didn't own a credit card. Worse, I loved Jack. While the Eleanora story was piercingly painful, I couldn't leave him. Deep in my soul, I knew that I should turn around and return to San Francisco, but I didn't have the courage.

When we arrived in Mexico City late that evening, we were met by a thuggish bodyguard whom Jack had hired to expedite the wedding. He rushed us to our hotel, the Camino Real.

Unfortunately, the judge who was to officiate had given up and gone home to bed. Jack staged one of his spectacular rages. With passionate argument and promise of a very expensive bottle of Napoleon brandy for the judge, Jack succeeded in sending the thug to wake up His Honor and persuade him to rise from his bed and come back to the hotel and marry us.

When the judge appeared at 11:45 p.m., he found a nervous group waiting in the coffee shop. This whole wedding had been predicated on the date of July 30, and we had only fifteen minutes left. Jack was in a state of high anxiety because of Carroll Righter's forecast, while I was depressed and in shock because of the news about Eleanora. Seeing Jack's agitation, the judge started to marry us right then and there, at the table surrounded by dirty coffee cups, soiled napkins, and old breadcrumbs. To everyone's surprise, I spoke up and refused to be married in the coffee shop. Later, that reminded me of my childhood nightmare, where I refused to be buried alive in a hat. Everyone was surprised to hear me speak, but we rushed up to our suite and the judge performed the ceremony there in Spanish, not a word of which either of us understood. Two bodyguards were witnesses.

The next day we hosted a lunch in the garden of a colorful restaurant for the bodyguards, their wives, and friends. Evidently this was part of Jack's contract. A lively mariachi band played as our guests spoke animatedly in Spanish and made numerous toasts, none of which we could follow. We flew back to San Francisco that afternoon and returned to our separate houses, with no one the wiser, and stayed that way for six weeks, until we formally announced our marriage. I should have believed in astrology and listened to Carroll Righter.

Margo's Revenge

Much to my surprise, after our secret Mexican marriage, Jack Warnecke decided to move into the large, charming, but slightly ramshackle old San Francisco house on Pierce Street that I had been renting and in which Charles, Adair, Kevin, and I were living. For our little family it had been large and spacious, with a big basement used as a playroom and storage area.

However, no sooner had Jack unpacked than the doorbell rang. His three younger children, Roger, Margo, and Fred, were standing at the threshold, unannounced, suitcases in hand. Jack must have known about this, but he had neglected to tell me. Massive rearranging ensued. Roger was in his second year at Stanford, and Margo was studying at Miss Chapin's School in New York, so Jack explained that they were only going to be home on vacations. Freddie, a sophomore in a local high school, was to live with us. He commandeered the big playroom in the basement. Another room went to Jack's cook, Hazel Hill, who evidently came with the package. A warm, nurturing black woman, she churned out three meals a day for the rest of our marriage.

Disorder and confusion seemed endemic in the new living arrangements of our extended family. The old electricity couldn't stand the sudden infusion of electronic equipment that arrived with my stepchildren. Fuses kept popping; my new husband's temper frayed. I felt as if the boat kept filling up with water and I was bailing as fast as I could just to keep afloat.

Working at being a wife to a successful architect thirteen years older than I was, caring for my three young children, ages seven, nine, and eleven, and being a stepmother to Jack's brood was challenging. Not only did my stepchildren bring the normal teenage problems into the house, for which I was totally unprepared, but all tensions were compounded because this was 1969 and the heyday of the Haight-Ashbury period in San Francisco.

In the ten years of his bachelor life, Jack's only daughter, Margo, had lived through his many girlfriends. Buxom, dressed in hippie fashion, one layer of patchwork or mismatched clothes piled on top of another, she looked older than her seventeen years. Men noticed her. She was smart and well-read. Although outgoing, at the same time she gave little away. She tolerated her new stepmother, but just barely. Jack told me how important it was for us to bond. "Margo needs a mother to fill the shoes of her own mother, who lives in Hawaii," he said. I never expected to play that part but hoped that, by my being kind and interested, Margo would come to accept me.

For many years, the high point of the social season for old San Francisco families was the cotillion, a formal ball that took place during Christmas vacation, at which young women of these families "came out" and were introduced to society. This event seemed particularly archaic and ludicrous in San Francisco in the heyday of hippies, sexual freedom, and drugs. I was taken aback to hear my sophisticated husband insist that Margo make a debut. Margo refused and protested vociferously, "Dad, you can't be serious. Debuts are a meaningless old-fashioned ritual. No one cares anymore. They're a thing of the past."

But Jack persisted in his usual steamroller fashion. "Your mother made her debut, and this is very important to your grandmother, who is old and may die soon. You can't let her down. As the only Cushing girl, you have to uphold the family tradition."

"No," Margo protested. "I won't, and that's that," and she left the house, slamming the heavy oak door, while I stood silently applauding in the wings.

Jack didn't drop the subject. His former mother-in-law, Mrs. Cushing, was a known San Francisco grand dame. Every time Jack talked to Margo, the argument resumed. I began to realize what the perceived status of marrying into the Cushing family meant to Jack. I felt that Margo shouldn't be forced into this outmoded ritual, but when Margo asked me for my opinion, I kept quiet. Newly married, I considered it my job to support my husband and not to contradict him in front of his daughter. Jack kept after Margo until one day, to my surprise, she capitulated. I never knew why but assumed that he'd simply worn her down.

Margo found her own revenge. As her debut escort, she chose my brother Christopher, sixteen years my junior and a student at the University of California at Santa Cruz. Margo was creating her own bonds with the Kennan family, but they weren't with me. Jack proposed that Margo and I should go together to pick out her ball gown, but Margo would have no part of that. "I'll go with a friend," she said.

Jack asked me to organize a small family dinner at our house before the cotillion. Much to his delight, Mrs. Cushing agreed to attend. This was the first time that she had been in Jack's house since his acrimonious divorce from her daughter, another Grace, eight years earlier. Jack fussed over every detail of the dinner and the décor, convinced that I would make a mistake or leave something undone. Was the wood in the fireplace properly stacked? Were there flowers on the table? Had I bought the perfect roast beef? What were we having for dessert?

He arranged that Margo, who had to dine at the cotillion with the other debutantes, would come by the house before dinner to say hello to her grandmother. The first Grace was in poor health in Hawaii and not coming back for this event.

The night of the cotillion, I greeted Mrs. Cushing, a dignified older woman, and installed her in the living room, wondering how I compared to her daughter. When the doorbell rang again, I opened it to see Margo—in a billowing white evening dress, with buttons almost to the waist and every button unfastened. Her overflowing bosoms were front and center. I stood speechless. Margo sailed by me and went upstairs to say hello to her father, who had not yet appeared.

Two minutes later an angry Jack, his untied bow tie dangling, stormed down the stairs into the hall, with Margo trailing behind. Glaring, he took me aside. "Tell her to button her buttons," he ordered, white with rage, and stomped back upstairs.

I don't know why I didn't respond, "You tell her. You are her father." Instead, in a conciliatory voice I suggested, "Margo, maybe that dress would look even better if you buttoned a few buttons."

With disdain, Margo looked me in the eye and said clearly, "Fuck you," then swept past me into the living room to meet her grandmother.

The evening had definitely taken a bad turn. I followed Margo and made polite conversation with Mrs. Cushing, trying to create some illusion of family harmony, while I felt Jack's unspoken fury.

With Mrs. Cushing in tow, we arrived at the cotillion and settled into the gold chairs in the family viewing area of the grand ballroom at the Palace Hotel. Each debutante, led out by her escort, came forward and curtsied to her parents. Margo and Christopher were at the end of the group. They had evidently sedated themselves with pot, so it would be more accurate to say they lurched out. Christopher had long curly hair to his shoulders, and Margo had made little progress with the buttons. There was an audible gasp. The family sitting directly in front of Mrs. Cushing stood up and marched out, saying, "We didn't come here to watch hippies come out." The next day there was an unfortunate photograph in the *San Francisco Chronicle*, depicting this incident for those not lucky enough to have been present. Mortified and angry, Jack didn't speak to Margo for five months. I felt guilty because I had not taken Margo's side.

Dinner with Jackie

Jack brought many new people into my life, including the Kennedy family. I knew, of course, that my husband and Jackie had enjoyed a romantic relationship at the time he was designing her husband's grave. In fact, Jack had spoken to me about his romance quite often, even comparing me—unflatteringly—to Jackie. "Jackie's house was always neat; why is yours so cluttered?" was the typical remark. But I stowed that information in a dusty niche in the attic of my mind.

After our marriage, Jack and I had spent considerable time redecorating an apartment on Park Avenue, a dramatic mélange of antiques, modern furniture, ornate screens, and Oriental rugs. To be more precise: Jack designed and acquired, while I tagged along and admired.

Although the apartment was roomy, he referred to it as "our pied-à-terre in Manhattan." Since Jack had a New York office, we spent quite a bit of time in the apartment.

However, the Kennedy connection didn't seem so distant when Jack appeared in our apartment one day to say that he had "run into Jackie" and had invited her to dinner three weeks from Tuesday. Had they really just bumped into each other? Somehow I questioned that the former first lady spent her time strolling on the streets of New York. But my more immediate problem was creating the dinner.

This meal loomed in my future as a momentous event. Our guests that Jack had invited were all well-known and glamorous New Yorkers, including Brendan Gill, the author and *New Yorker* columnist, and Lally Weymouth, who was Kay Graham's daughter. My anxiety level rose when Jack lectured me on how to properly organize this repast. Kathleen, our maid, would cook and serve, and her friend Sally would assist. That would be plenty of help for the eight of us. Jack reiterated that everything had to be perfect. "Don't you dare come out passing the hors d'oeuvres as if you are the maid. And, for heaven's sake, don't let Kathleen overcook the asparagus."

On the big night, Jack arrived home from his office, late as usual, and then announced he had to go out for a walk. I begged him to be back before the guests arrived at eight, but he strode out, saying, "My health is more important."

I was left standing alone, both scared and furious, when the first guest, Brendan Gill, arrived. I started jabbering about Jack's absence, but Brendan walked right up to me and, instead of giving me a kiss, put a hand on each of my breasts. Shocked, I pulled back to hear him say, "I just did that to stop you from being so nervous." It did take my mind off things. When Jack arrived late to his own party, I was almost beyond caring.

Then Jackie made her entrance. This was the first time I had met her other than at big events. Her legendary beauty was recognizable, but I was struck by her breathless soft voice, so low that one had to lean in to hear her. No one had prepared me for that. She was polite and gracious to everyone.

The dramatic use of mirrors magnified the unusual décor of the apartment—we looked more like sixteen than eight. Conversation was lively, but, to my horror, not a bite of food appeared. Slipping off to the kitchen, I found Kathleen and Sally white-faced.

"I'm sorry, Mrs. Warnecke," Kathleen said. "But we can't go out there. We are too scared. Look, our hands are shaking."

My heart sank. I went to the bar and brought them each a small glass of bourbon and insisted they drink it. "Pull yourselves together. I'm depending on you. You have to serve this dinner." Meanwhile, I took the plate of smoked salmon and passed it myself. Avoiding Jack's scowl, I kept circling.

Kathleen and Sally made their appearance a few minutes later, somewhat sedated by the bourbon. When we sat down to eat, the dinner conversation was stellar, and no one seemed to notice that the asparagus were indeed overcooked.

In the end, Jack considered the evening a success, while I was both proud and relieved that we had lived through it. For the next two weeks our doorman insisted on running the self-service elevator himself, wearing white gloves and regaling all the tenants about when Jacqueline Kennedy Onassis came for dinner. While I didn't wear white gloves, I told the story, too.

Turtle Soup and Lillian

It was the summer of 1972. While Jack and I were visiting friends at Martha's Vineyard, we were included in a casual Vineyard dinner party for twenty or so. Holding court from the sofa was an older woman, her face etched with deep lines, a hawk-like nose, and rather bulbous eyes. She definitely commanded attention. A guest whispered, "That's Lillian Hellman."

I had read her recent best seller, *Pentimento*, and was awed at actually seeing the author in the flesh. Jack, who loved celebrities and lacked inhibitions, soon wangled an introduction. He, of course, made much of the fact that I had been a book critic in San Francisco. For whatever reason, Lillian Hellman started talking to me.

I was frozen with shyness. I can't remember a word of that conversation, except that Lillian asked me to have lunch with her in New York sometime. "Oh, yes," I answered, convinced that the invitation would be soon forgotten. However, we ran into each other socially several times in the city, and eventually she invited me to her apartment for lunch.

At that time I was thinking of writing a book about authors, inspired by the writer interviews that I had done when I was the book critic for *San Francisco* magazine, and I thought that Lillian Hellman would be an ideal candidate for this project.

When the date neared, we turned out to be in Washington, but Jack, who liked even reflected glory, encouraged me to fly to New York especially for this lunch. He told me what to wear. I wanted to take the 9:00 a.m. shuttle, but Jack insisted that if I flew on the 11:00 a.m. shuttle I would be in plenty of time for our 12:30 lunch.

That morning I woke up to the clatter of pouring rain. Nervous, I called National Airport but was assured that the planes were flying out on time. Unfortunately, I hadn't called New York. When we reached the city, LaGuardia Airport was hidden by a thick umbrella of fog. Over the intercom, the pilot told us that LaGuardia was closed but we were going to "hang around for a while," in hopes that the fog would lift. Hanging around was evidently a euphemism for lurching about in a holding pattern in very turbulent air. My usual fear of flying, exacerbated by seeing my precious lunch with Lillian trickle away, made my stomach cramp, my hands sweat. Each minute seemed like an hour. Why hadn't I taken an earlier plane? Mashed back in my seat, hands clutching the armrests, I thought that this was probably my last hour on earth.

Just then the plane vibrated, made more ominous noises, and started heading down—to total destruction, as far as I was concerned. In fact, the plane was landing at Newark Airport. It was 12:30. I could still make it and be only thirty minutes late. But then I discovered that I didn't have enough money to take a cab from Newark. Precious minutes were wasted while I looked for a bank in the terminal—these being the days before ATMs. The bank had a long line, and I stood there mentally pushing the people in front of me, as if by massive concentration I could make the line go faster.

By the time I arrived at Lillian's apartment, it was 1:30. When she answered the door, Lillian seemed shorter than I remembered her—her intellectual stature must have added inches in my mind. She was sympathetic to my travel woes but harried, as she had a doctor's appointment at 2:15. Her dining room table was beautifully set for two, adorned with English china, silver, and crystal. Her incredible face—covered with a mass of lines, hollows, and pockets—was somehow still attractive. "So much character," I thought.

We sat down to lunch. Lillian was eating deviled ham on white bread, and I had a big bowl of turtle soup, "Remember the turtle story in my book?" she asked.

"Oh, God," I thought. I didn't, but I answered, "Yes."

She continued, "After the book came out, a man sent me a case of turtle soup. He said it was a very special turtle soup and

171

he thought I would like it. But two weeks later he sent a bill for four dollars a can."

"Did you pay him?" I asked.

"Yes. It seemed easiest in the end. But I thought about it for quite a while." Lillian made an abrupt change of subject. "Do you still see Jackie?" she asked.

I was surprised. Jack and Jackie's romance had always seemed very private, nothing I had ever confided to anyone. I definitely hadn't flown to lunch to discuss either turtles or Jacqueline Onassis. "No," I answered. "Jack and Jackie don't see each other. Their relationship didn't end badly. I think it just petered out." This conversation was definitely not going in the direction that I had hoped for, and I felt my authors project slipping away.

Lillian refused to let up. "That's typical of Jackie," she said. "She picks people up and then drops them. For a while she used to come by here quite a lot, but now she calls about twice a year. I don't think she has real friends. She needs new people. She must be very bored."

This type of conversation was much too sophisticated for me. I kept spooning the turtle soup, sipping cold white wine, and trying to figure out how to bring up my authors project. At last the subject veered to Lillian's writing. She was hoping to sign a contract that afternoon on her new book but still didn't know what the book would be about.

"Do you take advances?" I asked, naively wondering how you could take an advance on a book that hadn't been dreamed of.

"Oh, yes, I have to live on my writing," she replied. "Besides, I think it is a good system. It's the only way the publisher is guaranteed that you won't take your book to someone else and that you both have a commitment. Without an advance, there is no contract."

Hellman proceeded to tell me about her contract for *Pentimento*. For years, she said, she dealt with an elderly editor at

Little, Brown, and the contracts were very short and didn't have innumerable clauses. "He only specified that I was to write a book—no length or subject mentioned. However, he died before the contract was signed."

After the elderly editor's death, the new editor wrote a letter saying that this contract was highly irregular and that he wanted a description of what the book would be about. Lillian was angry and didn't care if they signed the contract or not, so she wrote back and said that she would guarantee to write them an epic poem. The editor wrote back a funny letter, attaching a contract in which Lillian guaranteed to write an epic poem.

I knew it was now or never. We had only ten minutes left. I haltingly laid out my authors project. Lillian replied that the *New York Times* had just done something similar.

"No," I argued, "mine will be much more in-depth."

"Well," said Lillian, "it might be of interest to libraries and schools."

Like the air leaving a balloon, my enthusiasm leaked away. The book began to look rather dull. I had been on the brink of asking her to be my first interviewee, but now I couldn't get the words out. Lillian started to talk about her upcoming trip to Sarasota, Florida. The opportunity was gone. I never wrote the book, and I realized she had asked me to lunch only to gossip about Jackie Kennedy. I had my fifteen minutes and I blew it.

To Russia with the Kennedys

"Jack," I called, after reading in the *Washington Post* that Senator Ted Kennedy was going to make his first trip to Russia with his family, as guests of General Secretary Leonid Brezhnev, "don't you think he needs an old Russia hand like me?"

Jack and I, with Adair and Kevin, had moved to Washington while Jack was overseeing the construction of his design for the Hart Senate Office Building. I was half joking, but Jack, who had signed up to be on an American Institute of Architects trip to China during that period, leaped at the idea. Having designed President Kennedy's grave site at Arlington National Cemetery, Ted Kennedy's house in Virginia, and Bobby Kennedy's pool house, Jack was basically the Kennedy family architect. "Write Teddy a letter and offer your services. After all, they won't have to pay you."

This was 1974, and the senator was the first major American politician to visit the Soviet Union following President Roosevelt's trip to Yalta in 1945 and President Nixon's trip in 1972. This trip had special importance for Senator Kennedy as a way of establishing his foreign-policy credentials; at the time, he was still thinking of running for president, which he ultimately did in 1980. He wanted to have his wife and children with him, especially because young Ted had recently had his leg amputated to remove a cancerous growth.

So I wrote a letter to the senator but heard nothing back and decided my offer might have been too presumptuous. Five days before departure, though, a call came from Kennedy's office: "Please send your passport over today—the Kennedys want you to go on this trip to help with arrangements and translation."

I was over the moon with excitement. I hadn't been to Russia for twelve years. Now I was finally going back, traveling with the Kennedy family and doing useful work. I paid no attention to the fact that the job description was very vague. I arranged babysitters for Adair and Kevin.

As it turned out, my first assignment was to pick up fourteen-year-old Kara and twelve-year-old Teddy in Virginia and bring them to Yugoslavia, where Ted and Joan were already visiting President Tito in Belgrade. The children's delayed departure was caused by Teddy's need for one more blood transfusion.

Nervous and tired, I arrived at the Kennedys' Virginia home at five in the morning and was greeted at the door by the two children, with their suitcases and a nurse. The nurse handed me a brown paper bag and cautioned, "The medicine and syringes are in here. If Teddy has any problem, you can give him a shot, can't you?"

I felt distinctly queasy. "I don't know how to give shots," I said. "Never mind," she said. "You'll find someone or figure it out."

Clutching the brown paper bag, I set forth for Dulles Airport with two children I had never met before. Luckily, I had no need for the medicine. Kara and Teddy turned out to be natural and amazingly unspoiled, which made the long journey a lot easier. But already I saw that my role on the trip would not be what I had anticipated.

We were routed to Belgrade via a change of aircraft in New York and an overnight in Paris. As we sat at Kennedy Airport waiting for our next plane, Teddy asked if he could walk around and stake out the airport. "Of course," I said, a little dopey from lack of sleep. My kids loved exploring new places.

About ten minutes later it dawned on me that I was supposed to be watching over the Kennedy children, not letting these possible kidnap victims roam around at will. With Kara in tow, I ran out of the waiting area and had a very anxious fifteen minutes—imagining the headline AIDE LOSES KENNEDY SON AT KENNEDY AIRPORT—until we discovered young Teddy happily riding up and down the escalators.

After spending a night in Paris with Kennedy friends Pierre and Nicole Salinger, Kara, Teddy, and I flew on to Belgrade. A Yugoslavian presidential aide was waiting for us at the tarmac and whisked us off for the trip to Tito's residence. We arrived at the end of an official lunch for the senator and Joan. While the children were reunited with their parents, I met the rest of the staff: Bob Hunter, Jim King, and Ken Regan, the photographer, all members of the Kennedy inner circle. We then returned to the private villa provided for our party by President Tito.

The next day we boarded an Aeroflot jet for Moscow. In 1974 the Soviet Union was still a closed society, and even the airplane felt alien. I heard that the Soviet soccer team was in the back section of the plane, elated from a victory over Yugoslavia the day before. When young Teddy found out, he asked, "Can I go back and get their autographs?" His father assented, so Teddy limped up and down the aisle, collecting autographs, while I followed behind, translating. The soccer players were full of questions. "Is the man in front really Senator Kennedy? Which one is the senator? Is that Robert Kennedy?" Ted Kennedy's face, so overexposed in the West, was unknown in the Soviet Union. In 1974 the Soviet press did not print pictures of American political leaders. Even though there were holes in the Iron Curtain, the curtain still hung.

The landing at Sheremetyevo Airport was a far cry from my bumpy wartime arrival. An official welcoming committee, bearing bouquets of flowers, met us. No need for passports, customs, or any of the usual aggravations of international travel. After a quick press conference, we were popped into a line of Zil limousines for the ride to town. We were accompanied by Soviet hosts (probably KGB, we were informed by the State Department), who stayed with us for most of the trip. Joan's Soviet hostess was a charming blonde who looked uncannily like Joan's twin, as if she had been chosen by central casting. Two police cars with sirens pulled in front and in back of the procession, and we were off.

We were Brezhnev's guests at a government villa. A large, solid yellow house up in the Lenin Hills, the villa was set in a grove of trees intersected by formal paths and patrolled by uniformed guards. A high wall enclosed the entire compound. The house was immaculate and well staffed with servants. In fact, the staff was so large that we joked that an army must have been camping in the basement. The residence had about ten bedrooms, a billiards room with an immense table and heavy ivory balls, paneled walls polished to such a degree that I wondered if they were really wood. The first morning I woke up to see the young guards marching up and down the tree-lined paths as snow fell on their heavy Russian capes. I felt I was living in a Tolstoy novel. As honored guests of the Soviet government, we were in true luxury and isolation.

We were given delicious food and had superb, if slightly impersonal, service. It seemed as if our little group came home every night to a private ocean liner, a self-contained world within its walls. When the senator wanted Kara and Teddy to see some films about the Soviet Union, the films and a projector magically appeared. Nothing was too much trouble.

Much of our trip was in the traditional pattern of a state visit. The Ted Kennedy on this trip was very different from the exuberant playboy that I had seen on our sailing trips. He was serious and let nothing get in the way of his mission. He paid courtesy calls on high government officials; he laid a wreath at the Tomb of the Unknown Soldier; we were given a private tour of the Kremlin. At night we were overwhelmed with hospitality at lavish formal dinners, presented with Russian extravagance. Numerous courses were offered, starting with caviar and washed down with unlimited vodka, wine, and champagne, and accompanied by endless toasts. Joan and the children did not join us at these dinners.

"Where's Joan?" I asked the first night.

"She isn't feeling well" was the explanation, although my offer to call the embassy doctor was turned down.

The high point of our trip was the meeting with Brezhnev. Everything led up to that event, and the senator felt that the success or failure of this visit depended on it. Like any audience with a head of state, it was run like a military operation, and punctuality was paramount. That morning, the security man from the villa, who normally knocked on our doors to wake us up, forgot. A strange oversight. There was a mad scramble to get ready, and everyone was tense.

Conferring with foreign-policy specialist Bob Hunter, the senator paced around, preoccupied and unreachable. Young

Teddy, coping with his new artificial leg, had trouble dressing. Despite heroic efforts, we left a few minutes behind schedule.

As we pulled out of the driveway, I saw a militiaman holding back all the traffic on our wide street. Within minutes we were heading for the Kremlin at sixty miles an hour through downtown Moscow. We could see cars pulled over to the side and a blur of staring faces. The gates of the Kremlin stood open, waiting for us. I flashed back to 1952, when my father was the American ambassador to the Soviet Union. Whenever an important Soviet leader was going to the Kremlin from Stalin's dacha, the cars sped down Arbat Street, a caravan of curtained limousines with eerie yellow headlights. All other traffic was stopped as these sinister corteges made their way down the street. It always sent shivers down my spine. Sitting in the limousine with Joan Kennedy, I could see myself standing against the wall twenty years ago, watching the Soviet leaders go by. Had Russia changed? At least we had no yellow headlights.

I was awed to be meeting Brezhnev. As we were escorted down the long corridors, I thought of all the historical figures who had traveled through those Kremlin gates. When we were ushered into the general secretary's office, we found the leader sitting at his desk. Behind him was a solid wall of photographers standing in assigned places—still photographers, movie photographers, television photographers—an incredible amount of photo power, focused on this one moment. The only person in motion was Ken Regan, our photographer, as the Soviet photojournalists were not allowed to stir from their spots.

In front of this photographic phalanx, Brezhnev seemed unexpectedly human. He had a warm manner, humorous eyebrows, and a good-looking face. He stood up next to his interpreter, Victor Sukhodrev, a handsome young man with flawless English. After we were all formally introduced, Brezhnev handed young Ted a beautifully wrapped present.

The senator did not miss a beat. "But, Mr. Chairman," Kennedy protested, "I have two children. What about my daughter?" There was quick scurrying among the aides, and an autographed photograph of Brezhnev was produced for Kara, which she accepted with good grace.

While the senator and Brezhnev continued with pleasantries, the Soviet senior aide took me aside and said, sotto voce, in Russian, "We know you're the daughter of Ambassador Kennan, and we want you to pass on to him how much he is respected here." I knew how much this belated recognition would mean to my father, after the pain of being declared persona non grata by Stalin two decades earlier.

Soon after, Joan, the children, and I were ushered out, leaving the senator with an unanticipated four-hour meeting with Brezhnev. The senator's agenda included promoting a full nuclear test ban treaty, a more relaxed Soviet emigration policy, and also an exit visa for the cellist Mstislav Rostropovich. Ted returned to our villa later that afternoon, triumphant and judging the meeting a success. Rostropovich did receive his exit visa.

Familiarity and change haunted me during the entire trip. One night had been scheduled for the puppet theater, especially for Kara and Teddy's benefit. The famous, almost life-size Russian puppets are manipulated from below and are capable of incredible physical contortions. The talented director, Sergei Obraztsov, had designed the puppets and written the plays himself. He had been doing this for forty years. His puppet shows—ostensibly for children but containing the only political satire allowed in Moscow—were enormously popular and sold out two to three months in advance. Our Soviet hosts had wanted us to see a classic called *An Unusual Concert*, but since we were busy the night of that performance, they arranged for us to see a different puppet play on our only free evening.

Arriving at the theater, we found the whole fifth row reserved for our party. A hush went over the audience as Obraztsov came out on the stage and announced, "We have sad news for you tonight. Our leading actor has taken ill, and we will not

be able to perform as scheduled. Instead, we will be present-
ing *An Unusual Concert.*" Not even a whisper of disappointment
was heard from the audience. I tried to imagine an American
audience that had bought tickets to see *Oklahoma!* two months in
advance being told that they were going to see *Carousel* instead.

When planning his trip, the senator had three major requests: to meet with Brezhnev, to appear on Soviet television,
and to speak at Moscow State University. The last request, so
normal for Americans, was a big stretch for our Soviet hosts.
At that time, the only American to have addressed students at
Moscow State University was Angela Davis, the African American human rights activist, more often described in the U.S.
press as a Communist and political troublemaker.

On our first night in Moscow, when the senator and his
aides had reviewed the program with our Soviet hosts, they
informed us that the speech at Moscow State University had
been reduced from a full-fledged lecture to a noon speech on
a Sunday, when the university was officially closed. It would be
held in an auditorium that seated only five hundred people.
Nevertheless, the senator agreed to the venue.

When we arrived at the university, there was a warm welcome from the rector, who was waiting outside to greet us, but
a noticeable dearth of students milling around. The security
men checking papers at the door made it clear that this event
was by invitation only. At least one-third of the audience was
over forty—hardly the students the senator had in mind.

Kennedy delivered an eloquent foreign policy speech, but
the audience looked stolid and unresponsive. Puzzled, I picked
up the earphones and started to listen to the translation and
realized why. Here was a major speech on U.S.–Soviet relations
being mangled in one of the most inept interpretations that I
had ever heard. Audible on the earphones were at least three
translators—two men and a woman—taking turns, in no pre-
dictable sequence, translating the speech. Because it takes longer to say the same sentence in Russian than it does in English,

the senator was outpacing his Soviet translators, who reacted by dropping off the ends of sentences when they got too far behind. Resonance, rhetoric, and considerable content were lost for the audience. I was sitting up on the stage with the official party, but far from the senator, so there was no way to reach him to tell him what was happening.

When the speech ended, the audience sat as wooden and impassive as they had been when the speech started. Senator Kennedy, however, was not going to be defeated. He decided to throw out a question to the audience, as he frequently did in the United States. The translator botched the first question, and the audience, surprised and uncomprehending, still sat on their hands. I wished that the whole podium would sink through the floor and we could all magically disappear. At that point, the rector of Moscow State University, a true host, salvaged the tense situation by taking over the microphone, explaining to the listeners what the senator was asking, and giving tacit approval to their participation.

The meeting took off. From then on, the question-and-answer period was very lively, with laughter and even spontaneous applause. The senator asked his questions about various issues, and the audience answered by a show of hands.

Just when the meeting was in high gear, one of our staff, worried about an impending meeting with Foreign Minister Andrei Gromyko, misinterpreted a gesture of Senator Kennedy's and cut the meeting short. He told the translator to tell the audience that the senator was not feeling well and had to leave. We exited rather quickly but were not "hustled out," as reported in the American press. We regretted that the press story of our rapid departure overshadowed this historic moment, the first time an elected American official had ever been permitted to speak at Moscow State University.

My role in this trip changed from day to day. Some of the time I translated for the senator or for the group; other times I made arrangements for Kara and Teddy. I also cataloged the numerous presents given to the Kennedys, as any gift worth over $25 had to be donated to the Smithsonian. On our last night in Moscow, I was given an unanticipated task: to distract and entertain the KGB when the senator and his staff went off secretly to meet with Jewish dissidents. The meeting with the dissidents had been set up through a back channel, and we knew that the purpose—namely, for the senator to hear the dissidents' stories—would be sabotaged if any KGB escorts came along. Kennedy asked me to make sure that the chauffeur, who was going to be dismissed for the evening, stayed around.

I snuck out and found Sasha, the driver, smoking in the courtyard. "Sasha, I know you are supposed to have the evening free, but something has come up and the senator might need you later. You absolutely must stay."

Sasha obviously thought this strange and said that no one—namely, our hosts and his bosses—had told him about a late meeting.

"No," I answered, "this has just happened. They don't know about it yet." I implied that I would go directly to General Secretary Brezhnev if Sasha left the premises.

After dinner, we sat around for a while with the staff and some of our Soviet escorts. One by one, Ted, Jim, Ken, and Bob went off, ostensibly to their rooms. Of course, I wanted desperately to be included in this trip, but instead my task was to sit up and entertain our Soviet hosts so that they would not be suspicious. I knew with whom I was dealing, but I sat, my hands cold and clammy, acting like the life of the party. When an agitated guard appeared and said the car had left with the senator and staff, our hosts looked at me with icy stares.

"Where did they go?" they asked accusingly. "I don't know," I answered.

They obviously didn't believe me, and all pretense of friendliness disappeared. The group turned their backs and strode out angrily, without saying good-bye. But I had done my job.

Joan Kennedy was with us for the Brezhnev visit, the Moscow State University speech, and general sightseeing, but much of the time she stayed in her room, saying that she wanted to write postcards to the nuns at her alma mater, Manhattanville College. I never could fathom why writing to the nuns was more important than seeing Moscow. I was unaware that she was fighting a battle against alcoholism, which was particularly difficult as she lived in the public eye. I accepted her frequent absences as a health problem, and no one made me any the wiser.

One day, when the senator was meeting with Gromyko, Joan and I were to go to the Bolshoi Ballet Academy, where the dancers of the famous Bolshoi Theatre trained. A talented pianist, Joan had also narrated *Peter and the Wolf* for the Boston Symphony. We were carrying her records as presents. The students were going to put on a special performance in her honor.

That day, Joan and I lunched at our guesthouse with some of the usual hosts. I noticed that, in addition to mineral water, there was vodka on the table, and our hosts started to pour. Joan accepted a glass. Every time she took a sip from her glass, one of the hosts refilled it. After an hour or so, Joan announced that she wasn't feeling well and would not be going to the ballet school. The hosts murmured a few hollow words of sympathy and said that they would cancel the visit.

I was mortified. I had been told that the children had been rehearsing for days for this special performance, and a cancellation of the event at the last minute would reflect badly on the Kennedys—not to mention that for me, a ballet aficionado, this was one of the high points of the trip. I drew myself up. "Well, it is a terrible disappointment to everyone that Joan is not feeling well enough to go, but I will go in her place. I studied ballet, I serve on the board of the San Francisco Ballet, and Mrs. Kennedy specifically asked me to bring the special present that she brought from Washington for the students." Of course, no one had any way of determining what Mrs. Kennedy wanted. So, feeling like an actress in my own play, I demanded, "Order the car." When we arrived at the school, the entire student body was lined up outside the building, each with a small bouquet of flowers for Mrs. Kennedy. I realized that no one there knew what Joan looked like, and I could easily have passed for her. I agonized over what to do. But if later the ballet director saw a photograph, it would be evident that Joan was a blonde and I was a brunette. So I entered, made Joan's apologies, gave the director Joan's recording, and sat in solitary splendor for a lovely and touching performance.

Years later, Joan and I were together at a Mexican health spa. When I started to reminisce about Moscow, Joan cut me short, saying, "Grace, don't you realize I have almost no memories of that trip?"

From Moscow we went on to Tbilisi, Georgia, and then Leningrad. Leningrad was a city of great vistas, long walks, and endless flights of stairs. The Soviet Union had no facilities for the handicapped. Our Soviet hosts noticed that young Teddy was visibly in pain while learning to navigate on his new prosthesis and offered to give us a wheelchair. But the senator declined. "He can't have a wheelchair. He must learn to walk with his artificial leg. We're not going to baby him," he explained.

The staff didn't dare contradict the senator, but we all suffered, watching Teddy struggle.

Finally, when we were going through the vast galleries in the Hermitage Museum at the Winter Palace, we couldn't stand it anymore. By this time young Teddy was visibly suffering. Behind the senator's back, I whispered to a guard to bring a wheelchair. I denied any complicity in this, but Teddy gratefully sank into the seat. The senator said nothing.

On the plane flying back to America, it occurred to me that for eight days I had not spoken with Jack, who was still in China. Normally he called me six times a day to check on my wardrobe, my activities, and our social life. I had deemed all that attention a sign of passion. But now I saw Jack as more of a puppeteer instead. He was controlling the strings, and I was the puppet dancing helplessly at the other end. As I drew closer to home, I felt those strings starting to fray. I knew life was going to be different.

Crashing a Coronation

We were still living in Washington in late 1974, but during the Christmas holidays back in San Francisco, Jack presented me with a new idea. He had read that the king of Nepal was to be crowned on February 24, Jack's birthday. As Jack was scheduled to be in Iran on business during that period, he decided that he and the king should have a simultaneous celebration in Kathmandu. After all, the countries are quite close, he argued.

Not for the first time, I thought Jack a little nuts, although I admired his spirit. "You don't just go to coronations," I protested. "You are invited."

But Jack, who still had true faith in the stars, didn't see it that way. "Look, the court astrologer picked the date two years ago as the most auspicious day for a coronation, so the portents of the planets must be equally lucky for my birthday. What better place to celebrate a birthday than in Kathmandu?"

Jack pitched his new idea not just to me but also to our beautiful blond San Francisco neighbor, Sarah, an amateur photographer. "Why don't you come with us? It will be an incredible opportunity for you to practice your photography. Grace," he added, "can write about it."

Formerly I would have been depressed by my husband's overt flirtation, but this time I was challenged. I suggested to Sarah that maybe we could do a piece for *British Vogue*. Never mind that *British Vogue* had never heard of us. I persuaded her that she and I should fly to Nepal a week early to "look over the situation," leaving our husbands behind. Despite the fact that we had no invitations, no hotel reservations, no press passes, we flew into Nepal—basically as coronation crashers.

Not only a tall, delicate blonde, Sarah also turned out to

have a convenient ability to cry on demand. After we landed in Kathmandu, our first stop was at the coronation press bureau. We introduced ourselves as representing *British Vogue*. When asked to present some *Vogue* ID for our press credentials, Sarah gave an emotional reply about how we had left the precious documents in London. We had nothing even suggesting we were journalists. With no other recourse, we stood there, smiling at one and all and explaining our predicament. The very polite Nepalese could not figure out how to dislodge us. The diminutive chief of protocol for the Nepalese government fell for the beautiful Sarah's charms, however, and we were given official press credentials.

Our next problem was to find a hotel. Of course, we had been told that Kathmandu was sold out and there was not a bed to be had. But now, flashing our press credentials, Sarah presented the visitors' bureau with a long tale about how we had been promised accommodations and then, with a pause as tears started to slip from her big blue eyes, "the person let us down, and here we are with no place to stay." Of course, the Nepalese housing authority did not want this weeping American, her friend, and their baggage on their hands, so after much discussion they found us temporary accommodations in the hotel for the flight crews that would be flying in the royal guests over the next few days. Within five hours, we were ensconced in our hotel. We had to promise to leave when the flight crews arrived, but I suspected, correctly, that we were there for the duration.

Kathmandu, dressed up for the coronation, was everything one could have imagined. All the temples and little houses were repainted in vivid colors, and in the evening the town sparkled with green and white lights. The twenty-three royal elephants— which can't live at Kathmandu's altitude—had been marched up from their jungle habitat and painted with eye makeup and gilded toenails. The Nepalese Army, its lancers and bagpipers in brand-new uniforms, kept parading the wide streets, rehearsing for the coronation procession.

Meeting people was a cinch. By dint of a daily drink or meal at the Yak & Yeti—an international bar-restaurant in an old Rana palace, run by former Russian ballet dancer Boris Lissanevitch—Sarah and I met all the resident foreigners and visiting press and picked up the day's news. The bar was much more effective as a news source than the Nepalese Press Bureau, which was full of goodwill but hopelessly enmeshed in bureaucratic tangles and brand-new Telex tape.

Sarah and I went to the airport, where she photographed the arriving VIPs. Prince Charles led the group in glamour, although he was outranked by the presidents of Pakistan and Sri Lanka. Imelda Marcos, wife of the president of the Philippines, arrived with a retinue of forty. Crown Prince Akihito and Crown Princess Michiko of Japan out-bowed and out-smiled even the polite Nepalese, and so were an instant hit. Our American delegation, headed up by Philip Buchan, a counsel to the president, looked lackluster in comparison, except for Cristina Ford, a blond bombshell and wife of the automobile tycoon Henry Ford.

By this time my husband's commercial flight had arrived. Sarah, now a hit with the international photographers, especially a handsome French one, barely had time to say hello to Jack before she hopped on the back of her photographer's motorcycle.

Jack asked, "Who is that?"

"Oh, just one of the other photographers," I answered. But I felt a bit smug.

Security began to tighten. We learned later that the king had read *The Day of the Jackal* and feared assassination. Roadblocks appeared everywhere, but with my press credentials we could still move around. All this, however, was not getting us in to the coronation.

The actual crowning of the king—with a two-million-dollar diadem of precious jewels, topped with a bird of paradise plume—was to take place at exactly 8:37 a.m. in the small courtyard of an ancient palace, with little spectator space. Even Jack admitted that there was no way of attending this event. But the afternoon part of the ceremony offered more possibilities. It was to be the traditional *durbar*—a really big show—with a procession of lancers, bagpipers, and incense bearers preceding the king and queen on the royal elephants. Their majesties were to dismount at a newly constructed pagoda, where they would receive honored guests and family.

Far away, off in fields, were fenced areas resembling cattle pens for all sorts of lower ranks of people: Nepalese government officials, diplomats, foreign residents, and Girl Scouts.

Jack busied himself getting his morning coat ready, then demanded that I put on an evening dress—the official coronation costume. Much to Jack's annoyance, I refused. I decided being trapped in evening dress among the local population, sacred cows, and rickshaws was not worth the gamble. More important, I was proud of my newly acquired press status. I was certain that the press didn't wear evening dress.

Jack procrastinated and delayed dressing, saying, "It's always best to arrive a little late for this type of thing." In disgust, I left him but went on alone, as Sarah had already joined forces with her French photographer. Jack had browbeaten me into giving him my press pass, so I found myself being gently but firmly pushed far from the action into one of the cattle pens—the one for foreign diplomats, as it turned out.

Broiling in the hot sun, unable to move, I watched the procession with the same perspective as from the last row of the top balcony in a large opera house. I could see the whole show but on a microscopic scale. "At least I'm here," I consoled myself. Suddenly that small comfort faded as I saw Jack's familiar tall silhouette, in his morning coat, suavely strolling across the parade ground, within twenty feet of the king and queen.

When we met up later that day, I asked Jack how he had done it. He told me that after passing through various barricades with my press credential, he and his friend, Ted Hartley, a partner in crime, had gone to the VIP entrance, where they chanced to arrive at the same time as the Indian ambassador, whom we had met the night before. Ted and Jack swept through the main gate and past the perplexed guards in the middle of the Indian delegation. The guards must have been curious to see two six-foot-tall Anglo-Saxons tagging along in the Indian group, but it enabled Ted and Jack to bypass the first hurdle without showing any credentials. Once inside, however, they realized that they couldn't settle down with the heads of state—who, by this time, were known to the Nepalese and to one another—or with the royal family, or with the Nepalese press in official uniform, or with the foreign press, all in blue jeans. So they maintained their precarious entrée by selective movement, always seeming to be in purposeful progress from one spot to another and looking in total command of the situation. They kept this choreography going as close to the royal pagoda as possible, calculating that for anyone to try to evict them so near to the center of activities would create an incident—something that the polite and ritualistic Nepalese would not want. While they didn't sit down, in essence they had front-row seats.

I was furious that Jack had ended up in the center of an event to which he was not even invited. Angry thoughts about chutzpah, astrology, and just common gall whirled through my head. I could imagine how my father, never a fan of Jack's, would have disapproved of this caper. But I had to admit that Jack never doubted that he was meant to be at the coronation, and so he was. I had doubted, and I ended up miles away in the cattle pen. Jack made fun of my ultimate placement, but he was also resentful that I had refused to join him.

After the coronation, Jack and I, with his friend Ted Hartley, flew to the jungle to stay at a famous resort named Tree-Tops. When our small plane landed in a clearing, we saw a line of elephants waiting to take us to the lodge. On top of each elephant was a platform with seats for three people. Ted and I ended up on the first elephant, but Jack lagged behind, fussing with his bag. The man in charge ordered our elephant to start and we took off, swaying in our lofty perch, on a fascinating walk through the jungle; I spotted crocodiles, hippos, monkeys, and exotic birds. Jack ended up on the next elephant. I was in a state of high excitement at my first trip to a tropical forest.

Jack's excitement was of a different nature. Angry and jealous that I had ended up on an elephant with another man—never mind that it was his friend and our traveling companion—he started to berate me as soon as we arrived. "How could you have gone ahead? Why didn't you wait for me?" His harangue was interrupted by dinner at the lodge, where Jack oozed his usual charm, but when we returned to our cabin, the tirade began again. "How could you get on an elephant without me?"

Previously, such arguments had ended with my apology and a reconciliation in bed, but this time I refused to say I was sorry and spent the night lying on a towel on the concrete floor of the shower. The glamorous trip had ended in a personal fiasco, but I felt the Bob Dylan song "The Times They Are A-Changin'" started going through my head. Was I going to spend the rest of my life sleeping in bathtubs or on shower floors?

Behind the Lens

I have always taken pictures. Maybe because of my family's nomadic existence, I craved reminders of where and with whom we had lived. From the time I received my first Brownie camera, I recorded much of the ephemera of my existence.

After watching Sarah take pictures at the coronation in Nepal, however, I became more serious about photography. When my friend Nancy heard how envious I was of the photographers in Kathmandu, she answered, "Well, do something about it. Go study photography."

Back in Washington, DC, I enrolled in a photography class at the Corcoran College of Art and Design, and I continued studying at the San Francisco Art Institute when we moved back to California later that year. In San Francisco the average age of the students was about twenty, and I was forty-three, the mother of three teenagers, ages seventeen, fifteen, and thirteen. My classmates' photos depicted nudes, decaying leaves, and street artists, while mine featured school sports and social events attended by people both clothed and well-dressed. A fellow student snidely commented, when my images were being shown, "Your life looks as if all you do is go to parties." But by and large the other students ignored me. The Art Institute in 1975 was a pretty hip place, and I hardly fit the profile.

When I read in the *San Francisco Chronicle* that President Gerald Ford was coming to town, a lightbulb turned on. I envisaged the crowd gathering to see the president exiting the St. Francis Hotel after his publicized luncheon speech. I dashed downtown, with two cameras and a light meter hanging around my neck, and positioned myself on the sidewalk opposite the side entrance to the hotel. Police and officials with badges, as well as the usual tourists, were milling around. I was happily shooting random crowd pictures when a burly TV cameraman came up to me and gestured up a tree. "You want a lift? There's room for one more person up there. My equipment's too heavy, but I'll gladly give you a boost."

I was a little leery but realized that his offer would give me a better vantage point. So his strong hands lifted me up and I nervously balanced on a branch. On a neighboring limb, an already ensconced young man glared at me. "Are you a professional?"

"Yes," I lied. There was no way I was going to leave my precarious perch. My neighbor continued to frown, and the branch dug into my side.

The president did not appear when promised, so out of boredom and discomfort my tree mate and I began to talk. We even compared light-meter settings but never got as far as exchanging names. The official press, including the photographers festooned with badges, stood in a line below us on the edge of the sidewalk.

With no warning, a platoon of police appeared and queued up in front of the press, effectively blocking the photographers and TV cameramen on the ground. After a moment the hotel door opened. More police came out, followed by the familiar figure of President Ford, about thirty feet away. A second later we heard a loud pop. I initially thought the sound was that of firecrackers. I swiveled in the direction of the sound and saw a woman with a gun. My lens was pointed right at her. Police streamed in all directions, the crowd started to run, and the area was cleared.

Frightened but almost in a trance, I kept photographing, somewhat hidden in my tree.

The Secret Service pushed President Ford into his limousine and drove off; the police were thinning out when I climbed down. I ran to the nearest pay phone and called Jack. "You won't believe it—someone just tried to kill the president."

"What the hell were you doing there?" he asked. Jack, who loved any kind of PR, immediately saw an opportunity for himself. "As soon as you get home, call Herb Caen. He'll want to put it in his column." But Herb Caen, the local columnist, did more than write a two-sentence item. He told me to sit tight, as a *Chronicle* car and a driver was on its way to bring me down to the paper with my film.

Kevin had just returned from school and asked if he could come, too. "Absolutely," I said. As we sped through town in the company car, Kevin's eyes were shining, and we both felt as if we were subjects in a TV program. At the paper, we sat nervously while they developed my prints, and then the editor came out, long-faced: "You had buck fever, kid. Yes, you have photos of Sara Jane Moore, but they are all out of focus. Sorry." Kevin and I were driven home, a dejected duo.

Nobody could have been more surprised than I was the next day: I opened the paper to see my photograph spread out over half of the front page and my name printed underneath it. It wasn't an image of the would-be assassin but one of the Secret Service springing into action and gently pushing President Ford into the back of his limousine. I quickly called Ken Regan, the photographer from the Kennedy trip, to boast about my photo.

His voice crackled with excitement. "What picture? Where is the film?" I admitted what had happened. "You idiot, you left it at the paper? It's yours, you know. *TIME* needs a photo. Get your ass back there, pick up your negatives, and get them to San Francisco Airport as soon you can." He told me that when the packet was on its way, he would send someone to meet the plane.

My image, with proper credit, was the lead photograph of the aborted Ford assassination in *TIME* magazine. I bought ten copies.

Overnight I became a professional photographer. From then on, I was never without a camera around my neck. My subsequent career included a wide range of subjects, from friends' children, to a cookbook called *No Pressure Steam Cooking*, to tall ships and public gatherings. I was named official photographer for the San Francisco bicentennial. Purely for fun, I photographed all the authors who gave readings at a local independent bookstore, Minerva's Owl, and as a result the owner gave me my first exhibition.

After that show, Heide Betz at the Van Doren Gallery offered me a one-woman show. I named it "Familiar Faces." After the opening, I phoned my parents to share my excitement, but my mother stayed true to form. Her comment was, "I can't imagine anyone paying $125 for one of your photographs." She hurt me, but I realized that she just didn't understand that photography could be a profession and that it happened to be mine. As usual, I made a joke of her reaction.

Photography brought me back to Moscow, working for *Newsweek* during the 1980 Olympics. These were the games that the United States boycotted as a protest against the Soviet invasion of Afghanistan, although our protest was lost on the average Russian, who never understood the purpose of it, and was a crushing blow to our athletes, who could not compete. A small nucleus of American press attended, largely to cover the much-anticipated races between two British runners, Sebastian Coe and Steve Ovett. Ken Regan had picked me as his backup photographer, and for seventeen days we covered every summer sport, including gymnastics, swimming, boxing, weight lifting, and track-and-field. Every night we rushed our film to the airport. All the photos published in *Newsweek* ended up being Ken's, but I had my second show at the Van Doren Gallery, of Olympics photographs. I was thrilled when a local critic wrote: "Grace Warnecke brings a fresh new eye to sports photography."

Photography also resulted in a collaboration between my father and me. In the summer of 1984 we were hired to do an article together for *House & Garden*. As we cruised up the coast of Norway toward Oslo, my father steered the boat and wrote the text, Mother cooked, and I took the pictures to illustrate the story.

In the course of that cruise, I learned how much sailing had brought to my parents' life together. In 1964 they bought their first boat, *Nagawicka*, but the boat was in Norway and I was in California, so I did not participate in these early sailing adventures, of which Christopher and Wendy were very much a part. By the time I joined my parents, they were on their second boat, the thirty-six-foot Nicholson, *North Wind*, on which we were presently cruising. To my surprise, Mother appeared in a new light.

Usually an indifferent cook, Mother was totally engaged on board. She prepared all the meals and served as my father's mate on many long, often uncomfortable voyages in the cold waters of the Skagerrak. Roaring winds and frequent rainstorms did not dampen her enjoyment. Sailing seemed to be a shared passion. And Mother had my father and the younger children to herself—there were no interruptions from the outside world, and my father couldn't retreat into his books. At high noon every day at sea, each adult drank a glass of sherry as a "propitiatory toast to Father Neptune." I began to respect my mother's contributions to their life on the water. She showed her Viking blood.

I loved being a photographer. Except for the *House & Garden* piece, that career was not related to being my father's daughter. My successes were my own doing. Photography used my eye, appreciation of art, and love of being part of historic events. I could be in the thick of things, and even push forward, but I was at the same time hidden behind the lens of the camera. The dual role suited me. Soon I had a third exhibition at the Van Doren Gallery, and over time I became increasingly secure behind the lens. In contrast, my marriage seemed more and more unsettled and out of focus.

On the Rocks

In the summer of 1975, after Jack's work on the Hart Senate Office Building ended, we migrated back to San Francisco. I wasn't looking forward to it. Our two years in Washington had been productive. Having my family nearby was nurturing after so many years apart. My three teenage children were all going through adolescent problems, not made any easier by Jack's rigorous travel schedule and his general indifference to them. They needed my attention, while Jack wanted me to devote all my time and energies to him.

In addition to my being his wife, he considered me an adjunct to his business. After each social event we attended, he gave me a printed form to complete, requiring me to note the names of all the guests, describe what was discussed, and then follow up: "Send a thank-you note to Mrs. X, a nice-getting-to-know-you note to Mr. Y, and flowers to the Z's." Eager to please, I initially performed these tasks without questioning, but as time went on I grew to resent them. No matter how hard

I worked, there was little recognition from Jack. After a dinner party up at the ranch, in honor of a *Vogue* editor, he wrote a memo listing eighteen mistakes I had made, such as "cheese too hard" and "fire improperly laid," and circulated it through his office. The humiliation stung. I felt that I was failing on all fronts—as a mother to my children and as the perfect helpmate that Jack demanded.

A low point of the first year back on the coast was a business trip to London. It included a magazine interview with both of us, the glamorous international couple, for a leading fashion magazine. Jack was always generous about buying me clothes, as long as he chose them. "You have no taste," he explained. "You're my wife and it's important that you look the part."

Maybe it was a secret rebellion, but the day before the trip, I went to Saks Fifth Avenue and bought a leopard-print pants outfit, the current rage in fashion. I really wanted it.

As we were packing, Jack glimpsed the smart outfit and exploded. "You bought that? Can't you see it makes you look vulgar? I told you not to buy anything without my seeing it first." He continued this tirade in the taxi to the airport and then kept fulminating on the plane, where I broke down in silent tears, hidden behind my dark glasses.

As we arrived in London, he looked at me, surprised. "My God, you look awful. You can't go out like that. Fix yourself up. Put on your makeup." Unbelievably, I did just that, because I understood that the magazine story was important for Jack, and I couldn't break away from the belief that Jack was the significant one, and I was only a prop.

I was living two lives: the public one as Jack's wife, and the private one in anguish. How could this marriage, begun with such passion between the two of us, end up with such estrangement? Why did I allow his demands to supersede my own needs and those of my children? Photography became an escape, and parties were another—anything that took me away from Jack. I started seeing a therapist and began to view myself from a new perspective.

At one of the last Washington dinner parties attended before returning to San Francisco, I complained about our upcoming move. Our Southern hostess, known for being outspoken, looked intently at me and drawled, "Well, honey, don't take it too seriously. I don't see you going into the golden years with Jack Warnecke." Her words reverberated in my head. I had always assumed that Jack was the star and I was lucky to be with him. But now it looked as if other people saw me as someone who mattered, too.

Back in San Francisco, I demanded that we go to a marriage counselor. After Jack monopolized the whole first session, it was clear that this was hopeless, that even in the therapist's office there was no room for me.

I finally asked Jack for a divorce. I anticipated the worst—a huge scene, threats. But his reaction was totally unexpected. Instead of the usual bullying, he morphed into a supplicant. He begged me to stay with him. He would give me anything I wanted if only I wouldn't leave. He would stay home; he would pay attention to my children. I discovered power, but it was too late. By this time, nothing could have brought us back together. On January 3, 1978, I filed for divorce. We had been married for eight years.

Jack begged. I found a lawyer and refused to back down. After many extremely unpleasant weeks, marked by incessant bickering, slamming of doors, and legal ultimatums, Jack moved out.

But I was very fragile. The day I learned that our separation would be reported in the *San Francisco Chronicle*, both in the Herb Caen column and the social columns, I flew to Los Angeles, because I couldn't bear reading about it or fielding phone calls. When I returned two days later, I was greeted by a big basket from the florist—four dozen long-stemmed yellow roses with a gift envelope in Jack's familiar sloping handwriting, addressed "Grace." I remembered that when we first started seeing each other, he sent me four dozen red roses, but now they had turned yellow. The yellow roses reminded me of Texas and the Kennedy assassination. Also, yellow was the color of cowardice. I threw the flowers into the garbage can and emptied it into the trash for good measure, hoping that the memories of Jack would leave the house as well.

That night there was an article about our impending divorce in the New York *Daily News*, obviously leaked by Jack, headlined: UNTIL CAREERS DO THEM PART. Careers were only the tip of the iceberg.

I was left rattling around in a six-bedroom rented house with Adair. Charles was living with his father. Kevin was a boarder at Trinity-Pawling School in Pawling, New York.

With the help of Gino Negroni, a photographer friend of my brother's, I set up a darkroom in the basement and we spent hours printing the photographs for my photo exhibitions. Gino cooked as well, so the smell of photo developer and spaghetti carbonara permeated that period of my life. But it was only temporary. By the end of the year, everyone was moving on. My divorce was granted, and I realized that I wanted to be nearer to my family on the East Coast. California days were ending, but what was coming next?

CHAPTER 7

New Waters

My new single life in San Francisco was jolted by a telephone call from John Wasserman, the funny and outrageous music critic of the *San Francisco Chronicle*, whom I barely knew. "How would you like to go to Russia with Joan Baez?" he asked.

He explained that Joan Baez was to be part of a much-headlined concert, with Santana and the Beach Boys, in Winter Palace Square in Leningrad on July 4, 1978. The Bay Area impresario Bill Graham was organizing the show. Wasserman was looking for an appropriate folk song for Joan to sing in Russian, as well as a Russian speaker to accompany her on the trip as a translator and companion. For me, this was an amazing opportunity. I was being given a free trip to the Soviet Union, an opportunity to brush up on my Russian, and a chance to be part of the inner circle of an American folk icon whom I had admired for years. I couldn't wait.

I rushed out and bought all of Joan Baez's records. As usual, I was flying blind. I did not know any Russian folk singers, so I called all my Russian friends and one came up with a song, "Circle of Friends," by Bulat Okudzhava, a well-known poet and bard. Often played and sung on the underground circuit, Okudzhava's works were just beginning to be officially published. He was, like Joan, a popular protester.

Sitting at the press conference when Bill Graham announced this concert, surrounded by musical celebrities, I relished being part of the rock music scene. My children were impressed. I treasured my passport with its hard-to-come-by Russian visa. A week before we were to leave, however, Grigory Romanov, second secretary of the Communist Party in Leningrad, abruptly canceled the trip. I was crushed.

A few days later, John Wasserman called to say that Joan Baez had a new proposal. Since Joan had cleared her schedule for this trip and we had our visas, why didn't the three of us take the trip, anyway, but go to Moscow instead of Leningrad? Joan wanted to meet with the famous physicist and political dissident Andrei Sakharov. Sakharov, known as the father of the Soviet hydrogen bomb, had shocked the Soviet government by coming out against nuclear testing and was now an intellectual hero in the West.

I accepted Joan's invitation but realized that this was a very different deal. In the original journey, with Bill Graham making the arrangements, there was a large staff seeing that everything was done for us; now *I* was the staff. John's role was to write a series of articles about the journey for the *San Francisco Chronicle*, not to mention keeping Joan amused. I was to take the photographs to accompany John's pieces, but I was also in charge of all logistics. While what we proposed to do was not illegal, I was acutely aware it would be viewed with skepticism by the Soviet authorities.

Joan was able to contact Sakharov's stepdaughter, Tatiana, who had recently immigrated to the United States and was living in the Boston area. Through Tatiana we received hand-drawn maps showing how to find Sakharov's apartment, because accurate Moscow city maps were not available at the time. Joan collected presents and letters for the Sakharovs, but I warned her that giving money was strictly illegal and could get us into serious trouble. Joan had already gone to jail in the States for blocking the entrance to an armed forces induction center, but I had no desire to end up in a Soviet prison.

The three of us set off on the long flight from San Francisco, routed via New York and Helsinki. John's suitcase, reflecting his macabre sense of humor, featured large stenciled letters saying VOYAGE OF THE DAMNED, attracting attention wherever we went. John availed himself of all the free drinks offered on the business class flight and was looking distinctly green by the time we arrived at Helsinki Airport. Sitting in the transit lounge, John roused himself from his stupor and whispered to me, "I think she's bringing money for the Jewish dissidents."

"What makes you think so?" I asked, my stomach suddenly tightening.

John gestured. "Notice that she is taking the guitar case with her to the bathroom. That's not normal. Why doesn't she leave it with us?"

I felt sick. Of course I could have made a scene and said that I wouldn't go if Joan was smuggling in money, but we were almost there and I didn't have the heart, or maybe the guts. We only suspected that there was money in the guitar case; we weren't certain. Besides, John was seriously hungover, so maybe this observation just reflected alcohol-induced paranoia. On the plane from Helsinki to Moscow, I agonized over the prospects, imagining a KGB interrogation about the contents of the guitar case. The message on John's suitcase seemed prophetic.

My knees were trembling as we stood in the dreaded customs line at Moscow's Sheremetyevo Airport. Then I heard my name called in Russian: "Greis."

I looked up to see the handsome face of Nikita Mikhalkov, a famous Russian film director, for whom I had recently translated at a Berkeley film festival. Nikita was returning to Moscow after receiving an Italian medal, Leone d'Oro—the Golden Lion—in Venice. I introduced him to Joan. Happily, he knew all about her and had heard her music. "It's ridiculous that you are standing in this queue," he said. "Come with me. I will introduce you." We trotted behind as he led us up to the head of the customs line. There he introduced Joan Baez as the famous folk singer from America, a great artist, and even added that I was the daughter of a former ambassador to the Soviet Union. It didn't hurt that Nikita's father was the composer of the Soviet national anthem. The customs official made a notation in our passports, gave a wave, and the next thing we knew we had crossed the border. None of our possessions had been examined. Nikita then invited us to a dinner the next night in his studio. Joan's trip was started, and my stomach relaxed.

We settled into the massive Hotel Rossiya, reputedly the second-largest hotel in the world, but Joan and I had to share a room, as the manager claimed that the giant edifice was full. Before that, our relationship had been formal, but now those barriers relaxed. Joan and I both suffered from jet-lag-induced insomnia, so we stayed up nights and she shared a lot about her life as a singer, her love affair with Bob Dylan, other romances, her marriage, political protests, and her beloved son, Gabriel. Somehow she wasn't so interested in Charles, Adair, and Kevin. I learned she had a wicked sense of humor, an uncanny ability to mimic people, and could turn a charm button on and off almost at will.

The second day in Moscow we set off, with the guitar, to visit a Jewish dissident group to whom Joan had an introduction through a peace group in Boston. They were expecting us. I located the apartment—not easy to do, as many apartment entrances in the older buildings of Moscow are off courtyards and poorly marked. Five or six men and women welcomed us into a tiny apartment. It seemed strange to see a bed pillow on the living room floor with a cord leading out from it, until a woman lifted up the pillow and pointed to the telephone that the pillow was muffling. The dissidents discussed their situation: they had mostly lost their jobs and were waiting for their exit visas, but they were uncertain whether they would receive them. As soon as Joan started to say she had brought something, I shook my head violently and handed her my notepad, on which I'd scrawled, "Write it down." As John and I suspected, she had brought money for the group and wanted to give it to them. The amount was large. The spokeswoman for the group became agitated. She took me into the bathroom and explained in a whisper next to a gushing faucet that if they accepted money from a foreigner they would risk imprisonment or worse. We soon left. While I was glad that we had not endangered any members of the group, I began to get that sinking feeling again. It was now definite that Joan was carrying undeclared money.

From then on, our life became a whirlwind. Andrei Konchalovsky, a half brother of Nikita Mikhalkov and a well-known film director for whom I had also translated in Berkeley, called and invited us to lunch at his mother's dacha. Joan's usual charm was muted, as she didn't like being dragged out of Moscow—a trip that would have been pure heaven for most Muscovites. What's more, this expedition took place before Joan Baez had confided to me that she suffered from a form of hypoglycemia, which required that she eat something every three hours or become cranky and withdrawn. The trip home from the dacha consisted of Andrei trying to make conversation and Joan staring sullenly into space. From then on, I carried food for her.

When we returned to our hotel that afternoon, there was a crisis with our room: the hotel manager announced we had to leave the next day, citing a regulation that foreigners were allowed to stay in Moscow for only three days. I went down to the front desk and successfully untangled this bureaucratic snafu by inventing an imaginary concert at which Joan was going to sing. This trip was definitely honing my improvisational talents. When I went back upstairs, I was stunned to see a line of maids in the hall outside our room, listening to the pure bell-like tones of Joan's voice singing "Imagine." Little housework was done that afternoon on the fifth floor of the Hotel Rossiya.

Through Nikita Mikhalkov, I obtained Okudzhava's phone number. I called and told the bard how much Joan wanted to meet him and how she had memorized his song. He invited us to his apartment. After some introductory back and forth, Joan sang his song, accompanied by her guitar. Each was instantly smitten with the other, and I felt that this trip was turning into a success.

Back at our hotel, the phone started to ring. Radio Moscow and various newspapers had gotten wind of Joan's presence and wanted interviews. One of these journalists was a young man; I'll call him Volodya. He had met Joan in Cuba and wanted to renew the friendship, even move on to a more intimate phase. Joan gave him an interview but did not welcome his attention. She told me that she did not want to see him anymore, and for the rest of the trip I found myself running interference.

The next day was the visit to Sakharov and the focus of our trip. We had been warned that the government had taken the house number off his building, as well as off each apartment on his floor. I felt very conspicuous as we set forth carrying the ever-present guitar. We took a taxi but asked the driver to drop us a few blocks away. By following Tatiana's map, we arrived at what we calculated was the right building, entered the door code, and went up to the designated floor. The lightbulbs on that floor had been removed, so the hallway was pitch dark. We counted the doorways by feel along the corridor.

Joan had assured me that Sakharov was expecting us, but when we knocked on the door, a very surprised Elena Bonner,

Sakharov's wife, peered at us through her thick dark-rimmed glasses. "Who are you?" she asked.

We stood awkwardly in the hall while I explained, and Sakharov finally approached the door and said, "Oh, yes, I did receive a call that someone was coming, but I didn't know who, and, besides, I thought it was tomorrow." We were invited in and sat down at the kitchen table, where we were offered tea. It was clear that Joan Baez meant nothing to them.

Joan started out looking for common ground by discussing one of her favorite causes—the plight of the people in Chile and Bangladesh—but Sakharov was not interested. The more they talked, with me feverishly translating, the further apart they seemed. He finally said, "You know, we have so many problems here that I am not interested in problems overseas or in what the American government is or is not doing. It was nice of you to come, but I don't see the point."

Joan, always quick to size up a situation, changed the subject. "Andrei," she said, "could I just play you a few songs?"

"Go ahead," he answered, pointing up at the ceiling. "Even they like music."

So Joan started singing and playing the guitar, and her melodic voice quickly made the direct contact with the Sakharovs that she couldn't achieve through mere dialogue. Afterward, we engaged in spirited conversation and Elena Bonner fed us a light meal. When we left, we exchanged warm hugs and good feelings. "Walk a few blocks and then turn onto another street," advised Sakharov. "The taxis have been told not to stop outside this building."

That afternoon my friend Andrei Voznesensky, the poet, and his wife, the writer Zoya Boguslavskaya, invited us out to their dacha in Peredelkino, the famous writers' colony. I had bonded with Andrei and Zoya during the Kennedy trip in 1974. While I fed Joan pilfered rolls from the hotel breakfast, a friend drove us out to the dacha.

In 1978, the famous poets in the Soviet Union had reputations similar to rock stars in the States. A big poetry reading would draw thousands. Unlike Sakharov, Voznesensky immediately took to Joan. After tea and a little wine, Andrei offered to read some poems. But in fact he didn't read, he declaimed. His sonorous voice reverberated through the small dacha, and soon Joan answered with her favorites—"Diamonds and Rust," "Imagine," and other standbys. It was magical. By the end of the evening, the Voznesenskys had offered to give a dinner for her in a country restaurant. Andrei promised to invite Okudzhava, ensuring Joan's attendance.

We were really on a roll. I was working flat out, translating for Joan's interviews, making arrangements, and taking pictures, while John Wasserman kept us amused and enjoyed all the hospitality. The Voznesenskys called and said that they had arranged for Joan to give a concert at the restaurant and had invited the cream of Moscow's intelligentsia to attend. I was nervous about the concert, because some of Joan's songs were difficult to translate properly. "Diamonds and Rust" was a good example.

When we arrived at the roadside restaurant in the woods, we found about thirty people waiting for us in a large private room on the second floor. Many well-known figures were there, including Brezhnev's handsome interpreter, Victor Sukhodrev, whom I had met on the Kennedy trip. After he and Joan conversed, he pulled me aside. "Don't worry," he announced with authority. "You can relax; I will translate for her." Greatly relieved, I sat down and became a guest and was able to converse with people on my own.

Eventually, Joan stood up and sang one song, eliciting rapt attention from the guests. "What a success," I thought. Then Joan put her guitar down and said she wanted to say something. "Thank you for this warm reception. I'm sorry, however; I am not used to singing in private rooms for the select few. I appreciate the dinner, but please excuse me, as I want to go downstairs and sing for the people."

Angrily, Sukhodrev turned to me. "From now on you can translate!" Everyone else looked as shocked as I felt.

Joan and I went downstairs, and I explained Joan's request to a startled restaurant manager. After a long delay, he found a microphone and some sound equipment, and to the total surprise of the restaurant patrons, Joan gave an impromptu concert, with me translating after each song. I was concentrating so hard that I only dimly remember some of the guests from above coming down. Joan was triumphant. The Voznesenskys waited for us, and it must have been two in the morning when we returned to the hotel. Our departure for New York was to be later that day.

The phone rang as soon as we got back to our room. It was Volodya. He already had heard all about Joan's impromptu concert and said the news was the sensation of Moscow. He wanted to meet us at the airport and interview Joan. I found this a great idea, since I was now worried about getting the guitar and its contents through customs without incident. Volodya was a well-connected journalist and I thought he could help.

Joan, on the other hand, was adamant. "I don't want to see Volodya. I've had enough interviews. Tell him no."

A few hours later, bleary-eyed and tired, we set off for the airport. As our taxi pulled up to Sheremetyevo Airport, sitting on the curb was Volodya. By now fear had given me courage to confront Joan. "Joan, you must speak to him. It is important. Don't ask why." She looked surprised but smiled at him and answered his questions. Volodya offered to escort us into the airport. We had a coffee and then he led us to the customs line. The next thing I knew, he flashed an ID that I couldn't see, mumbled something to the agent, and again we were given the VIP treatment, sailing through customs with no one so much as looking at the precious guitar case and its contents.

My photos were used as the backdrop when Joan was interviewed about the trip on the *Today* show, and they illustrated John Wasserman's articles in the *San Francisco Chronicle*. My future as a photographer seemed clear to me, but pieces in the puzzle soon shifted.

New York, New York

Looking down from on high at a maze in an English garden, one sees the lovely patterns, as well as the entrance and exit. But when in the maze, one sees only walls. The eighties were a maze for me. I moved back east in 1980 to be near my parents, siblings, and Kevin, who was at Trinity-Pawling.

My original plan was to move to Washington, where I had many friends, but after a two-week stay with an unmarried classmate who seemed to spend an inordinate amount of time nailing down an escort for a dinner party, I decided Washington was more suited for couples. Rather impulsively, I decided to relocate to New York. Theater, ballet, museums, and the sheer vitality of the city all appealed. In New York, I thought, you didn't need a date to attend a party.

Friends rented me a pied-à-terre, on the condition that I share it with a young male model while I looked for a place to buy. The two of us lived like strangers passing in the night. He was a habitué of the club scene, and I spent my time apartment-hunting and going to the movies.

After three months, I found the West Side apartment that is still my home. I planned to support myself as a photographer and assumed that I would pick up friends along the way. Neither happened. It took months to even get an appointment with a major photo editor, and it became clear that my reputation as a photographer in San Francisco did not follow me to New York City. Unless I was willing to move to the Lower East Side (much less expensive in those days than the Upper West Side) and give up restaurants, theater, and social life, I wasn't going to make it as a photographer. I felt as if an important part of me was being extinguished.

Meeting people was not the cinch that I had anticipated,

either. While married to Jack, I had lived in a world of movers
and shakers who quickly accepted us into their high-powered
milieu. Bill and Pat Buckley, Nan Kempner, David Halber-
stam, Jackie O—all were part of that world. We attended their
benefits and went to their dinner parties. But my identity was
as Jack's wife.

Moving back to New York as a single woman with little
money, I made the decision not to call anyone in that group.
I knew that they would all politely invite me to the occasional lunch, but I would only be a fringe part of their constel-
lation—the woman called when someone dropped out at the
last minute. I was not in a position to repay any hospitality.
So I cut myself off from my previous life and lived a solitary
existence.

That first summer was particularly hard, as even the few
people I had met disappeared on weekends. Walking around on
a steamy Fourth of July, I thought how awful the city was—op-
pressively hot, redolent of odd smells, its streets full of trash.
All the men seemed wrinkled, and all the women had roots
showing. I wondered why I had chosen to move to New York
from beautiful San Francisco. I could have eaten my loneliness
with a spoon.

I managed to get a temporary job taking the photos for a
book about toys; I enrolled in an exercise class and slowly made
a few friends. But after I had taken my last photo of "little boy
with dump truck" and "little girl with kitchen set," I sat looking
at a very uncertain future.

Financially, things were scary.

When an acquaintance from San Francisco, Stanley Weiss,
appeared in New York in 1981 and asked me to help him start an
organization called Business Executives for National Security
(BENS), I came on board, working part-time as a consultant.
With a new briefcase and my first business cards, I commuted
to Washington and traveled to Boston, Los Angeles, and San
Francisco. My responsibility was to establish new chapters for

this fledgling group concerned about how the cost of Cold War defense was affecting the economy. My cameras, lights, and tripods were tucked away at the top of a closet. It hurt even to look at them.

This was in 1982, when a campaign had started to achieve a mutual and verifiable freeze in nuclear weapons. Part of my BENS work was to represent the organization at various conclaves of the burgeoning peace movement and the nuclear freeze campaign. While not an antiwar organization, BENS was concerned about the scale and type of our country's defense spending.

During the same period, my father felt so passionately about the nuclear threat that he coauthored an article in *Foreign Affairs*, which attracted a lot of attention. I went out to Princeton and listened to my father railing against the horror of nuclear war. He had seen firsthand the devastation that the Second World War had caused in Europe.

For the first time, my father and I were promoting the same cause, albeit at very different levels. While he was writing and lecturing, I was struggling out of bed to represent BENS at early breakfasts at the back of the Brasserie restaurant, where those of us in associations active in the nuclear freeze campaign discussed issues on a much more nuts-and-bolts level. We were organizing lectures, fund-raisers, and marches.

The Brasserie group included a wide range of organizations, from reputable ones such as Physicians for Social Responsibility to fringe groups such as Pillowcases for Peace. The latter was the initiative of a peace activist who believed that if American and Russian children exchanged pillowcases, their dreams would bring peace to the world. After a while, the Brasserie breakfasts staled for me. Although I believed passionately in the cause, I thought we were preaching to the choir rather than breaking new ground. I consulted for BENS over a three-year period but resigned when my interests swung me in another direction.

With New York hotel rates sky-high, my apartment became a way station for visiting San Franciscans. My brother appeared one day, right after a couple had left the apartment a mess and the hostess exhausted, and lectured me on being too accommodating. "You're too generous. You take in anyone who asks. You're running a free hotel." As always, I took the criticism hard.

Christopher's accusation hit my secret feelings, probably seeded by my mother's criticisms, that underneath any success I might have lay an unorganized and inadequate person. I agreed to have fewer guests.

My resolve was soon tested. A few nights later, I picked up the phone to hear a young man, David Hoffman, whom I had met at an Esalen conference. Esalen, a modern-age psycho-spiritual retreat in Big Sur, California, dealt mostly with personal issues, but the director, Michael Murphy, had organized a small group that was developing practical initiatives to bring an end to the Cold War. Discussions were followed by evenings soaking in moonlit hot tubs.

David was calling because he needed a place to stay. He had no money and nowhere to go. Could he . . . ? Although Christopher's words rang in my ears, I heard myself responding, "Yes, but only for one night."

He stayed for three. When he left, he insisted that I must call him when I found myself in San Francisco. So, on my next trip west to see Adair, I rang.

Over dripping candles stuck in Chianti bottles, David started to talk about my future. "If you could do anything you wanted and money was no object, what would you choose?"

I thought and then replied that I would like to do something that combined my skill as a photographer, my ability to act as a catalyst for new projects, and my love of movies.

The next day, David called back. "I have just the job for you. I know this top documentary film director, Bill Jersey, who's based in Berkeley, and he's going to make a film about fifty years of U.S.–Soviet relations. He's looking for a writer. Can you see him today?"

I did, and soon I was hired to write for *The First Fifty Years*. BENS and the antinuclear campaign paled in contrast to the excitement of working on a film to which everyone involved was fervently committed. The camaraderie assuaged the pain of putting photography in the closet.

Bill Jersey was a teacher, a visionary, and an inspiration. He had the gift of leadership without being authoritarian. He listened to our small crew, but in the end his vision prevailed. His humor and wisdom defused the constant crises and small quarrels that pop up on any film set. As a boss he was constantly encouraging and gave me a sense of worth that I had rarely experienced.

Somehow Bill found out that I knew Harrison Salisbury, the *New York Times* correspondent, from the summer in Moscow when my father was ambassador. I was able to persuade Salisbury to be the on-camera interviewer for *The First Fifty Years*. Together, Bill and I lined up an impressive list of interviewees, including my father, former ambassador Averell Harriman, even ex-president Richard Nixon. My apartment became *The First Fifty Years* central.

One night I had dinner with Bill Wilson, a television producer and old friend of C. K.'s from the Stevenson campaign. When I excitedly described our work, Bill surprised me by saying, "What you're doing is what producers do. You are finding talent, searching locations, and opening doors. You don't want a writer credit. That means nothing in television." I demurred. I was proud of my writer status. He persisted: "If you don't ask for an associate-producer credit, I will never speak to you again." So on the train to Princeton, with my hands shaking in tandem with the jolting train, I stammered out my request. Bill Jersey acquiesced, and I became an associate producer.

We spent the afternoon in Princeton chatting with my parents before Salisbury interviewed my father. Noticing my father's slightly condescending treatment of me, Bill made an offhand remark to the effect that he was surprised at how old-fashioned my father was in his attitude toward women, especially toward me. I was shocked. It hadn't occurred to me that I was being patronized, and this became a turning point in my self-awareness. It was consequently a great moment when I was able to call my father and tell him that *The First Fifty Years* had won the Alfred I. duPont Award as the best independently produced documentary of the year.

"Very nice," he said.

With my new television credit, I was soon hired by Metromedia and was off to Moscow to work as associate producer on a series called *Inside Russia*. I went with an all-male crew—full of testosterone, bright ideas, and talent, but very little understanding of the country. We produced some beautifully shot and edited film, but the heavy anti-Soviet narration resulted in my inability to get a visa for several years. The "Kennan curse" had struck again.

After the Metromedia assignment ended, unemployment loomed once more. However, a good result of all my disparate jobs was that I had formed an impressive network of friends and acquaintances. Hearing of my plight, a friend from the peace movement rescued me, phoning to say he knew a rich Dutchman who was starting a foundation to bring journalists from the East and West together and was looking for someone to run his New York office. "He's a little eccentric," he said, "but you need a job and you're qualified. Do you want to meet him?"

Of course I did.

Within weeks, I became the U.S. director of the Alerdinck Foundation, which was based in a castle in Holland. My new boss, Frans Lurvink, was a buoyant, wealthy entrepreneur who had a new idea every five minutes. He set me up with an office and an assistant in the headquarters of his friend's bathing suit company in New York's Garment District. In a room festooned with oversize glossy posters of bikini-clad models, I worked to end the Cold War by bringing together correspondents from America, the Soviet Union, and Europe.

We attracted top journalists and organized some high-level conferences in Moscow, Paris, and New York. Frans, through some connections in the Soviet government, also succeeded in getting me off the Soviet blacklist so that I could help organize the Moscow conference. I was relieved and happy to be able to go back to the Soviet Union again, as without that possibility I was not going to be effective in what seemed to be my new mission: to end the Cold War.

Just as I'd succeeded in turning my nebulous Alerdinck job into a reality and had proudly received the first foundation grant that validated our work, Frans closed Alerdinck, as precipitously as he had founded it. It developed that he had lost considerable money gambling on the currency market. He left me the filing cabinet and the dictionary. It appeared that I'd hit another wall in the maze.

Back in the USSR

In the mid-eighties I embarked on a series of new jobs, often overlapping, some of which made sense and some of which I never should have undertaken. Two very contradictory traits—a lack of self-confidence and an astounding willingness to jump into the unknown—propelled me to accept many of these challenges.

One such project was the American Soviet Youth Orchestra. That incarnation started from a lunch. A friend, Edythe Holbrook, and her colleague, Tsugiko Scullion, both working for the American Field Service (AFS), were having lunch with Fred Starr, president of Oberlin College, to brainstorm ideas for some new initiative to bring the two sides of the Cold War together. As this subject was right up my alley and I knew Fred when he was director of the Kennan Institute, I was invited to join them. Fred, also a jazz musician, came up with the idea of a U.S.–Soviet youth orchestra. Music would penetrate the Iron Curtain. The young musicians could rehearse and practice at the renowned Oberlin Conservatory of Music, while AFS would manage cultural orientations and homestays. I was hired to do a feasibility study of such an orchestra and given an office at the AFS.

As usual, I started cramming. Despite a very musical father and sister, I had only an amateur appreciation of classical orchestral music. Two friends helped to inaugurate me into this new world, pointing out the difference between a French horn and a clarinet. I had a long way to go.

But then an even better offer came along. Rick Smolan, an editor of the *Day in the Life* series of photo books, asked me if I could go to Moscow for two months as an editor of their latest book, *A Day in the Life of the Soviet Union*. This would mean abandoning my half-completed feasibility study on the U.S.–Soviet youth orchestra. However, several things made Rick's offer irresistible. The most important was that my Russian language was fading, and I knew that without intense immersion it might disappear. I felt that my knowledge of the country was getting stale, as well, and would be revived by living and working there. I tried to persuade Fred Starr that this was only a temporary delay. I promised to find him the appropriate contact at the Ministry of Culture—an initiative crucial to the future of the orchestra. I found someone else for the feasibility study. As it became clear that I was going to Moscow no matter what, Fred went along with my plan, but he was not happy about it.

A Day in the Life's mission was to select and organize one hundred of the world's top photographers—fifty from the East and fifty from the West—who would have exactly twenty-four hours on May 15, 1987, to photograph the Soviet city to which they were assigned. We editors would research those cities, make assignments, brief the photographers, arrange for tickets and hotel rooms, and debrief them upon return, as all rolls of film had to be accompanied by identification and narration. It was a monumental task.

I met the rest of our seven-person staff at Kennedy Airport, all of us jittery and excited. This was still the Soviet Union. When we arrived at Sheremetyevo Airport, my compatriots all went through passport control, but I was asked to stand aside. One by one, all the passengers from the plane filed past, but I remained until I was alone in an empty hall. A uniformed guard pointed at a chair and said, "Sit down."

Rigid and with my heart thumping, I sat as stony-faced border guards paced up and down. Was this because I was born in Riga, and Latvia was now part of the Soviet Union? Were they going to claim me as a Soviet citizen? Could they have discovered the painting that I smuggled out for an artist friend a few years ago? Was I going to jail? What was my group doing? For what might have been fifteen minutes but to me was an eternity, I sat, glued to the chair.

Finally one of the guards walking by, still impassive, turned toward me and whispered in Russian, "Ne boites." "Don't be afraid." A few minutes later the control officer summoned me. Evidently my visa approval had been late in arriving. He stamped my passport with a bang, and I rejoined my apprehensive group.

The *Day in the Life* team was installed in hotel rooms and an office at the Sovin Center hotel complex. Twenty years older than anyone else on the staff, I tried to be part of the gang without joining in on the late night let-off-steam festivities, which were lubricated with a lot of vodka.

This was the sixth *Day in the Life* book, and by this time the editors and founders, Rick Smolan and David Cohen, had the system for the massive undertaking down pat. Twelve-hour days, six days a week, were the norm. My Russian language and geographical expertise improved exponentially, but my chances of keeping my promise to Fred Starr and finding a contact in the Ministry of Culture were fading, because we had virtually no time off.

The project came to life when our hundred photographers met for the first time in Moscow. Most of the Western photographers had worked together before, so screams of recognition sounded as each one entered our common office at the hotel. All the photographers had two days of briefing before they were scattered over the entire Soviet Union to take their pictures on May 15. As the only assignment editor who spoke Russian, I briefed the Russian and Eastern European lens men. It felt very strange to me to be briefing a Cuban photographer at a time when the United States had no relations with that country. Moreover, I had to come up with a description of the closed cities, places where foreigners were not permitted, which was difficult information to find. The stakes were high for these photojournalists, as the pictures that appeared in the book would be selected by photo editors in New York. No one knew who would make the cut. The book turned out to be not only a publishing success but also a historic freeze-frame of life in the Soviet Union shortly before the collapse.

One night toward the end of this extraordinary two-month stay, I was invited to have dinner at the apartment of an old friend, Tatiana Kudriavtseva, a well-known and respected Russian translator. Deciding that I deserved a cultural break at the end of this marathon activity, I accepted. When I arrived at her small apartment on Red Army Street, I found a crowded table set for eight. On one side of me was John le Carré, a literary hero of mine, and on the other side was Vladimir Kokonin, the deputy minister of culture. I couldn't believe the coincidence. Knowing that in Russia you would never talk business at a social event, I still managed to ask Kokonin if he would see me before I left the country. He gave me his phone number—invaluable in a country with no phone books—and the next day I was able to arrange an appointment at the ministry.

Very much emboldened by the success of *A Day in the Life of the Soviet Union*, I gave an enthusiastic speech about the prospects for an American–Russian youth orchestra. Negotiations, much to my surprise, started that day and we were soon on track. Fred Starr still didn't forgive my perceived defection, but the project moved forward, and I ended up as executive director of the American Soviet Youth Orchestra.

Creating an orchestra from scratch was an enormous job and doubly so for someone with no knowledge of the musical world. With the backing of the Oberlin Conservatory of Music and the AFS, I put together a prestigious advisory council. I met with the directors of prominent American conservatories to persuade them to encourage their students to audition.

But when I met with Joe Polisi, the director of the Juilliard School, he prophesied that our chances of success were very slim. *Only*, he emphasized, if we could get this one orchestra manager—and only her—did we have even a prayer of succeeding. The young woman, Debbie McKean, had toured the Far East with the New York Philharmonic. I found Debbie, and, much to my relief, she became our orchestra manager.

And so it continued—every day a new challenge. I signed a lease on Avery Fisher Hall before we even had a conductor; I also lived in constant fear that the whole project would implode.

Our goal was to have one hundred young musicians—fifty from the Soviet Union and fifty from the United States. This was a time of fifty–fifty formulas. In the end, we were able to persuade Zubin Mehta to be our inaugural conductor at the Kennedy Center in Washington, DC. However, he refused to conduct Mahler's First Symphony without a 110-person orchestra, so we had to add ten more American musicians, ruining the symmetry. These new musicians also greatly added to the budget and, thereby, to my anxiety and workload, since most of my time at the orchestra was spent fund-raising.

The rehearsal period was at the Oberlin Conservatory of

Music. Because the Russian minders were a little under the weather due to jet lag and a bibulous welcome reception, we were able to place each Russian with an American in a dormitory room at Oberlin, and that proved a huge success. The roommates all had little dictionaries, and with their shared love of music they managed to communicate.

As the familiar bars of Tchaikovsky's *Romeo and Juliet* sounded throughout the auditorium at our first concert at Oberlin College, tears of joy dampened my cheeks. The next day I held back tears of rage when Fred Starr informed me that he had decided to take my place on tour while I was to sit at the AFS office in the stifling July heat and raise more money.

Although the youth orchestra ended up being an unexpected success, I was happy to resign when the first tour ended in the fall of 1988. The orchestra continued for another fifteen years, under the leadership of Edie Holbrook. For me it had been a stressful experience. But new projects were already in motion and new lives were about to start.

Valya

"You won't believe it," I heard my father's voice over the telephone, "but the most amazing thing just happened. We received a letter from Valya. You're going to Russia next week, aren't you? But don't get too excited. The message is seven years old." This was 1985, and I had just been offered the job to go to Russia as an associate producer with Metromedia.

My father explained when I dropped by to say good-bye to my parents that a Princeton University dean had called to inform him that she had met a woman named Valya at the House of Architects in Moscow. Valya asked the dean if she knew of a George Kennan, and the dean replied that she knew him by reputation and, as she lived in Princeton, she could certainly find him. She took Valya's hastily scrawled name and phone number on a scrap of paper and stashed it in a drawer, where it lay for seven years. Only now had she brought it my father. "Can you believe she only just found it!" My orderly father was outraged.

Valya had been my friend in School Number 131 in Moscow, and I had invited her to our embassy apartment a couple of times. My parents immediately liked her and even invited her to visit them after I had gone back to the States. I corresponded with Valya, as well, but our letter-writing languished as my Russian language ability faded. I blamed myself. It had been almost forty years since I had heard from her.

Contacting Valya wasn't as easy as I had foreseen. My Metromedia delegation was working flat out. We were shooting a documentary and evening news segments. As the interpreter, I was on call every minute—from breakfast until the staff went to bed. In those days, waiters spoke little English, and menus were in Russian, so without an interpreter the group couldn't order. Knowing that the hotel telephones were tapped by the KGB, I planned to call Valya on a pay phone away from the hotel, but opportunities to do so were slim. To look less conspicuous, I asked our young soundman if he would go out with me one night after dinner. Of course, that was the night that everyone wanted "just one more for the road," but finally we escaped and found a faraway public phone.

My heart pounded as I dialed the number. A young female voice answered. After I asked for Valya, the girl identified herself as Valya's daughter, Irina, and said that her mother was at the theater. Could I call back? I explained that I had known her mom many years ago at School Number 131.

"Oh, yes, I know all about you," she replied. "You are Grace. I read your letters."

We set up a call on the following night. The soundman and I went out again, and this time Valya answered. We agreed to meet. But where? She said that she couldn't come near my hotel, so could I meet her at a subway stop? I agreed, then had a panic attack. What if this wasn't Valya? What if the note was a trap written by the KGB? What if this was a setup and I was falling right into it? This was still the Cold War in 1985, and the Soviet Union was our enemy. I tossed and turned most of the night.

The next day, with much trepidation, I walked to the Pushkin metro stop. A woman with short gray hair, of indeterminate age, stood there. She came toward me and, without saying a word, put her arm in mine, and we started to walk. I didn't recognize her. She looked nothing like the black-haired, sharp-featured young girl that I remembered. I felt very tense. We strolled up and down the streets of Moscow and talked in Russian. She asked me about my parents, my sister Joan, the farm, and the school. She told me that they called me a camel because I wouldn't use the bathroom, and then I felt sure that the KGB couldn't have known that. Clearly this was Valya. We compared lives and found some surprising similarities. We had both been married twice. We both had daughters born the same year. She and my former husband were both architects.

Years dropped away, and I realized that the pull that made us friends in the first place was still there. Finally she asked, "Do you remember where my apartment was?" I didn't. She added, "You knew where it was, but you were never in it. Would you like to see it now?"

"Yes," I answered, again getting nervous. Soviet citizens were not encouraged to have foreigners in their apartments and risked questioning by local authorities. People had gone to the gulag for less in the past. If Valya was willing to have me, how could I say no? I felt my father at my back. Once you have agreed to something, you can't renege. Courage is often interpreted as a choice, but for me, courageous choices mostly happened because I saw no alternatives.

When we entered the building, Valya instructed me not to speak until we were in her apartment. Inside the crowded small flat, Valya made tea. It turned out that this was her parents' apartment, where she lived when we were schoolmates. She had lived there all her life, first with them, then with two sequential husbands, and now with her daughter, who worked for Canadian television and spoke beautiful English.

Like most Russian apartments, it was jam-packed. Felt slippers of different colors and shapes lined the hall—Russians don't wear shoes inside the home. Two doors led into a bifurcated bathroom—one to a toilet, and one to a bathtub and sink. The two main rooms were full to the brim with a lifetime of belongings. The living room doubled as Valya's bedroom. What appeared to be a sofa also served as her bed. A bookcase with glass doors, crammed with books and memorabilia, took up one wall. Little china figurines, including a camel, marched across the top. I wondered if the camel was me. The small kitchen, with a table that could squeeze four, was where we sat and talked. Valya showed me a neat pile of letters tied up with ribbon, and I recognized my familiar handwriting.

As we sipped our tea, the doorbell rang. Valya went to the door and greeted her neighbor, who was obviously dropping in for a chat. When the friend saw me, she blanched—I had never seen anyone actually turn white before—and started to back out. "No," Valya said, "you must come in. I want you to meet my old schoolmate, Grace, from America." But the neighbor's fear was palpable, and she left without sitting down. It was a stark reminder of how dangerous it was for Russians to consort with foreigners.

That fear was even clearer when Valya explained why our letters had stopped. It had nothing to do with my Russian language. After Valya and I had corresponded for a year, the KGB called her father down to their headquarters and told him that they had been tracking our letters. His daughter must never write to her friend again. If the epistolary exchange between the two fourteen-year-olds didn't end immediately, he would be in big trouble.

After this reunion, a visit with Valya became a regular part of every trip I made to Moscow. She opened a window to a closed society and enabled me to look inside. These meetings with her were precious, and I had so many questions. I asked if she had ever been abroad. She looked at me with a little smile and said that she had lived for a year in Cuba, as an architect for the port of Havana.

"That must have been interesting, such a different climate and culture. Did you learn Spanish?" I asked.

"You have no idea," she answered. "We were not allowed to socialize with Cubans. We Soviets lived in a separate building and only mixed with one another." I had an uncomfortable flash to the American embassy compound in Moscow, which I frequently visited and in which Americans mostly mixed with their compatriots.

Valya's parents had died, but I asked about the rest of her family. Did she have cousins, nieces, nephews?

After a long silence, she answered with a rather matter-of-fact tone. "We came from the Caucasus." Now I understood her black hair and slightly Asian appearance. "I had two uncles. They were both shot in the thirties. My uncle in Georgia was drinking and made a joke about Stalin, and that was the end of him. The other uncle, a scientist, a party member, lived in Moscow. Well, there was no explanation. He and my aunt had gone to the Bolshoi opera one night. He wore his best leather gloves, laying them on a table when they returned. The night 'they' came for him, they even took his gloves. They had no right to take the gloves. Pigs they were." She sounded almost more upset about the gloves than about her uncle. Her family learned later that after some months in prison, the uncle was shot, too. But Valya added incredulously that her father, an engineer and a good Communist, never had any doubts about the system, despite losing a brother and brother-in-law. It was very clear from Valya's indignation that she did.

During another visit, I was reading the memoir of Galina Vishnevskaya, a famous opera singer, who was married to the cellist Mstislav Rostropovich. I told Valya their dramatic story—how they had been exiled and stripped of all their medals and honors and were now living in Washington, DC, where he was conductor of the National Symphony Orchestra.

She stopped me. "Can I borrow the book, please? I must read it."

"But you don't read English."

She was insistent. "Don't worry; my daughter will translate it. This is very important." I ended up leaving her the book for three days, and when she returned it, wrapped in a new brown-paper cover, she smiled. "Someone has been reading this book every minute since you gave it to me. My daughter and her friends took turns staying up all night reading it to me. We had no idea what happened to the cellist Rostropovich."

Valya's experiences were often revealing, sometimes surprising. When her daughter, Irina, was married and about to have a baby, this happy prospect did not please Valya. "I am going to be a grandmother," she announced in a sepulchral tone.

"But aren't you pleased?" I asked.

"No," she replied. "This means that I have to quit my job to take care of the baby. From now on I'll just be a baby nurse. Irina has a good job, and I can't deprive her of a future. Your life is different. You're American. You travel all over the world. But I will never leave the playground. With us, when you become a grandmother, life is over. No man will ever look at me again." I realized that she was losing not only the camaraderie of her job but also that of her club, the House of Architects, which served as her social center.

The last time I saw Valya, she was planning to leave the apartment in which she had lived all her life. Irina and her husband had a new flat in a massive apartment complex out in the drab suburbs of Moscow, far from the center. They were going to trade apartments.

"How horrible," I commiserated. "You're going to miss this apartment. It's so central and you can walk everywhere, especially to the theaters and concert halls that you love."

Yet again she surprised me. "No, it will be all right. Yes, I'll be far away, but the air. I will have fresh air." Fresh air is a Russian passion.

She moved in 1999, and we haven't seen each other since. My stolen hours with Valya were always separate from my work, yet the content of our discussions about the plight of Soviet women at that time framed the outcomes of the work I later did. Much of what I know and learned about Russia came from Valya, over the endless cups of tea in that apartment. And much of what success I had working in Russia was because of her insights.

Minding My Own Business

The riskiest—and most rewarding—of my many ventures was starting my own business-consulting company. It was all Renee's fault. When I met Renee, she was newly single and had just arrived in New York. We became instant friends and spent evenings testing inexpensive restaurants and discussing men, movies, and the problems of our daily lives. This was the spring of 1988. My job as the executive director of the American Soviet Youth Orchestra had entailed frequent trips to Moscow, all on the Pan Am direct flight from Kennedy Airport. The length of the trip plus the trepidation felt by most first-time travelers going to the Soviet Union were great levelers. Passengers shared their concerns. On these planes I met many CEOs and was soon informally briefing my new friends, heads of impressive companies, on what to expect and how to operate in the Soviet Union. I was amused and was proud of my newfound expertise.

Renee listened with interest to my stories, until one day she interjected, "People pay a fortune for the knowledge that you are simply giving away. You should start your own consulting company. You could make a lot of money."

Although the money part sounded appealing, I was not

convinced. "First of all, I don't know anything about business," I told her. "I have no graduate degree. And I'm not very well organized."

But Renee kept up her persuasion. "I have an MA in urban planning. I know all about small business. You have the country knowledge and I'm very well organized. We'll be a good team."

I was impressed by her master's degree and wowed by her self-confidence, a quality I seemed to be missing. Now that we were talking partnership, everything sounded more plausible, but I was still reluctant. "We don't have any money. It takes money to start a business."

Renee swept away my reservations. "It doesn't take that much money. My friend, Mary, will give us office space for six months, and I'll pay for the incidental expenses. After that, the money will be flowing in. You'll see."

So after I left the youth orchestra, Renee and I opened SOVUS Business Consultants in 1989. SOVUS was short for Soviet–U.S., and although it had no particular meaning in Russian, it sounded as if it did. We didn't anticipate that the Soviet Union would fall apart in three years.

After we printed stationery and business cards, our first SOVUS project was to take an exploratory trip to the Soviet Union, since Renee had never been there. She couldn't operate as a consultant about a country she had never seen. With high hopes, warm coats, and smart hats, we flew to Moscow.

I was excited about showing Renee the city of my childhood—moonlight over Red Square, red stars twinkling on the Kremlin towers, guards goose-stepping back and forth in front of Lenin's tomb. How could anyone resist? But, to my shock, Renee disliked Russia from the start. She seemed to perceive Moscow as an olfactory assault. "They smell," she said after we exited a crowded public elevator. "It's disgusting. Don't they take baths?"

My retort—"When you have ten people sharing a communal

apartment with one bathroom, it is not so easy to commandeer the shower"—fell on deaf ears.

Out on Gorky Street, she kept complaining: "I don't understand how people can live here. Moscow reeks of gas; I think it is very unhealthy."

It was true that the cheap little Lada cars emitted some questionable gas odors, but I was used to them. By the time we returned to New York, the honeymoon was over. As I said to a friend, "Renee and I are getting a divorce before the marriage." We parted amicably. I would be damned if I was going to waste our handsome new SOVUS stationery and business cards, though, so I moved SOVUS into my apartment. Little did I know that my apartment would double as an office for the next ten years.

I wrote to all my friends and contacts about my new company and sat back, praying for the phone to ring. But it didn't. When I was close to admitting defeat, a call came from the International Human Rights Law Group in Washington, DC. They had heard about SOVUS from a friend, Joan Bingham, who served on their board. Could I organize an election-monitoring group for the first Russian elections? The delegation needed visas, tickets, hotel reservations, election-monitoring credentials, and a week of meetings with party leaders, and, oh, yes, the election was only ten days away.

"No problem," I said, wondering how I could possibly put this all together so fast.

Lying in bed that night, unable to sleep, I suddenly remembered a charismatic young man from Siberia, Gennadi Alfarenko. I had met Gennadi on my last trip to Moscow, at the late night soirees of a friend, Tanya Kolodzei. He was alive with excitement about the changes beginning to occur in the Soviet Union and had moved from Siberia to Moscow to be part of the action. "If you ever need any help, call me," he said, as he gave me his phone number. At 4:00 a.m. New York time, I called.

Gennadi didn't seem the least bit surprised to hear from me and, true to his promise, swung into action. Ignoring the fact that my communications bill would swallow any possible profits, Gennadi and I plotted by phone. He was proud of Russia's new democratic leanings and wanted to prove that foreigners could function in the new Russia. In the end, a successful trip took place, satisfying the demands of the International Human Rights Law Group.

I had stepped onto a rapidly moving treadmill that I wouldn't get off for a decade. Little did I know that the learning curve would be so steep, with every new client and the pattern of that initial job repeated again and again. I soon realized I needed a backup person in the office. As this preceded my feminist awakening, I thought a male voice was necessary to make SOVUS sound professional. I hired a young man named Sean Woods, a Russian major and recent college graduate looking for a job. He was happy to accept a low salary with an impressive title: "SOVUS Associate." And he had a mellifluous telephone voice.

By the time someone called from Auto Radiator Sales in Buffalo, New York, Sean and I were ready. "Of course we can find a partner in the USSR with whom you can joint-venture your machine tooling and dying," he said.

"What's machine tooling and dying?" Sean and I asked each other.

By dint of extensive combing and exploitation of the Rolodex, we found a perfect partner in the Estonian Soviet Socialist Republic for Auto Radiator Sales. We acquired more clients and another employee. The three of us held weekly staff meetings, more like pep rallies, where we planned new projects and worked on the existing ones. One of us appeared at every conference devoted to U.S.–Soviet trade, and we produced a smart brochure advertising our almost nonexistent experience.

One day a journalist called and asked to interview me for an article he was writing on spec for a business weekly. I didn't know who was fooling whom. No one was more surprised than I was when the article appeared in the press and SOVUS was described as a thriving consulting business. My parents did not share my enthusiasm. Both of them would have liked to see me in a steady nine-to-five job for a reputable organization, with benefits.

As it happened, I had started a business at a very auspicious moment. The period just before the breakup of the Soviet Union was an intensely exciting time in Moscow. The first McDonald's had just opened; joint ventures were springing up like mushrooms; massive demonstrations were taking place, with speakers criticizing the government. Every day there were new developments. The monolithic Soviet Union resembled a giant ship that had just hit an iceberg and was beginning to sink.

Most of my business turned out to be in Leningrad, soon to be renamed St. Petersburg. One of my clients requested that I meet with Anatoly Sobchak, the charismatic mayor of St. Petersburg, to promote his project, long since forgotten. I had contacts in Sobchak's office, so I had a good chance of meeting with the mayor. But at the last minute he was busy, and I was shunted off to meet with the deputy mayor, whose name was Vladimir Vladimirovich Putin.

I had read that Putin came from the KGB. I walked into the office of a compact blond man with chilling blue eyes. We were alone. All I could think of was how I would not have wanted to be on the other side of an interrogation by him. He had none of Sobchak's charm, and I was not successful in getting what my client wanted. If someone told me that I had just talked for thirty minutes with the future president of Russia, I would have thought the person delusional.

After a trip to Moscow, I wrote an article about the underground revolution that was taking place and compared the new Moscow with the city I had known as a child and young woman. Feeling I had nothing to lose, I submitted it to the *New York Times* and the *Washington Post*. I don't remember ever being as excited as the day, Saturday, March 3, 1990, when I opened the *New York Times* and there was my article on the op-ed page, accompanied by a huge photograph. Underneath was the caption BY GRACE KENNAN WARNECKE, PRESIDENT, SOVUS INC. Against all odds, SOVUS and Grace were launched.

CHAPTER 8

The Soviet Union and Another Breakup

The same year, a Russian Peter Pan flew into my life and remained there for the next sixteen years.

Several years before, at a conference at the Esalen Institute in California, a Russian American poetess named Vera Dunham had fascinated me: Large in all respects, Vera had an immense body and dramatic emotions, as well as an enormous vocabulary and a vast store of poetry in both languages that put the rest of us more academic Russian American specialists to shame.

Back in New York, Vera invited me to visit her for lunch one Sunday in Port Jefferson, Long Island. Among the guests was Tanya, whom I soon learned was the sister of Evgeny Porotov, nicknamed Zhenya, a well-known Russian TV journalist and on-air reporter for Leningrad Television. At the time, Zhenya was visiting Tanya, but he did not attend the lunch. Vera soon made it clear that my new mission was to assist Zhenya in selling his films of the burgeoning democracy movement in Russia to American television. I was not convinced but agreed to meet him.

Tanya and Zhenya appeared at my apartment within days. He was not what I expected.

Instead of a typical stocky Russian, a slim, rather Parisian-looking man in a belted gray tweed winter coat and beret came into my apartment. He spoke Russian so quickly that I only understood about half of what he said, but I gathered that he had film clips of crowds defiantly rallying behind Mayor Anatoly Sobchak in the Leningrad streets. This description piqued my interest, as we had heard rumors of unrest in Leningrad, but nothing specific.

Tanya had to go back to work, so she left Zhenya with me. We walked around the Upper West Side, with me speaking in hesitant Russian. I was puzzled and fascinated by this Soviet man, so different from the dour, cautious Soviet diplomats I had met. Back at home, I discovered Zhenya's address book in my apartment. I knew he would be back.

The meetings that Zhenya had been filming took place at the beginning of the "democracy" movement that ultimately fueled the collapse of the Soviet Union. Most of these demonstrations were unrecorded, as Soviet television journalists were issued cameras for specific assignments by the state-controlled television, and photographing dissent was not on that agenda.

But Zhenya had his own professional video camera, given to him by Tanya, so he was able to film forbidden meetings and demonstrations, at considerable personal risk. Some of his films had already been smuggled out of the Soviet Union and had been shown on both the BBC and Danish television but not in the United States. As a result, Zhenya himself was journalistic news at the time and had just been interviewed by Peter Jennings on ABC's *World News Tonight*. When Zhenya reappeared in my apartment to retrieve his address book, he arrived with film clips of his work. I was able to screen them on the special adapter for Russian films that I had bought for SOVUS.

One of Zhenya's most moving films was shot at the Leningrad Film Studio, where, for the first time, a group of gulag survivors had been amassed for a collective photograph. Zhenya had been invited to film the group picture for TV but hung around after the survivors were dismissed. One by one the former prisoners (many of whom had been incarcerated as relatives of "enemies of the people") came to Zhenya, thrusting out photos of executed relatives, and spilled their stories with such intensity and passion that my eyes welled up. "Of course, Americans must see this," I said.

Fueled by my own emotion, I exploited my network of contacts. I called everyone who might be interested. Soon, and much to my surprise, Zhenya and I found ourselves showing his film to Robin MacNeil and his executive producer, Les Crystal. "Voices from the Gulag" aired a few days later on *The MacNeil/ Lehrer NewsHour* on public television. As we watched the program together, Zhenya announced very solemnly, "Now you are my agent." With no experience and no background, I became one. We started assembling and editing his films, giving them titles, which I translated into English, and showing them to anyone who would watch.

Zhenya was a gadfly—playful, impish, and eternally youthful. He twinkled. But there was a courageous, tough side to him, as well. A former officer in the Red Army, and subsequently a war correspondent, he had faced death so often that he was fearless. One of his pet sayings was: "The bullet you hear is not for you." His strong, lithe body helped. Early one morning on his way to my apartment in New York, he was jumped by three men, who tried to steal his video camera. He beat them all off and appeared at my apartment, grinning triumphantly at this victory.

That first year, I worked intensely with Zhenya on his several forays to America. I made him a business card, with my phone number, and wrote him a résumé that mystified him. "Why would anybody care where I went to university?" he asked. I introduced him to everyone I thought could help him, and I translated as best I could. My Russian–English dictionary was always at my side. Zhenya never learned to speak English, although he eventually understood quite a bit. Zhenya always addressed me very politely, using the Russian formal "you," and was never in any way flirtatious. At that time, when the Soviet Union was considered "the enemy" and former president Reagan had called the country "the evil empire," it was inconceivable even to think of a personal relationship with a Soviet. Also, Zhenya had told me about his wife, another Tanya, and their three children, Sasha, Gosha, and Dasha. And I was dating a man named Bob. On a business trip to Leningrad, Zhenya arranged for me to meet Tanya, who struck me as pleasant if a little shy. She was thirty years younger than I was.

In the fall of 1990 Zhenya reappeared in New York, and we agreed to meet at an art gallery featuring an installation by a famous Soviet dissident artist, Ilya Kabakov. Kabakov had transformed the entire Ronald Feldman Gallery into a re-creation of a Soviet communal apartment, and it was quite a sensation. Each room had hundreds of little scraps of paper on which were written imaginary sentences uttered by the room's inhabitant. They dangled from the ceiling, attached by little pieces of string. It made me dizzy. But the disorienting mood of this claustrophobic apartment didn't leave me; I sensed that I was moving into a new world.

From the gallery we went to dinner at the apartment of a friend, David, an American also fascinated by everything Russian and thus by Zhenya. David was dressed all in black, and the apartment was lit and decorated with flickering candles. Some bottles of vodka and a large bowl of tired potato chips sat on a low table. Dinner, I figured. Among the guests was a striking Japanese American, Anka, billed as David's girlfriend. I questioned this designation when Anka sidled up to Zhenya and started a largely nonverbal flirtation, interspersed with his few words of English and her small vocabulary of Russian.

Suddenly I was angry. "How dare she," I fumed to myself. I walked over to Zhenya, with whom I had the advantage of language, and used the familiar "you." Soon we were the only two people in the room, and I was engulfed in feelings swirling around like the papers hanging in Kabakov's communal apartment. The world refused to sit still. We went back to my apartment and soon tumbled into bed.

The next morning, we both awoke with a start. "Oh, my God, I have slept with an American lady," Zhenya said, staring at me.

"And I've slept with a Red Army officer," I answered. We both laughed in amazement. The Cold War was coming to an end. I broke up with Bob.

A week later Zhenya moved in, and what had started as a moment of passion gradually changed into a long-term relationship, totally different from any I had ever known. We were joined at the hip professionally. As his agent, I was part of everything he did in America and much of what he did in Leningrad. He helped me with my endless SOVUS projects. Everyone knew that we were colleagues.

Conducting a love affair, however, was quite different. First there was the age gap. When we met, he was forty-four and I was fifty-six. Then there was the awkward fact that he was married. Never mind that by now I knew the marriage had taken place because of a pregnancy, that during this marriage he had fathered two illegitimate children, whom he supported with the knowledge of his wife. I did not want to have to explain this unusual situation to one and all. The fact that Zhenya refused to learn English meant I had to translate for him, which cut down on our social life except with Russian-speaking friends. We couldn't go to theater, movies, or even watch television, because of the language problem. Zhenya was too proud to let me pay for him in restaurants, so we ate at home. Since he loved to shop and cook, that became an adventure. He never used recipes but just picked up whatever appealed to him and created a dish; he did more things with sausages and turnips than I ever imagined possible. We lived in a cocoon of our own making, creating a special intense intimacy. In our bubble, life was grand.

Zhenya loved to create little surprises, and I never knew what I to expect. When I first knew Zhenya, Soviet citizens were not allowed to register in a hotel in the Soviet Union without a special permit or to visit foreign guests in hotels without permission. One time when I was staying in a Leningrad hotel, Zhenya persuaded me to sneak him in. He wanted to see what was forbidden to him. I had to go out to a meeting and left him in my room. I was, as usual, uncomfortable about breaking rules. When I returned from my business appointment, I was startled to see my high-heeled shoes lined up across the top of an ornate gilded mirror and Zhenya standing, flushed with pleasure. Another time I came back to the New York apartment, and Zhenya, unexpectedly, wasn't there. I called, looked everywhere, until I heard a muffled laugh from the fireplace, where a naked Zhenya was grinning at me from behind the fire screen.

Of course, these moments of togetherness were few and far between. More often there were the long separations, punctuated by short notes or e-mails, always open to interception. Our e-mail was stilted and in code, as his children used his computer. That computer was also subject to frequent breakdowns and often out for repair. Phone calls were even worse. Even at the end, Zhenya remained in some ways a product of the Soviet world—and answered the telephone with suspicion and in monosyllables. A typical call went like this:

Grace: "How are you?" Zhenya: "Fine."

"How are the children?" "Fine."

"Are you going to be traveling?" (By this I meant coming to the States.) "I may have a business trip." (But no indication where to or when.)

I would hang up the phone and often scream with frustration at the end of one of these exchanges.

Our meetings, however pleasurable, were sporadic and often short. Out of necessity we lived in the moment, and since those moments were few, we rarely fought or quarreled about minor things. I slowly developed a trust in a relationship unlike any I had ever known before. One time I brought up the fact that our love affair was unbalanced, that he had a family and I lived alone; I might want to remarry. He said, "Remarry if you want, but I will be with you until one of us dies."

He kept his word. We stayed close until he was burned to death in a fire at his dacha in 2006. It has never been determined whether the conflagration was arson or accidental, but a bright light was extinguished that night. Russia lost a brave journalist, and I lost a best friend.

On Soviet Soil

As the Soviet Union was opening up, SOVUS rolled along, acquiring clients and gaining credibility. But other consulting companies were emerging, and I knew we had to do something special to keep SOVUS ahead of the curve. At a SOVUS staff meeting, I came up with an idea.

"Why don't we put on our own conference here in New York? But we have to have an original subject, something different." We came up with "Real Estate Opportunities in the USSR." We were proudly plowing a new field.

I learned the names of the leading officials in Moscow and Leningrad who controlled land use. If I could attract them to the United States, I figured, American businesses would flock to our conference to meet these influential figures. I flew to Moscow to find the appropriate Soviet officials and arrange meetings with them, and I was amazed not only that these men agreed to see me but also that six of them signed on to be speakers at our conference, scheduled for March 1991. Delta Airlines gave us a special price on air tickets. The U.S. Trade Council signed on as cosponsor of the conference. We were elated.

Six weeks before the conference date, my assistant, Sean, appeared at work, obviously upset. "Have you seen the television this morning?" I hadn't. "The U.S. is bombing Iraq. We are at war. What will happen to the conference?"

"Iraq is not Russia," I answered firmly. "We should be all right. We still have time."

But I didn't anticipate that the threat of terrorism during the Gulf War would cause the State Department to issue a moratorium on nonessential air travel even within our own borders, so no U.S. government employees could be reimbursed for attending such a conference. All similar symposiums were canceled, and very few people signed up for ours. My six Russian speakers, however, seemed unaffected by the Iraq War. I stood fast. I told my staff, "We can't let our conference participants down. If we cancel, our reputation will be ruined." So we invited everyone in New York and Washington who had anything to do with Russia as "special"—or nonpaying—guests, knowing that they could come by car or train.

The conference ended up being well attended, received good press, and was a public relations success for SOVUS, but the lack of paying participants made it a financial disaster. I decided to take out a loan to pay off the loss, but, despite their hesitancy about SOVUS, my parents had a horror of debt. They came to the rescue and bailed me out. I was mortified at having to accept their help, but SOVUS stayed afloat.

After my father's death in 2005, I was stunned to find a copy of a letter that he wrote to my children during this crisis, asking for their financial support. It pierced my heart. "I do not regard her present situation as primarily her own fault. She has worked very hard. She has carved out for herself a remarkable and unique place in the pattern of private Soviet—

American exchanges. She knows her business. She has more friends and contacts in Russia than has anyone else in the game. And when she has met with ingratitude, or has found herself exploited, as so often happened, she has always bounced back with great courage and with that special sort of gallantry for which we all love her." If only I had known how he really felt. What I always interpreted as disapproval was probably genuine concern for my future. My parents worried about financial insecurity all their lives, probably as a result of the hardships that they suffered in the early years of the Depression, and I was continuously traveling down some new, not remunerative path.

Among readers responding to my op-ed piece in the *New York Times* was a woman with an engaging voice, who introduced herself on the telephone as Alexandra Chalif. She asked me to join an organization she had just founded called the Alliance of American and Russian Women (AARW). The goal of AARW was to help Russian women engage in the business enterprises that were starting up under Mikhail Gorbachev's reforms.

I declined. "I can't possibly. I have just started a business of my own and have no time for any volunteer work."

"Well, would you be my guest for lunch and tell me all about SOVUS? Maybe we can do something together," she appealed.

Saying no has never been my strong point, so I accepted. Alexandra, nicknamed Sasha, was a Connecticut psychotherapist with Russian grandparents; she wanted to explore her roots as well as help Russian women. She also tapped some latent guilt I had for always working in a man's world and never doing anything special to promote my own sex.

Sasha had great sales talent. Within weeks, not only had I joined AARW but I was also named the vice president, though I made it clear that SOVUS business would always have priority.

Sasha organized the alliance's first group of twenty American business and professional women to fly to Moscow as business trainers and role models at a conference with Russian women. Then, with an American sidekick nicknamed Pasha, she located some young women in Moscow eager to work with AARW. High on enthusiasm and low on money, we housed our group of American participants for a week's stay in a converted dormitory named the First of May Hotel, while our Russian women commuted from home. The hotel was way below Fodor's radar screen: an hour from the center of town, with no soap or toilet paper, threadbare rugs on cold concrete floors, and the smell of boiled cabbage wafting up from the cafeteria, which soon temporarily shut down rather than meet the demands of the American women. But despite the culture shock, our plucky group moved ever forward. By contrast, my SOVUS clients, all men, usually stayed in downtown Moscow at the American-owned and expensive Radisson Slavyanskaya, with its smart restaurants and creature comforts. I ricocheted back and forth between these two worlds. From the stories of our young Russian coordinators, I also learned more about the travails and everyday life of the average Russian woman.

Sasha and I soon realized that a lot of the training we were offering was useless. I still cringe when remembering a lecture given by one of our American participants on "Dress for Success" at a time when many of the Russian attendees, still living in crowded communal apartments, hand-washed their laundry—including sheets and towels—in the bathtub at night and appeared every day in the same newly washed white blouse. But the alliance women learned quickly and thrived in the unsettled but exhilarating atmosphere of Moscow in the last years of the Soviet Union. Training grew more targeted to our audience; friendships developed between Russian and American participants. On future trips we upgraded to better hotels nearer to the center of the city. Despite some physical hardships, we were caught up in the excitement of it all.

Still, when I traveled to attend a conference or to make new contacts for SOVUS, I had to pay my way on the company's meager budget. On one such trip to Leningrad, Zhenya found me a cheap apartment out in a suburb—a steal, he boasted, at only $15 a night. He drove me out there to drop off my suitcase, and the apartment, while minuscule, looked cozy and comfortable in the daylight. It was dark, though, when I returned alone that evening after a day of appointments and meetings, in a new yellow suit, carrying my shiny leather briefcase. The ten-watt bulb that should have lit the hall was out, and the entry was pitch-black. I stumbled over an invisible step and fell into a puddle with a terrible odor, which I quickly identified as urine.

Lying immobile in the puddle of piss, my suit stained, my briefcase ruined, I wondered what had ever impelled me to work in this country. Why hadn't I looked for the respectable job that my parents so wished I had?

After washing and ironing my smelly suit, I paid a courtesy call the next day to Sharon Miles, the wife of our consul general Dick Miles, in their residence, a former royal palace. I always kept in touch with State Department representatives, partly out of respect for my father, and also because it was an easy and inexpensive way to keep my finger on the pulse of the constantly shifting political situation in the country.

Sharon and I had a polite and rather formal talk over tea, after which she offered to drive me to my next appointment, which was to meet Zhenya at a subway stop in the distant Leningrad suburb where he lived. I demurred but probably not very forcefully. Sharon persisted, and off we went. We became hopelessly lost looking for that faraway subway station, but we talked about Russia, about Russian literature, about Russian women and the chaos around us. We became fast friends, a friendship that has lasted to this day.

A few years later, when her husband became deputy chief of mission of the U.S. embassy in Moscow, Sharon insisted that I stay with them on my frequent Moscow sojourns, which was a joy and a great relief. Sharon became an effective early booster of the Russian women's movement. She even invited women leaders and activists to meet in her house in the American embassy compound, as most Russian apartments were too small and too crowded with family members to house such gatherings. She made significant contributions to the success of the Alliance of American and Russian Women.

Living in the American embassy compound as a guest of the Mileses was not only comfortable, but it also made my life seem less fragmented. While the embassy was not in the building where I had lived as a child, it still had a familiar ambiance; I felt that threads of my life, formerly scattered in all directions, were being woven into a more manageable pattern. But there was still a bumpy road ahead—how bumpy, I didn't know.

An Empire Crumbles

Whenever I read memoirs from observers of the Bolshevik Revolution in St. Petersburg, I was struck by how ordinary the writer's life seemed while a cataclysmic change was taking place. Little did I know that one day a Soviet revolution would be a backdrop to my own humdrum daily affairs.

It was August 18, 1991, when Sasha and I arrived in Moscow with our latest group of twenty-two American women eager to share their expertise as participants in an AARW conference. For most, this was their first trip to the Soviet Union. They were nervous, and their fear was not assuaged when they saw our dreary accommodations—a guesthouse of the Uzbek Republic Mission. Sasha had chosen this large, colorless building located on the other side of the Moscow River from the Kremlin and downtown Moscow because it was cheap, but we soon began to question the choice. Our delegates were dismayed, as most rooms had no telephones and no television. At this time Moscow had no air-conditioning except in expensive foreign-owned hotels, so the rooms were hot and stuffy, as well.

The hotel's clientele seemed to be composed mostly of Uzbek families, trudging in and out, carrying large striped bags of clothes and with food that presumably they ate in their rooms; the smell of it permeated the corridors. The small cafeteria was depressing, and our group was soon grumbling that the food was inedible. But Sasha and I knew that the food outside could be as bad or worse. This was a period of enormous food shortages, and people stood in line whenever anything appeared.

Sasha and I commandeered the two suites—the only rooms with telephone and TV—since we had to be in touch with our local conference organizers. On the day of our arrival, however, our women were exhausted, so everyone went to bed early.

Early the next morning, young Lena, our Russian coordinator, telephoned. "Have you turned the TV on? Something is happening." She explained that we had better be on guard; there had been an announcement on the radio of a "declaration of Soviet leadership" by a renegade group of Communists, who were opposed to Soviet president Mikhail Gorbachev's recent economic and political reforms commonly known as "perestroika" and "glasnost." While Gorbachev vacationed in the Crimea, a state of emergency was being declared. Elite tank divisions were in the streets. No one seemed to know what all this might mean, but Lena offered a warning: "I think that we should be careful. I will cancel the sightseeing tour today."

We gathered the ladies into our suites and huddled around the TV, but there was no English-language station, so we could only see various functionaries speaking. I called my contact at the American embassy, who ominously announced, "They are registering all American citizens at the Slavyanskaya Hotel in case of an evacuation—you had better sign up your group."

Leaving our women behind munching on their supply of energy bars and trail mix, Sasha and I collected everyone's passports
and walked across town to the designated hotel. We fell into
line at a table in the lobby where Americans were being registered. Everyone was comparing rumors:

"It's a revolution."

"Gorbachev is very ill."

"The hard-liners are taking over."

"The Army is coming in to maintain order."

"Have you seen the tanks? There are rows and rows of
them."

"Red Square is blocked off."

But there was no real information. After guiltily enjoying
a rare salad at the hotel's Mozart Café, Sasha and I ran back
to our Uzbek hideaway. En route we agreed that we had to
downplay this event, as these women were our responsibility
and there was no point in scaring them to death. We were well
aware that, even in normal times, changes in travel plans could
take an inordinate amount time, thanks to Soviet bureaucracy.
Thus taking the next flight out of Moscow was not an option
in this confusion. Luckily, we had only a short time left before we'd be moving on to St. Petersburg. But how could we
still put on a conference in Moscow tomorrow, in the middle of
such chaos?

Back at the hotel, we found our group unhappily huddled
around the television, which was inexplicably showing a performance of the Bolshoi Ballet dancing *Swan Lake*. I placed calls
to the United States for our nervous delegates. This was still
a time when each call had to be placed individually through a
long-distance operator. "Please tell them that you are fine, and
safe," Sasha and I begged, although we weren't the least bit sure
they were. I prayed that I was doing a good job of masking my
own frayed nerves and fears.

That night, with the goal of getting more information
on the situation, four of us decided to risk going to the Hotel

Baltschug Kempinski, an elegant German hotel overlooking the Kremlin but on our side of the river. We didn't want to risk crossing any bridges, as they were easy targets for attack. Why we abandoned our fellow travelers is incomprehensible to me now, but the rationale seemed to make sense at the time. When we arrived at the Kempinski, we had a drink, sampled the fine buffet in the dining room, and chatted with guests who were just as confused as we were. So much for our fact-finding mission.

When we left the hotel, we were startled by the sound of gunshots. Looking up, we saw some snipers on a nearby roof. We ran as fast as we could until we were out of range, terrified and praying that each shot was not aimed at one of us. When we arrived back at the hotel, we found that the power was out. The last in our foursome, I groped my way down the pitch-dark inner corridor to find my room, hoping that no strange body would jump out at me. What a fitting coda to a harrowing day.

Our conference the next day was in an educational institution far from the center of town, chosen because it fit our budget—a blessing in disguise. We shepherded our group into the relative safety of the subway, with no idea how many people we might find at our meeting on the other end. Amazingly, about two-thirds of those registered showed up, and we blocked the political crisis from our minds and kept the workshops going. At day's end, one of the Russian attendees took me aside and said, "We wouldn't have missed the conference for anything— never mind the revolution."

From the conference we returned to the hotel by subway, ensuring that our women never saw the tanks in the streets. At the hotel we collected our bags and then headed to the railway station to take the Red Arrow midnight train to Leningrad. You could almost hear the collective sigh of relief as the train slowly pulled out of the station, the brass band playing a typical Soviet farewell.

We had no idea how this crisis had been played at home, and one of our surprises was how worried everyone's friends and relatives had been. Except for my mother. "Oh, we weren't worried," she said. "We knew that you would be all right." She never knew how hurt that made me feel.

When the Soviet Union finally collapsed four months later, on December 26, 1991, I was sitting safely on my bed in New York City, watching it on television. I cheered, then called my father to congratulate him on foreseeing this forty-five years earlier. But he was not as celebratory. "This is all happening too fast," he said. "You'll see. It will bring more trouble in its wake."

Dancing in the Snow

Thankfully, not all of the SOVUS clients were of the machine-tool-and-die variety. One of the most colorful was the National Dance Institute (NDI). Jacques d'Amboise, the founder of NDI and former star of the New York City Ballet, hired me to take him and his photographer wife, Carrie, to Siberia to audition and recruit two young dancers from the coldest place in the world. The young dancers would be featured in an NDI production about children who lived in climatic extremes.

Yakutsk, Siberia, was chosen as the coldest place in the world large enough to have a cadre of child dancers. Part of my contract was that Zhenya would come along as a cameraman.

Jacques, Carrie, Zhenya, and I flew off on May 1, 1993, to this city built on permafrost. The few concrete tall buildings were sinking slowly and irregularly into the ground, as the indoor heat gradually melted the ice underneath the edifices. Zhenya described Yakutsk as a city built by a collective of drunken architects, and his description fit. Buildings were tilting every which way. Jacques, whose buoyant spirit never seemed to be dampened, was soon training and auditioning a hundred little Yakuts. They, in turn, passed the training on to their neighbors. Walking through town one day, Zhenya and I saw children in every courtyard practicing Jacques's steps.

One night, while we were dining in a local restaurant, a man with a bulging briefcase stopped at our table. Yakutsk was the center of a gold-mining region, and he wanted to show us gold. We were not about to look at gold in a public restaurant, though, so we suggested that the salesman come by the hotel the next day.

Before breakfast there was a loud knock on my door. Expecting one of the group, I opened the door in my bathrobe, and in strode the gold man. Without a word or a request, he opened his briefcase and poured gold necklaces, rings, brooches, and bracelets all over my unmade bed.

Frightened at having a $100,000 worth of gold in my room, I phoned Zhenya and Jacques. They appeared quickly and were quite amused by the whole episode. I think Jacques bought something for Carrie, but I couldn't wait to see the unexpected guest depart.

Before going to Yakutsk, Zhenya had asked me to bring two sets of American makeup "just in case." I thought this an odd suggestion but did so without questioning it. Then one morning, while I was with Jacques, who was rehearsing the winsome young dancers, Zhenya came in and nudged me. "Quick," he said, "go to the hotel and get me the makeup."

"What's wrong?" I asked.

"They're claiming our flight is overbooked and we can't leave Yakutsk for two weeks." For Jacques and Carrie, a two-week delay would have been a disaster. I ran to the hotel for the makeup. Later, I was relieved when I learned that Zhenya's bribery to the airline representative—in the form of a mascara wand, lipstick, and rouge—did the trick, and our plane took off as scheduled, with us on board.

Volkhov Ventures

Perhaps Grace—who is now going to a Russian school—will get
deeper into Russia than I have been allowed to get.

— Letter from George Kennan to his
sister Jeanette from Moscow, 1944

Back in New York, recovering from the slightly surreal experience of watching children dance in the snowy streets of Yakutsk, I received another life-changing phone call from Sasha
Chalif. It was 1994 and while I was in Siberia she had escorted
a group of AARW women to Leningrad. She excitedly gave me
an update:

"We visited this town called Volkhov where the mayor is a
woman. Imagine! Her name is Nonna Mikhailovna Volchkova.
I signed an agreement for AARW to collaborate with the city
of Volkhov on the creation of a small-business incubator, especially for women-led businesses. I figured that you and Ida
Schmertz would organize it."

Ida, who had recently left a high-level position at American
Express, had business expertise and the vocabulary that went
with it. Sasha spoke with her usual infectious enthusiasm but
was vague on the details. All I could think was, "What is she
talking about? What on earth is a business incubator?"

I soon learned that a business incubator is a facility in which
fledgling companies pool resources—telephones, copiers,
computers, and staff—to lower the overhead costs of launch-
ing a new business. The start-up businesses benefit from the
encouragement of a communal setting, shared experience,
and, often, an educational program. The Volkhov mayor had
recently seen an incubator in Finland and thought that her city
would benefit from one too.

It was easy to see why Sasha chose us: I had fluent Russian, a
background in Russian history, physical stamina, people skills,
and a willingness to jump into the unknown. Ida, with her

valuable business background, was a hard worker and a perfectionist. She believed if you could get something right in three tries, six attempts might be even better. This drove me crazy, but our differences made us effective as partners.

On our own money, we studied and visited over twenty business incubators from Milwaukee to Poland, each unique with different problems. How long should a business stay in the building before it moves out? How large a staff? Should educational courses be included?

I'll never forget my first trip to Volkhov, a far cry from familiar metropolises of Moscow and Leningrad. A city of 50,000, Volkhov was eighty miles east of Leningrad; three hours by car on narrow, ill-maintained roads. A railroad junction and the site of the first hydroelectric station in the Soviet Union, the flat, symmetrically laid-out municipality had been built after the revolution to service this station, so it was without the onion-domed churches or older buildings that gave many Russian towns their special charm. It lacked history, theaters, or restaurants (the only two were smoky Mafia hangouts). Because of its strategic position, Volkhov had been closed to foreigners until the fall of the Soviet Union. I was often the first foreigner a resident had ever met. When I told Zhenya what we proposed to do there, he laughed. "What makes you American ladies think you can do anything in a town like Volkhov? You don't begin to understand the problems you will face. After two days in Volkhov you will be begging to leave. And don't even think about having a woman director. That will never work."

But we persisted. When the United States Agency for International Development (USAID) called for a Request for Proposal for four business incubators in all of Russia, AARW, spearheaded by Ida, Sasha, and me, came up with a lengthy proposal. Triumphing over 132 competing organizations, AARW received one of the four grants awarded: $1.5 million for a three-year period, later extended by a year. In a fax to my parents from Moscow, I wrote, "I've been so excited that they had to tie me down with weights, so I don't float straight to the moon."

Excited though we were, our grant came at a chaotic time in Russia. The Soviet Union had collapsed only three years before, and the new Russian government was trying to cope with high expectations and old, irrelevant institutions. The old joke about perestroika also applied to the new situation. "Perestroika is like a society where people are switching from driving on the left side to the right side—gradually."

The mayor of Volkhov, Nonna Mikhailovna Volchkova, an engineer by training and one of a handful of female politicians in Russia, was the only one who managed a city of this size. Now in her fifties, this small, sturdy woman had been mayor since 1985. "If the Kremlin ran its military operations like Nonna Mikhailovna runs this city, we'd have taken those Chechen rebels in a matter of days," asserted a director of the local aluminum factory.

When USAID announced our award I drove to Volkhov to give the mayor and her staff the news. They took me to inspect the building chosen for the incubator, an empty abandoned warehouse on the edge of town. Standing in the unfinished, cold structure, I told the small group of city officials about the grant, talking fast about what we hoped to accomplish and how wonderful this would be for the city. Scared to raise expectations and fearing we might become a Mafia target, I avoided mentioning the grant's monetary value. When the welcoming committee left, I stayed behind to photograph. As I took pictures of this crumbling concrete structure, I remembered the bright, well-maintained incubators Ida and I had toured. The enormity of it all hit me. What had we taken on? How were we ever going to make this into a working incubator?

Ida and I were project supervisors, commuting from the United States, which, USAID calculated would take 60 percent of our time. (I was still running SOVUS in the remaining 40 percent.) After a long search, and against Zhenya's advice, we hired a woman, an energetic young, University of Michigan MBA, Rachel Freemen, to be the site director for the first two years. Although inexperienced in incubator management, Rachel had phenomenal energy and worked with whirlwind speed. She also made smart personal decisions that helped her move into the community. She adopted a puppy and made friends among the dog walkers. When she discovered that there was no girls' sports team at the local school, she organized an indoor field hockey team and became the coach. She brought the players red T-shirts from the United States, with VOLKHOV written in English and Russian. The peppy red-shirted girls became an unofficial greeting committee for the incubator, giving tours, hanging coats, and serving refreshments.

Ida and I each made four to five trips a year to Volkhov, sometimes together and sometimes separately. We rented a one-bedroom apartment in a Khrushchyovka (a name for the cheap, hastily erected apartment houses that Khrushchev had built) for $75 a month. We busied ourselves hiring a local staff, fixing up the incubator building, designing an educational program, ordering the needed equipment, and dealing with USAID Moscow.

The highs and lows of Volkhov often came in pairs. One winter day I wrote my parents: "It snowed hard for two days, so Volkhov is covered with about two feet of snow—believe it or not, it looks like a Tyrolean mountain resort. Everyone is out with dogs, sleds, skis—it is quite festive. Apartment a little less so—as stove leaks gas and we can no longer cook."

An unforeseen problem was that most people in this isolated town had never seen a small business, and even those who wanted to start one had no idea of what the possibilities were. Rachel came up with a "Competition for New Ideas." Anyone was welcome to contribute ideas for a new business, and we placed their proposals in an album to inspire new applicants. Businesses born in the Volkhov incubator ranged from a bakery to a refrigerator-repair concern. (Yes, people dragged their small refrigerators in to the incubator.) Later, to engage the city with the incubator, we sponsored a competition for our logo, and a twelve-year-old boy won. As he proudly stood at the presentation ceremony receiving his Sony Walkman, I misted up. Somehow we were succeeding.

Volkhov life was primitive. There was no laundromat in town or washing machine in our apartment. Newspapers appeared so irregularly that we often had no idea what was going on in the world. Our television set had such a grainy screen that it functioned more like a radio with a lot of static. One day I half-listened to a grave account about the death of a princess, only to learn an hour later that they were talking about Princess Di. I wanted to kick the TV in frustration.

It was a time of unpredictable and serious food shortages, so one never knew what would be found in the grocery store. Almost every food item was rationed; however, when one took ration coupons to the market, the shelves were often bare. I wrote my children in September of 1998: "Just arrived in Volkhov—bitter cold, no heat, and rain, but the warmth of the welcome definitely compensates. Imports have been almost cut off because of the banking crisis—whole categories of foods and goods are disappearing. Many shelves are totally empty. The staff just bought the last bottle of mineral water for me. However, one can endure these privations for a few days—it's the rest of the population that is stuck with it."

I nursed that bottle of water for four days and supplemented it with tea. Of course, in spring and summer it was the opposite: our grateful farmers would come by with more bags of fruit and vegetables than we could possibly eat.

To help the farmers, we launched an innovative leasing program, which was not a normal incubator service. At the time, most farmers had no way of getting their goods to the big city, so the road from Volkhov was lined with farmers' wives, each with a rusty scale, selling potatoes, onions, apples, and other local produce out of worn buckets. Apple by apple, they sold their wares. Our leasing program allowed a local farmer to buy a truck, with the cost to be paid off over the next two years with money made from selling his goods at the market in St. Petersburg.

The leasing business ultimately spun off to become a very successful commercial company that still functions today. One of my greatest victories was that Zhenya ultimately became an incubator fan. When he finally came to scout it for a television program, he was amazed and impressed by our progress.

Quite the contrary, one day we had an inspection visit from a "very important person" sent by USAID in a special air-conditioned limousine from St. Petersburg. He spoke Russian, but was aggressive, rude, and verbally attacked everyone he spoke with including me, until someone mentioned that I was ambassador George Kennan's daughter. He then made a total about-face and embarked on an oration about my father for whom he had evidently been an escort officer in Berlin. In summation, he proclaimed "Your father is my God." At my wits end, I answered, "Well, I am only the daughter of God." So much for showing off my work.

Ida and I were careful to keep the oblast government officials in Leningrad informed about the incubator. The first two years they were polite but their skepticism was noticeable. Zhenya wasn't the only person who had doubts. USAID, based in Moscow, also left us alone, largely because it was a long trip to Volkhov and no one wanted to go there. This allowed us to weather the difficult early stages with little supervision, a great blessing. But by the end of years three and four, even the USAID bigwigs were coming to see this unusual incubator, distinguished by the leasing program, our community involvement, and the red T-shirt welcoming committee. Our knitwear atelier was happy to put on a fashion show at the drop of a hat, and the bakery nourished everyone with fragrant fresh bread.

My four years at the incubator were challenging and frustrating. It became a period of constant learning and endless traveling. I ended up with the experience that my father regretted he never had: living in Russia side by side with Russians. He had been largely confined to the embassy and the regulated diplomatic life, while I was spending days in a hick town in the Leningrad oblast. Later he admitted how much he envied me. I felt in some way vindicated.

CHAPTER 9

Ukraine

The economic collapse in Russia in 1998 hit SOVUS hard. American companies no longer wanted to do business there. At the same time, the Volkhov incubator grant ended. The phone stopped ringing, and I was mired in credit card debt. I wrote to everyone on my Rolodex who worked with Russia, announcing my availability as a consultant, but responses were hardly pouring in.

During this fallow period, I received an invitation from First Lady Hillary Clinton to attend a celebration of International Women's Day at the White House. In the security line at the presidential residence, I ran into Sheila Scott, from Winrock International, a Rockefeller Foundation, who had been working in Russia and Ukraine. Flushed with the success of the incubator, I regaled her with excitement and pride about our adventures and accomplishments in Volkhov.

To my total surprise a Winrock representative called a few months later and offered me the job as chief of party, or director, of a new women's economic empowerment program (WEE) in Ukraine, a three-year commitment. Although I could ill afford to do so, I declined. Ukraine loomed as an unknown world. My only previous trip there was largely memorable for an eight-hour bus ride to Odessa in a conveyance with no springs, and leaving me with the feeling, "Thank God I never have to go back there again." Now, Ukraine was an independent nation, but three years in this unknown country seemed interminable.

The representative wrote back, asking what she could offer to induce me to accept the job. I came up with a short list that included a car and driver and a cell phone. To my surprise, Winrock immediately agreed to my requests. I was committed. When my friend Meredith praised me for taking this big step, I answered, "I am an adventurer." That bit of bravado was pure bluff. In reality, I was scared and felt that I was on a forced march, that there was no choice. I was leaving my aging parents, adult children, and friends, but for what?

The descent into Borispol Airport in Kyiv (Kiev) in February 1999 reinforced my feeling that this was in some way a Siberian exile. All I could see was white—no line separating the earth and the sky. I had landed in a cotton ball in a totally new country. Ukraine, even when a Soviet republic, always had its own very special character.

Formerly called "the bread basket of Europe" the country was agricultural rather than industrial, and food played a different role than in Russia. I grew to love Ukrainian borscht, the dumplings called *vareniki*, and endless cakes, although I never was able to eat *salo* or white pork fat, which was considered a delicious regional specialty.

Central Kyiv had never permitted the ugly Soviet highrises, and remained a picturesque European-looking city with no building higher than the cathedral of Saint Sophia. After a lonely month in a dreary dark brown apartment, I found a light, newly modernized apartment furnished with smart Italian furniture, and a balcony overlooking the rooftops of old Kyiv. The building had actually been built in 1911 and the first tenant of my apartment was a wealthy merchant. My living quarters had morphed into a communal apartment during the Soviet period and I imagined a family of four living in my bedroom. After independence the apartment somehow ended up as the property of a government official whose daughter had renovated it and become my landlord. History was always near at hand in Ukraine.

Our office was inconveniently situated in two former residential flats, a block apart. In the cold Kyiv winter, I had to don a coat, hat, scarf, boots, and gloves to slog through the snow each time I needed to meet with the other half of the all women staff, most left over from the previous Winrock project. The project was challenging in all ways.

I had to flesh out and run WEE's six major projects: short-term (three-day) trainings; a grants program; advocacy seminars; a microcredit program; study tours to Poland; and six women's business support centers in different Ukrainian oblasts.

All projects reported to me. As the WEE project was designed to help women in the outlying areas, not in Kyiv, my job called for almost constant travel by an overnight train; day trains were virtually nonexistent. I described my first trip to Simferopol in the Crimea in a letter to my father:

> Just returned from Simferopol, where I had gone to observe and participate in a two-day training in business for Crimean Tartar women, sponsored by the Danish Council and UN High Commission for Refugees. Three of us—two of my Ukrainian trainers and I—left Kiev in early evening, arriving in Simferopol at 1:00 the next afternoon. I bet the train hadn't changed much since you were there. A tattered old Oriental rug on the floor; some blankets that seemed left over from the Crimean War; slippery little mattress pads that kept sliding off the beds; and a rather foul smell. Windows did not open. Overheated. Bathroom—best not described.

> Like everyone else, we brought our food and had a picnic dinner
> of pickled seaweed, cooked perch, black bread, fruit, and chocolate.

While I dealt with all aspects of the Winrock program, I had the most input in the women's business support centers. Once I selected a city that would give our activities the best chance to succeed, I hired a director, rented space, supervised activities, and doled out the money to keep the center running. Each center offered four intensive three-month courses in "How to Start Your Own Business," limited to twenty-five students. They were free but available on a competitive basis. We had up to eight candidates for every vacancy.

Trying to ensure that we selected our candidates on a fair and competitive basis, I double-checked one day with the Kharkiv director. "How do you choose the women who end up in your classes?" I asked her.

"Oh," she said proudly, "I look in their eyes."

I omitted that in my report to USAID and was amused when President Bush seemed to use the same principle on his first meeting with President Putin.

We ended up with centers in Chernihiv, Kharkiv, Donetsk, Nikolaev, Simferopol, and Ivano-Frankivsk, cities I now know well.

When WEE's first three-month course ended, I was invited to address our Kharkiv graduates, in Russian of course. I worked hard on the speech and told a story about starting SOVUS and all the excitement and challenges that accrue from running one's own business. I stressed how women are often better than men at the multitasking entailed.

My talk was such a hit that rumors soon circulated: if Grace gave the graduation address, the women were more likely to be successful. Since our full complement of business centers held twenty-four graduations a year, this was an impossible goal. Neither USAID nor Winrock considered my role as a graduation speaker very important, but I gave these talks as often as I could. This was only nine years after the collapse of the Soviet Union, and Communist cartoons of the evil capitalist, usually depicted as a fat man with a cigar in his mouth, still lurked in the back of our students' minds. If these women were going to create viable small businesses, I knew that psychological empowerment was just as important as business education. Our graduates needed to understand that businesses could be respectable and contribute to the social good.

While the trains were still old-fashioned, I was in Ukraine at a time of intensive change and modernization. I remember the excitement when the first supermarket opened in Kyiv and I no longer had to go to four separate stores to buy food for dinner. Everyone was thrilled when the first Asian restaurant opened, when the first woman on my staff received a driver's license, when you could buy French cheese or even peanut butter. The whole city seemed to be in a state of metamorphosis. It was a time of hope.

Nonetheless, there were problems—one of the biggest, language. Although most people on the street spoke Russian, the State Department and USAID recognized Ukrainian as the official language, and many Ukrainian diaspora who were flocking back to their motherland from the United States and Canada spoke only Ukrainian. While the languages have many identical words, the grammar, some letters of the alphabet, and much of the vocabulary are different.

I started to study Ukrainian, learning enough to understand simple language—welcoming phrases, directions, and food. My tutor turned out to be an ultranationalist, however, and liked only Ukrainian writers such as Taras Shevchenko and Ivan Franko. When she belittled my beloved Chekhov, Tolstoy, and Dostoyevsky, I ultimately gave up on speaking Ukrainian, fearing that I would speak both languages badly. Instead, I spoke Russian and studied Russian classics with a Russian-language teacher.

The language problem never went away. Every day there

had to be decisions regarding the language for each meeting, conference, or interview. I was frequently on Ukrainian television, where I spoke in Russian, but on the radio Russian was forbidden and I had to speak in English and talk through a translator. Most Kyivites spoke both languages, and it was not uncommon to hear someone start a sentence in Russian, insert a phrase in Ukrainian, and then finish it in Russian.

A far larger problem was money. When I arrived in Ukraine, all financial transactions were in cash—rent, salaries, business centers—everything. The full horror of it hit me when I had to go to the bank with my accountant to pick up the monthly allotment that had been wired to my passport. After we counted the money, bill by bill, we would walk out as casually as possible—with as much as $40,000 in cash, mostly converted into Ukrainian hryvnia, tucked into my large purse. I had sleepless nights, dreading these visits to the bank, imagining being jumped on by Mafia operatives. Back in our office, we stashed the cash in a small safe, which any self-respecting burglar could easily have made off with. The next day our center directors would arrive, by night trains, to carry their allotted funds back with them on their persons. Miraculously, we never had any money stolen.

Being separated from my family for so long was hard. My children, my father, and I corresponded by fax. Winrock authorized two trips a year to the States, but, as Ukraine was designated a "hardship post," they had a liberal six-week vacation policy. By dint of taking advantage of that policy and paying for some trips myself, I returned to the States between three and four times a year. I always went to Princeton, where my parents listened to my stories with both fascination and bewilderment.

They were impressed that, at the age of sixty-seven, I had finally landed a regular paying job. They didn't see that running my own company had been an invaluable preparation for directing a twenty-five-person staff in Ukraine. My parents did not resent my absence, however, the way many families might have because, following in my father's tradition, I was working for my country.

I explored Ukraine in many different ways. One of the most memorable trips was to Chernobyl. While in Ukraine, I came to believe that the Chernobyl event contributed to Ukraine's move to independence at the time of the breakup of the Soviet Union. The explosion of the nuclear reactor in 1986, and the consequent radioactive fallout had traumatized the country. Particularly upsetting was that six days after the incident, local children were forced to march through the polluted atmosphere in the May Day parade. Many childhood thyroid cancers resulted.

Hearing so much talk about the subject, I decided I had to see it for myself even though the reactor was still in operation. Zhenya and two American friends, Joanne and Roger Pugh, decided to go with me. We had to receive special government permits and have a private escort with a Geiger counter. We were tested for radiation exposure when we left and were very relieved to see that we had not been contaminated. Writing about this experience in the English-language newspaper, the *Kyiv Post*, I said:

> What struck me most about Chernobyl was the absence of sound. Never have I been to a quieter place, and the silence was eerie. No birds, nor traffic, nor all the industrial hums and screeches that we are accustomed to. A second impression was how intangible radiation is—one cannot smell it, eat it, see it or touch it, but it is everywhere. It is also very spotty. One can be standing at a place in the center of the exclusion zone where there is virtually no radiation but two feet away from the road the radiation level can be 1,000 times greater.

The stresses of my first years in Ukraine were mitigated by the visits of my three children, who appeared one by one. Adair came first and we spent a long weekend in Crimea, sightseeing and playing cards, at which she excels.

Next to come was Kevin, who arrived in January 2001 to see Kyiv decked out in New Year's finery. While I had been working in Volkhov, Kevin was exploring new frontiers of his own. A lifelong sports enthusiast, he had spent more than a year organizing a consortium to buy the Pittsburgh Pirates baseball team. On Valentine's Day 1996, he called me in New York to tell me that he had become, at age thirty-three, the youngest managing owner in baseball history. I was puffed with pride. The whole family was dumbstruck and elated at this news, no one more so than my father. My SOVUS staff sent me the Pirates' score every day that I was away from New York. For the next eleven years, all Kennan family members festooned themselves with Pirates' regalia and made many trips to Pittsburgh. At the same time a dark cloud overshadowed the baseball years. My first Christmas home from Ukraine, Kevin had confided in me that he was gay, but he warned that this must be kept between us as homosexuality was anathema to the world of sports. So I even invented imaginary girlfriends and other unlikely scenarios, suffering because of the emotional toll that keeping this secret exacted from Kevin and from me.

And last, appearing in September, was Charles, who in contrast spent his time mostly chasing Ukrainian girls. Occasionally he asked me to serve as his translator, much to my embarrassment.

One afternoon during Charles's visit, Ella from my staff came to my office: "Grace, there's something you should know. I was listening to the radio, and an airplane has crashed into a building in New York City."

Charles and I rushed to my apartment to look at television. My sister-in-law, Jean McClatchy with a young friend Nicole were visiting and I was giving a dinner for eight in their honor that night. The four of us watched in horror as the nightmarish images of the planes hitting the twin towers repeated again and again on the screen.

"Do you suppose anyone will show up for dinner?" Nicole asked.

We had no idea. But not only did everyone appear, two additional American friends appeared self-invited. "We can't stand being alone," they explained. That night seemed surreal, but the true frightful tragedy only came through during the next days when we learned more details, such as the acrid smell and images of trapped victims jumping out the windows.

A deluge of flowers and letters of condolence from all over Ukraine poured into my office. The U.S. ambassador, Carlos Pascual, organized a moving memorial service in a church, and I finally was able to cry as we sang "America the Beautiful." Never had I felt more American.

Everyone was stranded for the first five days as planes were forbidden to fly from Europe to America, but Charles, who was renting an apartment, decided he loved Ukraine and ended up staying for six weeks. I saw more of him in Kyiv than I did in America.

As time went on, our business-center graduates opened more and more small companies. Cafés, beauty salons, accounting firms, health-food stores, translation bureaus, coffee shops, furniture shops, and a myriad of other little businesses sprang up, many of which I visited. I loved this aspect of my job. One of my favorites was a café in Kharkiv, an academic city with seventeen universities. A woman named Valentina, who was enrolled in our class, told us that her husband had stopped speaking to her, as she was wasting her time on "this silly course" and not tending to him. Upon graduation, and with money from our microcredit program, she opened a simple café with home-cooked food, named Valentina's, in a university neighborhood. It became an instant success. Soon the husband came to her: "We have to talk. It's not fitting that you, a woman, can work ordering provisions and buying equipment—why don't I do that?" He became her business partner, and their daughter served as hostess.

Of course, it wasn't always that easy. Another of my successful entrepreneurs informed me that as a result of the education
she received, she had started her own business and was getting a
divorce. She explained, "He beat me. Now I can afford to leave
him." I envisioned headlines such as USAID PROJECT RAISES DI-
VORCE RATE IN UKRAINE. Happily, that didn't happen.

In the end I lived in Kyiv for four and a half years, making
many friends both Ukrainian and ex-pat. I had always dreamed
of living in London, Paris, or Rome and enjoying the expatri-
ate life described in so many books. Instead, Kyiv became my
moveable feast.

Hostage Crisis: The Nord-Ost Siege

It was October of 2002. I was in Kyiv, packing for a three-day
visit to Moscow, when my colleague Olga called, her voice full
of concern. "Are you sure you want to go?" she asked in Russian. "Aren't you concerned about *zalozhniki*?"

I was too proud to admit that I didn't understand what
zalozhniki meant, and since Olga was a congenital worrywart, I
paid scant attention.

Somewhat impulsively, I'd decided to fly to Moscow for a
long weekend, because Ambassador and Mrs. Vershbow had
invited me to a special concert at their residence, Spaso House,
featuring young soloists from the Bolshoi Opera. I was eager to
revisit the yellow mansion, our home when my father served as
ambassador in 1952.

On the flight, my young American seat companion immediately asked, "Aren't you scared?" "No, why should I be?" I
replied.

I learned only then that the audience watching the musical *Nord Ost* at Moscow Ball Bearing Plant's Palace of Culture—known as the Dubrovka Theater—was being held hostage
at gunpoint by a group of Chechen terrorists. Now I realized
that *zalozhniki* meant "hostages." My seatmate was worried about

what we would find when we landed at Sheremetyevo Airport. As only a year had passed since September 11, I became frightened, too. I assumed that the musical evening, which I had so anticipated, would be canceled, and I would be sitting alone in a Moscow hotel during this crisis. But upon landing, I called the embassy and learned that Ambassador and Mrs. Vershbow had decided to proceed with the evening. I questioned whether this was a smart move.

On arrival at my hotel, I sat glued to the television, focused solely on the human drama being played out so close by. I saw the theater entrance, with masked gunmen armed with Kalashnikovs occasionally peering out the door. It was hard to pull myself away from this live drama in order to go and listen to opera singers. I was even more startled to arrive and find Spaso House ablaze with lights. Instead of hiding itself as a possible terrorist target, the old mansion lit up the quiet residential street and pocket park on which it is situated. No one could miss it.

When I walked into the white ballroom of Spaso House, I could see three-year-old Christopher playing with his trucks; my mother dancing at my so-called coming-out party; and the upstairs living room where the bug was found in the seal of the United States. Ambassador and Mrs. Vershbow greeted me warmly as a former resident.

After guests had gathered in the new music hall created in the back of Spaso House, the ambassador welcomed the audience, perched on little gilt chairs, and spoke reassuringly about not letting terrorists control our lives and that the arts are especially important during crises like this. He was followed by a magnificent concert of six young opera singers, most of whom had been with the Bolshoi for only two to five years. Unlike the overweight divas of Kyiv, these artists were beautiful and had remarkably fresh voices. The most memorable, a soprano named Lolita Semenina, made shivers go up and down my spine, especially when she performed the part of Tatiana from the last act of *Eugene Onegin*. I was not surprised to read later that she was one of the soloists at the reopening gala of the Bolshoi Theatre in 2011. The performance was followed by a reception for the young soloists in the ballroom, and what had initially appeared frivolous suddenly felt life-affirming in this troubled time.

The next day the hostage crisis was still at a stalemate, so I decided to walk to the Pushkin Museum. Nearby Red Square was closed. The whole center of the city bristled with military and police vehicles, while strange unmarked cars with blue flashing lights streaked by. It was a solace to see the familiar Impressionists, but I didn't stay long: I felt compelled to get back to the hotel and to the television, where I sat glued, imagining the seven hundred or so people sitting in the Palace of Culture auditorium, without food and only little water. Jumping channels, I saw that, for once, Russian television had the most complete coverage. The rainy, gloomy weather on TV and out my hotel window seemed to tie us all together but also made me feel especially far from my family.

My friend Ray Stults, music critic for the English-language *Moscow Times*, had invited me to see *42nd Street* that night, one of a new wave of American musicals recently imported to the Moscow theater scene. The producer, Boris Krasnov, a talented and flamboyant Russian set designer, had announced that morning that he, like Ambassador Vershbow, had decided that "the show must go on," although other theaters canceled their performances for that evening. However, Krasnov took precautions, and when we arrived at the Moscow Youth Palace, newly hired security guards frisked each person at the door and checked purses and bags, delaying the opening for over an hour. The inconvenience was for once reassuring.

The young American and Canadian cast danced and sang with amazing grace and pep. From the first bars of the catchy, rousing overture, eyes were shining and feet were tapping in the audience. Somehow the musical, which had been cheerful and fun when I saw it in New York, acquired a special luster in the tense atmosphere of Moscow.

After the show, a friend of Ray's invited us, along with three young dancers from the chorus, to eat and relax at a loud and garish karaoke bar. I noticed that in Moscow one is always assaulted by contrasts, such as the pure young operatic voices and the croaking karaoke.

The dancers turned out to be not as carefree as they had appeared onstage. They were young and scared to be so far away from home. Their fear had been exacerbated by an eyewitness report from two of their dressers, who had been trapped in the Dubrovka Theater. Locked in a windowless room at the back of the theater, one of the dressers had been able to phone for help on his cell phone. He pinpointed their location so precisely that the militia was able to drill a hole in the outside wall, through which the two dressers managed to wiggle out. When the dressers came back to work with the *42nd Street* cast the next night, one of them gave her firsthand account to the young actors, only raising their already high stress level.

Yelling over the noise in the karaoke bar, the American and Canadian dancers spoke of their experiences as strangers in this foreign land. Housed in a hotel miles from the theater, they endured unfamiliar food and found few people who spoke English. Their tap shoes were still locked up in customs, which seemed particularly odd: American tap shoes were considered suspect, but forty Chechen terrorists had flown to Moscow unnoticed.

Mostly, however, we talked about the hostage crisis. Ray had just heard that, starting the next morning, the Chechen terrorists planned to kill ten hostages an hour, a prospect hard to comprehend. We all compared this crisis with September 11 and agreed that, while the effects may have been similar for the helpless bystanders, these hostages were living through something quite different. The gray weather underlined the general gloom. It was dark even at midday, as if the heavens were also in mourning.

The next morning I awoke to find the crisis technically over. The security forces had stormed the theater, and about sixty-seven hostages were announced dead. The Chechen terrorists had all been killed. The surviving hostages who were assisted out of the theater looked almost unconscious. There was none of the joy one expected. We soon learned that the audience had been gassed by Russian security forces, which accounted for the listless and enfeebled demeanor of the survivors. What was the point of all this? If the goal of the Chechens had been to bring their war to the attention of the world, they had been successful. However, as far as changing Russian policy toward the Chechens, the hostage-taking, if anything, made the situation worse.

The next day I was back at my desk in Kyiv, doing daily tasks. But I felt as if I'd come out on a sunny street from a very powerful movie: for a while everything seemed flat and one-dimensional after those intense, dark days in Moscow.

Madame Director

My time in Ukraine was divided in two. The first half was a learning period, where I was always climbing a very steep mountain, only to see another hill every time I reached the top of a rise.

The second half was easier in the sense that I knew what I was doing, but harder in that I was weighed down by new responsibilities. When it was clear that we were not going to reach our goals in three years, I applied for a two-year project extension, which was approved. My time in Ukraine was going on longer than anticipated.

In my third year, I was promoted to country director for Winrock, which meant that I now was overseeing two anti-trafficking projects, as well as the WEE program. This meant more meetings at USAID and the embassy and trips to the anti-trafficking centers, as well as representing Winrock at conferences all over Eastern Europe. Of course, I loved these excursions to Sofia, Bucharest, Dubrovnik. Cities that had been only names came alive for me, as did the rich and violent history of the region.

By now I had learned that in Ukraine one must never shake hands across a threshold, as that brought bad luck; that it was customary to sit down and have a moment of silence before going on a trip; that open windows were a no-no, despite how hot the weather was, as any kind of draft made you sick; and that going out without a hat in winter was certain to bring on some dreaded respiratory ailment.

I also learned how to cope with the stream of entrepreneurs who wanted to sell their wares in our office. It had started with the orange man. One day I returned from lunch to find a man with a sack of oranges and a portable scale, doing business in our reception area. When I complained, my staff protested. They said they needed vitamin C in the winter, and this was so convenient. "We work long hours here and don't have time to stand in line at the grocery store," someone said. "Besides, we are supposed to be helping small businesses, aren't we?" So the orange man was allowed to come at lunchtime once a week, soon to be followed by monthly visits from an underwear company and a silver designer. These items seemed to be essential, too.

The longer I stayed, the fate of the Jews during the Second World War, an ugly part of Ukrainian history, kept surfacing. Western Ukraine had been a big part of the Jewish pale. During the war, much of the Jewish population was killed or shipped off to camps, but a conspiracy of silence covered this iniquitous period. One day I went to the town of Uzhgorod, near the Slovakian border, and read in an old guidebook that the town had a famous synagogue, now used as a concert hall. When I called on the mayor, I asked if I could see it.

"Well, it's no longer a concert hall, we have built a new one. Are you Jewish?" the mayor asked.

"No, but could I see it anyway?" I persisted. "I read it was a famous building."

Much to my surprise, the mayor found a custodian, who unlocked the door but refused to enter with me. I walked into a large unfurnished room, but it wasn't empty—I felt the presence of hundreds of spirits resonating through my whole body in a strange, mystical way. I stayed awhile, said a prayer, and emerged very shaken. Knowing the answer, I purposely asked the guide what had happened to the Jewish population. "Oh," she said. "They left."

Another time, I was in the town of Zhitomer as an election observer. The local escort, whose name was Popov, from the committee of voters, out of nowhere pointed to a square. "This was the Jewish market. That building was the synagogue," he said sadly. "It is now a porno movie theater. Zhitomer was the jewelry- and silver-making center of the country so all Orthodox church candlesticks and candelabra were made here, ironically by Jewish artisans."

Popov had a sense of history and was angry at the desecration that the Soviet government had caused in his city. Jewish history had no connection to my work, but I became fascinated by the area's history. It created a special bond between me and my Ukrainian friends. Their biggest compliment was: "You're not like others. You are one of us."

My job entailed much public speaking, all in Russian. I had spent hours composing and rehearsing my first speeches, fighting acute stage fright, but as I became busier I had to learn to write them quickly, and finally to ad-lib. One time, as I sat onstage at an advocacy forum, looking down at three hundred eager faces, I feverishly wondered, "What am I going to say?" Suddenly I remembered a small dinner in New York City where a woman named Betsy Barlow told us how she started the Central Park Conservancy to save the park when it was falling into decrepitude and was the home of derelicts and drug addicts. I told Betsy's story. My remarks must have been a success, because a few weeks later, at a forum in Donetsk, a woman raised a hand and asked, "Can you tell us the story about the lady who saved the park in New York?"

On my Christmas visit to Princeton in 2002, after seeing my father, now ninety-eight years old, so frail and quiet, and my mother, fading away into dementia, I realized that it was time to go home. After four years in Ukraine, I wanted to be with both my parents in the short time that remained to them. I also missed spending time with my children. I trained an efficient and inspiring Ukrainian staff member, Natalia Karbowska, to take over my job and in mid-June, I left. Reflecting the usual Ukrainian sense of over-the-top hospitality, I exited on a tidal wave of good-bye parties. Listening to the tributes to both my accomplishments and me, I realized I was not the same person who'd arrived on that snowy day four years ago. Everything had finally come into focus. I had become someone who made a difference.

CHAPTER 10

Circling Back

Back in New York, life was unexpectedly a little bleak. Standing in line at the bank or the post office, I missed my friends from Ukraine and the time we had for one another. I felt nostalgia for the slightly crazy but also romantic world of Kyiv—old babushkas wielding their brooms of twigs, in contrast to New York's young, svelte, miniskirted girls tottering around on their high heels. In Kyiv, my warm supportive staff had served as a family—ersatz, maybe, but sustaining nonetheless. Now it was time to reacquaint myself with my real family and attend to some unresolved issues.

The mother and father that I found were not the ones I had left four years ago. Dementia had made major inroads on my mother's mind. Still well-dressed and dignified, Mother was now a submissive patient, told what to do by the very helpers she once directed. The surprise that greeted my every arrival was genuine, as she couldn't remember being told that I was coming.

Each visit, we sat and watched her favorite DVD, *The Sound of Music*. It gave her endless pleasure, as if each viewing were the first time. Sadly, she would never be able to answer the questions that I was finally brave enough to ask. On the other hand, the mother who had been so hard on me as a child now loved me wholeheartedly.

Mother had always been extremely reserved. While capable of charming eminent scholars and heads of state, she rarely divulged her own concerns and never shared her insecurities. It was hard for me, rarely knowing what she was thinking. Now I wished that I had tried harder to penetrate those barriers she had built. On reflection, I realized that despite all the resentments that had piled up over our lifelong relationship, I'd never stopped seeking her approval or yearning for the kind of mother—daughter closeness that I often read about.

How many hours of my life had been spent in a psychiatrist's office, trying to unravel this complicated relationship. I found myself revisiting a particularly painful session in San Francisco. For a full hour, I had reviewed my litany of grievances—how my mother farmed me out to relatives as a child, how she called me fat, how she panned my performance in the school play, how she didn't attend my weddings or the births of any of my children or support me when I was divorcing C. K. As the hour wound down, the doctor stopped me and asked, "Have you ever considered that your mother didn't love you?" I was stunned. This was not possible. Maybe she didn't like me, but of course she loved me. That's what mothers do, isn't it? How could he suggest that she didn't love me? Did that mean she actually hated me? I rolled this theory over and over like a bitter hard candy on the tongue. Maybe the doctor was right— she never had loved me. For a brief period I even enjoyed the drama of myself as an unwanted, unloved child.

More recently, I've come to understand that I was born before my mother was ready to have me. She barely knew her new husband when I came along. One time she confided to me that she had had a legal abortion in Riga between my birth and Joanie's, because she wasn't ready to have another child. So while her mothering fell far short of admirable, she probably did the best she could.

Now all that was in the past. After leaving Ukraine behind and resettling in New York, I fell into the habit of spending holidays and occasional weekends with my parents. It was a pleasure to leave my small Manhattan apartment for the spacious and comfortable Princeton house, where Mother presided as the lovely chatelaine, despite her memory loss, where meals appeared on time, and where my father enthralled all our guests. My parents had good help, and I appreciated the sanctuary my mother had created.

Spending more time with my parents, I began to recognize how ill-suited they had been, although in later years my father would have been lost without her. My mother never trod the intellectual paths that lured my father, although he often tried out his new ideas on her. He did not share her interests or favorite pastimes, either, taking a particularly patronizing tone when he remarked on her penchant for shopping and interior design. These were "women's activities," he would explain, and not worthy of his participation. When Mother was a young bride in Moscow, she came home one day with a forty-eight-piece set of original Meissen china, bought at a commission shop. Father often complained at this example of mother's extravagance until later a friend told him what a rare find she had made.

What I grew to respect the most about my mother was what she sacrificed to be the wife of my father for more than seventy years. He was not an easy man to live with, and Mother put up with all his tantrums, moods, and impractical ideas. He would never have become the famous man he was, never have written twenty-one books, without her at his side, keeping the outside world at bay so that he had time to write. She maintained her unwavering support through long, painful separations, constant moves, and unanticipated turns in the road. She always put him first. Her sacrifice included neglecting her children at times, but now at least I can appreciate her efforts. I realize that, although I was not first in line, she loved me.

My father was fading, too, but his transformation was more physical than mental. When I came home, it was a shock to see him with his legs failing. Even a short walk was a major effort. His hypochondria became more pronounced, and every day he relayed new symptoms of some dread disease. It was painful to see this extraordinarily active man now almost a prisoner in the wing chair in his bedroom.

He loved my stories from Ukraine, and I now had my captive audience. Our roles had gradually been reversed, and I saw my father through different eyes. Always quick to criticize my mother, I had been much slower to recognize my father's male chauvinism and see how much we three Kennan daughters had been affected by it. My father greatly admired women but felt that they were there to tempt, entertain, and support men. For a long time I accepted second-class citizenship, although at the same time I resented being put in this category. My father's gender bias first became clear to me when Christopher was born and anointed the family crown prince. Only then did I realize that I might be a beloved daughter to him, but he didn't consider me his intellectual heir. That never stopped me from trying, however. Even when I attained some notoriety and success as country director for Winrock, my father's comment on this promotion, delivered with evident pride, was: "You know, you would be the ideal social secretary in the Moscow embassy."

I was both admiring and critical of my father. At times, within the confines of the Princeton house, he demonstrated a petulant, demanding side of his character that never appeared in public. But his knowledge of history, his beautiful prose, his analytic mind, his mastery of foreign languages were all exceptional. His gifts left me with feelings of inadequacy that took a lifetime to combat, but he passed on to me his identification with Russia, his love of literature, appreciation of the arts, and eagerness to explore the world.

Despite his aches and pains, Father was determined to live to see his hundredth birthday in 2004. He loved ritual, and he planned to participate in this one. His birthday celebration started with an event in his honor given at the Institute for Advanced Study, where he had worked for so many years. He felt poorly that morning and said that he didn't think he would make it, so the rest of the family went to the institute auditorium and sat in one of the front rows.

Suddenly Joanie tapped me on the shoulder. "Turn around; look who's coming."

And there, propped up by Tony, the housekeeper, and Wendy's son, George Pfaeffli, was our father, slowly, carefully walking in. My heart was in my throat, I was so nervous. He then gave what turned out to be his last speech—a little rambling and with diminished voice, but still beautifully worded and making sense.

On my father's actual birthday, February 16, Princeton University hosted a large gathering in his honor, although, to everyone's disappointment, Father was too weak to attend and stayed home.

The keynote speaker was Secretary of State Colin Powell, who gave an eloquent tribute. Powell asked us after lunch if he could call on the honoree. We phoned Tony to warn him. We learned later that Father insisted on getting out of bed, dressing, and was standing erect when the secretary walked in. That was his best birthday present.

The whole family assembled at the Princeton house for dinner on his birthday; all four of his children and seven of his eight grandchildren were present. Only Christopher's son, Oliver, was missing, as he was in the hospital with pneumonia. Dressed in an elegant suit, Father made it down the stairs and sat at the head of the table. As we waited for some words of wisdom on this momentous occasion, he smiled and looked slowly around the table. "If you think living to be one hundred is a great accomplishment, it's greatly overrated."

When he died a year later, peacefully at home, he was ready

to go, while the rest of us suffered the loss. For me, the world seemed very empty after he left us. After his demise and true to form he left us a file, "To be opened after my death." He wanted a small family service in the Episcopal church in Princeton, followed by a memorial service at the National Cathedral in Washington. At first we thought such a public remembrance was too much to undertake for someone who died at 101 and whose close friends had all preceded him, but when six hundred guests appeared at the cathedral, we realized how much he meant to so many people, including many who never knew him except through his writings. Our mother died three years later, also at home, at the young age of ninety-eight. They are buried side by side in the Princeton graveyard.

New Beginnings

Having spent four years empowering Ukrainian women, I came home deciding it was time to empower me. The insecurities that had plagued me for so long—fear that I wasn't smart enough, that I wasn't competent, that someone wouldn't like me—were finally quelled. I liked to joke that all those overnight Ukrainian trains shook them out of me. I was able to stop worrying about being broke, since my children shared their inheritance from their deceased father and had arranged a monthly stipend for me, in addition to the money I had made and saved in Ukraine. I bought a house in Martha's Vineyard, together with Adair and Kevin, so that we could have a home for family and friends.

Still, going into retirement was not my style. Why waste those newfound managerial and organizational skills that I never dreamed I had? After returning to New York, the most significant step I took was to sign up for a class called Memoirs from the Middle, taught by an inspiring poet named Veronica Golos. Now when people listened to my stories and said, "Oh, but you must write them down," I could answer, "Well, now that you mention it, I'm doing just that!"

The course was life changing. I started to chip away at an unwieldy knot of memories clamoring to be a book. Each class started with a prompt. Who would have guessed that being asked to write about "my first secret" would have led to my description of throwing my clothes overboard on my way back to the States after the Second World War? Four other Veronica Golos alumni joined me in forming our own writing group. We have met weekly for the past ten years—one of those years with Veronica, until she moved to New Mexico. She remains a chip in our brains.

After so many years of commuting to Russia and Ukraine, I was also eager to explore other parts of the world. When our U.S. ambassador to Kyrgyzstan, Marie Jovanovitch, a friend from Moscow and Kyiv, invited me to visit her in Bishkek, I leaped at the chance. During the visit, I saw some of the earth's most striking mountains. I also spent a day with Rosa Otunbaeva, who was later elected president of Kyrgyzstan and the first woman president in Central Asia. I ventured to Tasmania and Kangaroo Island in Australia, archaeological ruins in Western Turkey, and the pampas in Argentina. Before long, I had worn out my suitcase, but I never saw an itinerary that didn't whet my appetite for further explorations. Preparing for the day when I might no longer be able to traipse all over the world, I indulged the foodie in me and enrolled in cooking classes. Not only did I want to upgrade my culinary skills, but I wanted to evoke the smells, spices, and tastes of succulent dishes I had savored in various countries.

Looking back on my life has been a revelation. Traits that once seemed liabilities now feel like strengths. Maybe jumping unprepared into new situations isn't irresponsible but courageous.

Maybe peripatetic ways aren't mere restlessness but reflect a lust for life. What all this has shown me is that it takes a lifetime to paint a self-portrait, and mine, thankfully, is still unfinished.

AFTERWORD

My children have been mostly absent from this memoir at their request. They all have their own stories. But I think readers deserve an update.

Charles, my Number One Son as he calls himself, continues to battle a host of addictions, with varying degrees of success. His story changes from day to day, without reaching clear resolution. High hopes of recovery have been continually dashed. I pray that someday he can free himself from his demons.

Adair, my strong, feminist daughter, came out at an early age and never looked back. She and I have had our painful separations, both physical and psychological, but we are now intimates, and I rely on her. She lives in San Francisco, with her partner, Marla, Marla's son, Miles, and a dog named Holiday. Her house is a social center, which she controls like the queen bee but at the same time she is active in many social causes as well as managing family properties.

Kevin finally came out in a *New York Times* interview in 2012 in order to protest the homophobia in major-league sports, I was immensely proud and also relieved, both for him and for myself. This was one big secret that we no longer had to carry around. I felt certain that my father would have admired him as well for being courageous enough to risk social ostracism and to fight for his own beliefs. Kevin, now happily married to Jack, is chairman of the McClatchy Company. They recently had a son, Connor, born in March 2017.

As for me, I am now chairman of the board of the National Committee on American Foreign Policy and led a delegation to Taiwan, China, Korea, and Japan on their behalf in 2015. While meeting with the president of Taiwan I couldn't help thinking how fitting, if ironic, that I am now working in my father's field, and trust he would be proud. But I am especially fortunate to be blessed with my children, my siblings, and their progeny, all descendants of George and Annelise Kennan and from a happenstance meeting in Berlin.

INDEX